Beyond Heart Mountain

Alan O'Hashi

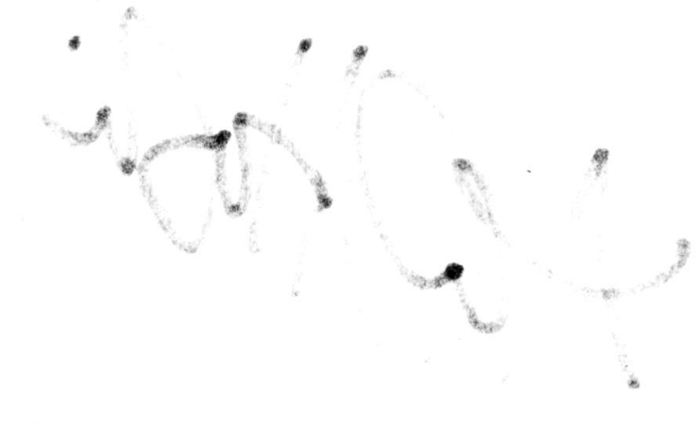

Winter Goose Publishing
45 Lafayette Road #114
North Hampton, NH 03862

wintergoosepublishing.com
Contact Information: info@wintergoosepublishing.com

Beyond Heart Mountain

First Edition: 2022

Cover Design and Formatting by Winter Goose Publishing

ISBN: 978-1-952909-14-6

Published in the United States of America

To my parents Frank O'Hashi and Sumiko Sakata-O'Hashi,
grandparents Jusaburo "Joe" and Toki Sakata,
Toichi "George" and Natsu "Mary" Ohashi

FOREWORD

I first met Alan O'Hashi when he was a graduate student in Political Science at the University of Wyoming in 1975. He was an intern at the Wyoming State Legislature when I was the House Majority Whip.

He "learned the ropes" as a young man and used those experiences and skills working for local governments in Wyoming. We continued to work together while Alan was a member of the Wyoming Uranium Mill Tailings Task Force, and I was a US Senator serving on the Subcommittee on Nuclear Regulation Committee on the Environment and Public Works.

After one meeting we had in 1987, I was later successful in convincing the US Department of Energy, the state of Wyoming, and the Nuclear Regulatory Commission to remove the Susquehanna uranium mill tailings from the inactive site on the Wind River Indian Reservation.

Over the years, I also became well aware of Alan's interest in his Japanese-American heritage and the Heart Mountain Relocation Center between Cody and Powell in northwest Wyoming.

Alan and I share a common interest in the Heart Mountain relocation camp. As a Boy Scout from Cody, I had the opportunity to spend time participating in scouting activities with the troop from California. During that time, I befriended fellow Scout Norm Mineta, who was relocated to Wyoming from there.

Norm and I remained in close contact. He was elected to the US House of Representatives, and I was elected to the US Senate. While in Congress, we sponsored the Civil Liberties Act of 1988. The act issued a formal apology to survivors of the relocation camp experience and paid financial reparations.

His book Beyond Heart Mountain is really about civility. He writes from his own deep experiences growing up in Wyoming as a Baby Boomer after World War II and how those memories flavor his work ethics today. He has always been an able collaborator, and it has been a sincere pleasure to know him.

I am pleased to add these words to his fine work as we both work toward a better future for the coming generations.

Alan K. Simpson
US Senator, Wyo. (Retired)
1979-1997

INTRODUCTION

Beyond Heart Mountain is an offbeat Western. The story started out as a survey of Japanese residents and business owners who inhabited two blocks on the west side of Cheyenne, Wyoming, from the 1920s through the 1960s.

The project grew into a modern-day Cowboys and Indians story told through my eyes. I'm a Baby Boomer and third generation Japanese from Cheyenne who has roots in this tiny neighborhood. My grandmother worked as a cook at City Café, which was a culinary mainstay, and my grandfather owned a pool hall next door on West 17th Street.

After I dug into Japanese history in Cheyenne, it led me to wonder how my family that lived in Wyoming during World War II affected my upbringing. I'm a Wyomingite through-and-through and relate to you my experiences in the context of Wyoming history.

After growing up in Cheyenne during the Cold War, being uprooted to Laramie, working my first job in Gillette during the coal boom and another in Lander during the uranium bust, I regained my roots with the Northern Arapaho Tribe on the Wind River Indian Reservation. But it wasn't until last year that I circled back to my Cheyenne roots with this writing project.

Following the bombing of Pearl Harbor on December 7, 1941, the US government classified Japanese people who lived on the West Coast as threats to the national security. The following spring, President Franklin D. Roosevelt issued Executive Order 9066 that forced these Japanese to leave their homes and transfer to one of ten relocation camps scattered around the interior of the United States, including the Heart Mountain camp in northeast Wyoming.

According to the 1940 US Census Bureau, there were around a hundred and twenty-seven thousand Japanese in the country. The Bureau estimated that between a hundred and twelve thousand and a hundred and twenty thousand found themselves in relocation camps.

The Japanese internment effort administered by the War Relocation Authority spent an estimated one hundred and sixty million dollars over the course of World War II that also established a vast bureaucracy comprising three thousand employees to administer the ten relocation camps.

The few Japanese who lived in middle-of-nowhere places, like my family in Wyoming, were considered interned in place. The xenophobia, racism, and distrust experienced particularly by my mom and dad affected them in profound ways, which rubbed off on the socialization of myself, and presumably caused my sister to adopt Superman's Truth, Justice, and the American Way.

Beyond Heart Mountain is about civility and a different American way. There's nothing inherently wrong with Superman's American way. It is where bigger is better than smaller, winning is better than losing, and people are accepted based on assimilation. But what if the American way was achieved by a better balance between individual needs with those of the wider community, acceptance of all based on who they are, and success measured by collaboration and sharing?

What if we take the outcomes of the past and learn from the Japanese internment camp experience and apply a new vision of the American way to the treatment of Muslims in the aftermath of 9/11, and immigrants seeking entry through the southern border of the United States? The World War II Japanese internment and the recent immigrant family separation and detention circumstances are different, but the mainstream attitudes about both are the same.

Beyond Heart Mountain examines the historic roots of racial and ethnic cultural homogeneity dating back to colonial times in the United States, and the subsequent reasons attitudinal adjustments happen slowly despite the rapidly occurring social and cultural changes now being experienced in America.

As an adult and now in my twilight years, I've come to realize the effects assimilation has had on me. Despite how well I learned to fit in with the American way and live in two worlds, I still find myself isolated from my Japanese roots.

Although I'm mostly used up, I'm doing what I can to bring about more civility as I work to bridge racial and other cultural divides as an individual, as member of various groups, in my neighborhood, and nationally.

I believe the world would be saved by now if each of us had more spare time.

Alan O'Hashi
Boulder, Colorado

ONE: Where Were You?

It was an unusually hot day in September. I must have been in a hurry because I didn't bother to turn on The Today Show or Morning Edition on Colorado Public Radio while getting ready for my commute to work in Denver. This particular morning, I took the Regional Transportation District (RTD) route 205 bus from the stop near my Boulder condo to the RTD Walnut Street station in downtown Boulder. My bus stop was next to the convenience store, where I stopped most days for a cup of coffee.

"Looks like it's going to be a good one out there." I don't think the clerk understood a word I said about the glorious weather predicted for the day. He grinned and handed over my change. I clunked a couple cents into the plastic leave-a-penny/take-a-penny tray on the counter and cut through the gas pumps to the bus stand.

Living near the corner of Valmont Road and 28th Street was convenient—walking distance to the liquor store and the Asian market. The condo complex was a converted 1970s-era apartment building. Across Goose Creek was a vintage plumbing store called Rayback that stocked ancient brass fittings for minor maintenance jobs.

From the downtown Boulder bus station, few passengers waited to catch the B Express bus to Denver. There was no free parking. I was okay with transferring from a local bus downtown to get the seat of my choice, which was one with extra legroom toward the middle of the cabin a couple rows ahead of where a wheelchair would be parked—similar to the exit row seats on an airplane.

By the time we reached the last Boulder stop at the Table Mesa Park-N-Ride, the seats were filled with commuters rattling their morning papers, cramming for college classes at the Auraria campus, reading books, listening to music on iPods, catching up on sleep.

This was well before laptops, internet hot spots, and smartphones. I had a cell phone. It was a Kyocera with a personal digital assistant (PDA) built in, and it was the size of a small box of Velveeta cheese.

"Did you hear what happened in New York," the guy sitting next to me asked. When I told him I hadn't, he said, "An airplane crashed into one of the Twin Towers."

He shrugged when I asked him what kind of plane it was, but other passengers murmured about the news and I overheard, "It was a small plane, like a Cessna." Hmm, a small plane, nothing to see here, folks, and soon we all returned to being immersed in ourselves.

The bus pulled up to a stall in Market Street Station. We disembarked and made our ways up the stairs and escalators to the 16th Street Mall.

My connection was for the eastbound RTD 20 bus that dropped me off near my work in a converted single-family home in an older neighborhood.

I walked up the steps and creaked open the wrought-iron screen door before winding my way up the staircase towards my office.

"You can go home if you want," my boss told me at the top of the stairs. "Two planes hit the World Trade Center. There isn't much more information, but all the air traffic is grounded."

My colleagues had all gone. I had the longest commute to and from Boulder and was the last to hear. I walked back to the bus station and noticed the eerily quiet streets—no car engines, no airplane noise, few people out and about. When I stood waiting for the light at Broadway and the 16th Street Mall, I glanced up at the Denver World Trade Center that I later learned was a similar target to its namesake in Lower Manhattan.

The bus back to Boulder was abuzz with rumor, but I didn't engage.

TWO: The Day the Earth Stood Still

There is a movie called *The Day the Earth Stood Still* (1951) that stars Michael Rennie and Patricia Neal. It's about a flying saucer that comes to Earth and warns the earthlings that unless humans quit fighting amongst themselves, the planet will be destroyed. As a demonstration of their cosmic abilities, the aliens neutralize electricity and offer an ultimatum that people better live in peace or face annihilation.

Not much explanation is necessary about what happened on September 11, 2001, other than it was a day the Earth stood still. You likely know where you were and what you were doing that day. My unremarkable commute to work that summer morning is one I will always remember.

When the World Trade Center and the Pentagon were hit by three weaponized commercial passenger jets, and a fourth crashed in a Pennsylvania field, those terrorist attacks would fan the flames of racial and ethnic xenophobia in America that was sparked similarly when the Empire of Japan bombed Pearl Harbor in Hawaii on December 7, 1941, and drew the United States into World War II.

After that attack, in February 1942, President Franklin Delano Roosevelt (FDR) signed Executive Order (EO) 9066 that ordered, among other things, Japanese—particularly those living on the West Coast—to uproot themselves from their homes and businesses. There was fear that there may be Japanese spies embedded within the general citizenry on the West Coast.

The federal government reorganized, and new agencies were established to manage somewhere between a hundred and twelve thousand and a hundred and twenty thousand men, women, and children of Japanese descent who were sorted out in fifteen assembly centers before being herded up and shipped by rail to one of ten makeshift war relocation centers constructed in remote places within the interior of the United States.

To say that EO 9066 dug a cultural trench between Asians and Caucasian America is an understatement. While researching this story, I learned the American quest for cultural and racial homogeneity dates back to George Washington in the Eighteenth century and continues to Donald Trump in the Twenty-first century.

The US government didn't always prop up a xenophobic culture. After the United States left Vietnam in the capable hands of Communists in 1975, thousands of "boat people" travelled to the free world, including the United States. The military set up detention camps at several army bases to house Vietnamese refugees on a temporary basis. The week before Saigon (now Ho Chi Minh City) fell, US Navy ships and the Air Force evacuated ninety-five thousand South Vietnamese. Later in 1975, another hundred and twenty-five thousand refugees left South

Vietnam and were received at US military bases in the Philippines and Guam before being transferred to other domestic installations where they lived in preparation for permanent resettlement.

At the beginning of the mass exodus, there wasn't a strong consensus among Americans around whether South Vietnamese refugee resettlement in the United States was a good idea or not. But despite the split public opinion, the US Congress approved the Indochina Migration and Refugee Assistance Act that President Gerald Ford signed into law in May, 1975. The president also allowed Vietnamese refugees to enter the United States under a special status, along with four hundred and five million dollars in resettlement aid.

The earth is still standing still.

THREE: Civility and Superman's American Way

My favorite heroes growing up were mortals like Zorro and Batman who used their cunning to save the day. I made a mistake and ironed my Superman cape thinking it was indestructible.

I called my mom to talk about 9/11 after news sources established that al-Qaeda, the extremist Islamic network founded by Osama bin Laden and Abdullah Azzam, was responsible for the attacks. We exchanged a few pleasantries and condolences about what happened.

"Thank god no Asians were involved," she said.

Both my parents and their families had firsthand experience and knowledge about racism toward Japanese and, by association, all other Asians following Pearl Harbor.

"I feel for Muslims, but now they'll be watching all of us." My mom referenced how anyone with brown skin would be scrutinized by the dominant culture.

"You be good. You'll be noticed if you aren't," my mom always warned me. "That's just the way it's always been. Don't draw attention to yourself."

Civility. Civility is more than being polite, but in the context of Beyond Heart Mountain, it is also about disagreeing with respect and finding common ground, rather than entrenching into unwavering personal beliefs.

Civility begins with each of us taking on the daunting task of rewinding tape recordings of our pasts (I'm dating myself), and how our experiences and upbringings define who we are. The hard work begins as we change our perspectives and view the world not only through our own eyes, but through those of others who may be tremendously different from ourselves.

The Adventures of Superman was a 1950s TV program that boys, including myself, watched religiously. The narrator at the beginning of the show set the story backdrop: "Faster than a speeding bullet, more powerful than a locomotive, able to leap tall buildings in a single bound. Look up in the sky—it's a bird, it's a plane! No, it's Superman. Yes, it's Superman. Strange visitor from another planet who came to earth with powers and abilities far beyond those of mortal men; Superman, who can change the course of mighty rivers, bend steel in his bare hands, and who, disguised as Clark Kent, a mild-mannered reporter for a great metropolitan newspaper, fights a never-ending battle for truth, justice, and the American Way."

Superman's American Way exemplifies a society that is, in theory, civil, fair, and provides opportunity for all, regardless of individual or group identity. It is characterized by a continual reach for high material success, rugged I-can-do-it-myself individualism, and acceptance of others based on assimilation.

What if we re-envision Superman's American Way to reflect civility in the multi-cultural nature of the United States, and we strive for truth and justice based on collaboration, decisions made by consensus that value opinions of the few, and acceptance of everyone?

Beginning in the Eighteenth century, pundits metaphorically characterized the United States as a "melting pot" in which races and ethnicities would learn English and assimilate themselves into homogenous Americans. This concept was largely espoused by J. Hector St. John de Crevecoeur in his *Letters from an American Farmer*, where he stated, "He is an American, who, leaving behind him all his ancient prejudices and manners, receives new ones from the new mode of life he has embraced, the new government he obeys, and the new rank he holds."

That was true when the pot contained white cheeses like Swiss, Edam, Gouda, Parmesan, and Feta. They blended together to make a mixed pot of assimilated white cheese. It was true until western expansion bumped into indigenous people and those who migrated northward from what is now Mexico and eastward from Asiatic areas.

Over time, immigrants from Europe had the benefits of Superman's American Way to look forward to after they learned English and easily blended into the dominant American cultural pot of white cheeses that melted on the East Coast stove stoked by founding fathers and mothers from Europe.

As America became more diverse, other immigrant groups didn't have the social and cultural benefits ahead of them because of public policies that limited immigration, and sometimes prohibited immigration, particularly from Asian countries.

Regardless of America's long history of striving for homogeneity, the country has become racially and ethnically multicultural because of immigration.

Today, the blended food metaphor would be more like a "tossed salad" that has separate ingredients unified with a common dressing, while our country becomes more culturally diverse and socio-economic gaps continue to widen.

If each of us intentionally is more civil in our interactions with others and alters our personal beliefs about people unlike ourselves, divides can be narrowed. There's no telling what will happen when Millennials and their kids are in charge and change things. A Millennial mom explained to me that when her kids grow up, their melting pot would consist of M&M's, Reese's Pieces, and Skittles being blended together.

FOUR: Inciting Incident

The last building standing in the former downtown Cheyenne Japanese neighborhood was 509 W. 17th Street.

My upbringing in Cheyenne's Japanese community certainly wasn't like it might have been in a Little Tokyo you would find in, say, New York City or Los Angeles, or Japantown in San Francisco, but how these two blocks evolved from vibrancy into parking lots is a cautionary tale.

I had forgotten about my childhood time on West 17th Street. Well, I hadn't actually forgotten, but when I saw John Dinneen giving an interview on the local TV news, I was reminded of it.

John and I were classmates at Cheyenne East High School (EHS)—the class of 1971. He and his family have deep roots in Cheyenne. They sold cars—Lincoln and Mercury—at least in the 1960s.

My dad did quite a bit of business with the Dinneens over the years. One of our memorable family cars was a 1963-or-so Monterrey sedan that had a rear window called the "breezeway" that rolled down. We also had a big avocado-green Mercury "family truckster" station wagon with the fake wood paneling on the sides. The family truckster, of course, is the car the Griswolds drive from Chicago to Wallyworld in the cult classic *Vacation* (1983), starring Chevy Chase and Beverly D'Angelo.

When John and his brother Jim got out of the car business, they were left with the original and historic dealership and automotive repair garage, which was repurposed into an office building anchored by a steak house. There is the land where their car lots were located. They sold some property, but one old, nondescript, long-vacant building at 509 W. 17th St. was still standing. They acquired the land and building, hoping to raze it and construct ten townhomes, which are under construction and soon to be occupied.

The structure in question was over fifty years old and found not to be architecturally significant by the Cheyenne Historic Preservation Board, but rather, an historic place because it was the last building standing in what the heart of the Cheyenne Japanese community was.

John's TV interview followed a hearing before the Preservation Board. His demolition request was approved but with a condition that a cultural and historical survey be completed of Japanese-operated businesses and downtown residents. Some on the board wanted the building preserved because razing it would remove the last vestige of Cheyenne's Japanese community.

On this site, the 400 and 500 blocks of West 17th Street are largely vacant. The residents who hustled and bustled around the neighborhood left forty years ago. The landlords, unable to keep their buildings occupied, razed them after they became empty.

Based on my renewed interest in the neighborhood, John asked me to do a survey of past denizens and land uses. That survey work is the basis of this book.

The Japanese neighborhood's demise was, in my estimation, a combination of a cultural identity crisis and urban sprawl that occurred concurrently and culminated during the late 1960s into the 1970s.

With my family being a part of the Japanese community, I have wondered about how my assimilation contributed to the two blocks turning into a sea of parking lots.

My sister and I are third-generation Japanese American and Cheyenne natives. Back when Lorinda and I were growing up there, being a Baby Boomer wasn't a thing. We were just kids. I didn't even self-identify or notice that I was Japanese.

My family often drove to Salt Lake City, Utah, to visit my dad's sisters, Marie and Amy, for Easter break. Marie was one of the youngest of my dad's siblings. She left Cheyenne and went to college at Weber State in Ogden, where she met and married her husband Masao "Mooch" Matsukawa. She taught school and Mooch was a social worker. They lived in a suburb called Murray and had two kids, Matthew and Mauri.

We all attended Easter services together at their Japanese Church of Christ. It was always fun to go there because afterwards we could walk to the Church of Jesus Christ of Latter-Day Saints (LDS) Temple Square where the Mormon Tabernacle and Mormon Temple are on a beautiful campus.

Our visits included meeting up with one of Dad's older sisters, Amy. She and her husband, Ichiro "Ich" Doi, lived in the Salt Lake City suburb of Bountiful. They ran the Deluxe and the Excellent dry cleaner shops. They didn't have kids. Amy had kidney disease, which eventually took her life. Dialysis was just being developed.

I enjoyed going to work with Amy and Ich. Their storefront was always humid and warm. Dry cleaners have a distinctive odor. Customers dropped off clothes that eventually soaked in a chemical solvent that somehow clung to clothing crud. When the garments tumbled in dryers, I imagine they vented most of the solvents out into the outside air. That which remained on the clothing was steam-pressed out.

During a visit in the summer of 1962, Auntie Amy introduced me to live theater. I went along reluctantly to be courteous. And my mom made me go. Little did I know the tickets were for *The Music Man*, the theme of which had an enormous influence on my outlook on life.

On those weekend trips, I was immersed with other Japanese but didn't realize it. My mom even told a story about the first time we attended an Easter service with the Matsukawas, when I looked around the congregation and wondered, "Why is everyone here Japanese except us?"

After agreeing to help the Dinneens with their historical survey of the neighborhood, I began to realize the importance of my past and how it influences my present life.

As a citizen, I was expected to act certain ways, but I was always conflicted about how I fit into the American way because regardless how hard I tried to be like everyone else, I was still viewed as different.

FIVE: Revisionist Wyoming History

This is my sister, Lorinda, and I in our grandparents Ohashi's backyard. Being from Wyoming, it was hard not to self-identify with the Wild West.

Wyoming is best known for being a place that epitomizes a standard ballad about the wide-open spaces where bison herds were plentiful, and pronghorn antelope roamed under clear blue skies. "Home on the Range" (circa 1872) became the anthem of the American West.

"Home on the Range" was a poem written by Dr. Brewster Higley, who settled in Kansas on property granted to him by the Homestead Act after pioneering west from Indiana. His friend, Daniel Kelley, set music to poem.

The Wild West was being tamed when President Abraham Lincoln signed the Homestead Act during the Civil War in 1862. The law encouraged any adult citizen, or intended citizen, who had never fought against the United States, to occupy the frontier and gave them a hundred and sixty acres of surveyed government land. In exchange for the land, the act required pioneers to build a home and farm the land which were once the traditional homelands of Native Americans. Congress amended the law in 1916 with the Stock Raising Act that enlarged the allotments to six hundred and forty acres to encourage ranching.

This version of Wyoming's past is about all I learned in my history classes, and the movie production industry that once flourished in the state perpetuated this Wooly West view of Wyoming.

Shane (1953) was filmed in Jackson Hole and starred Alan Ladd as a dashing former gunfighter who moves to a homestead, only to be called back to action when a conflict develops with a big cattle rancher who wants to drive other settlers off their land. The movie showed off the splendor of the Grand Teton mountains.

Gary Cooper played *The Virginian* (1929), a ranch hand near Medicine Bow in south-central Wyoming. The story is based on the novel by Owen Wister, who wrote the novel in his cabin located across the street from the Virginian Hotel on what's now US Highway 30, also called the Lincoln Highway.

I am working on a documentary project about cowboy actor Tim McCoy who lived in Lander and Thermopolis and worked closely with the Northern Arapaho and Eastern Shoshone tribes on the Wind River Indian Reservation. McCoy's first job, as a casting director, was to recruit two hundred tribal members—mostly Arapaho—to be background actors in an epic silent movie, *The Covered Wagon* (1923). The story is about settlers moving west in a big wagon train, complete with fending off Indian attacks and evading a buffalo stampede.

The romantic West continues to be this vision of Wyoming. "Wyoming is where the untamed spirit of the West and majestic natural beauty open your mind and invigorate your senses to release your own inner freedom and sense of adventure," according to the Wyoming Travel and Tourism Office.

As a student, the school district required fourth graders and seventh graders to take Wyoming history classes. I learned about mountain men like John Colter being chased, naked, through the woods during the winter by cunning savages, and Catholic missionaries like John DeSmet proselytizing the heathen red man. I don't recall learning anything about the World War II Japanese relocation camp where thousands of Japanese residents from the West Coast were interned near Heart Mountain in northeast Wyoming, nor about the Wyoming Alien Land Act prohibiting Japanese from owning land. It wasn't until the 1980s, when I was living in Lander, that I learned anything about the Heart Mountain Relocation Center between Cody and Powell in northeast Wyoming and that it was one of ten constructed around the interior of the United States during World War II.

"Center" is a misnomer. Tall barbwire fences surrounded each compound, with towers constructed around the perimeter manned by armed guards. Based on conversations with my parents and their contemporaries, they referred to them as "camps" where several thousand Japanese were interned after being herded up and transported from their homes, mostly on the west coast of the United States.

While researching this story, I found some sources refer to the relocation centers as "concentration camps" and internees as "prisoners." I chose not to use those characterizations because, I think, the terms race bait and are inflammatory. My mission is to inform and entertain.

That being said, the CST reported in late 1942 a group of internees protested the barbwire fence and the guard towers, saying "we are not prisoners of war" (POW) in a petition to the War Relocation Authority (WRA). FDR subsequently issued EO 9102 that charged the WRA with managing the Japanese ordered into relocation camps.

In the early 1980s, I met a Japanese woman named Mrs. Honkawa on a commuter flight from Denver to Riverton. She was on her way to Worland for a family funeral. We chatted about her experience as a young woman at the Heart Mountain camp.

Her story intrigued me. I was a "stringer" for the local paper, the *Wyoming State Journal* (WSJ). I wrote some occasional columns and covered sports. The publisher,

Bill Sniffin, asked me to do more writing. That's one of the great things about small towns. Unexpected opportunities arise.

I drove up to Park County with one of the other WSJ reporters named Diana to find the place. The Heart Mountain site wasn't very well marked. We were looking around the Buffalo Bill Museum in Cody and asked at the information desk about it.

"Drive ten or twelve miles towards Powell. You can't miss it," the attendant said. "There's a tall chimney. Look for a turn off the road to your left, and then after the railroad tracks, you drive up a hill."

When I first rumbled up the uneven, dusty dirt road to explore the ruins, the Bureau of Reclamation (BOR) stored a rolled-up orange plastic snow fence in one of the abandoned barracks. Those original structures look much the same today.

The BOR was established in 1902 as a part of the US Department of the Interior (DOI). The BOR provided infrastructure for the newly settled lands by constructing dams, installing power plants, and digging water delivery canal systems in seventeen western states. These projects promoted and supported the economic expansion and encouraged homesteading in the otherwise arid western frontier.

After the war, many Heart Mountain camp barracks were repurposed around western Wyoming. Some of the pitched-roof wooden structures were refurbished into single-family houses. Those are the subject of a documentary film, Moving Walls, by my colleague Sharon Yamato. I helped her record interviews with people who currently live in the renovated barracks near Heart Mountain. Some barracks were moved north of Riverton and became the Cottonwood Cottages.

The physical landmark of the area is Heart Mountain. It's a limestone and dolomite geologic feature that protrudes 8,123 feet through the Big Horn Basin floor and overlooks the relocation camp.

The weird thing about Heart Mountain is, the rock that pokes up out of the top is three hundred million years old, but the underneath part of the mountain is fifty million years old, give or take a few million.

I didn't quite know what to make of my first visit to the Heart Mountain camp ruins or how I felt about being there. Looking at the vast and open terrain, it was hard to believe thousands of people lived there. I understood it intellectually, but I wasn't sure how I felt emotionally.

I wrote about my conversation with Mrs. Honkawa and the subsequent trip to northwest Wyoming in a newspaper column titled "Beyond Heart Mountain."

While writing this book, and with the advancements in research technology, I hoped to have a follow-up conversation with Mrs. Honkawa. I looked her up on Ancestry.com, only to learn that she passed away years earlier.

Local and national anti-Japanese propaganda shaped attitudes and opinions about the news that Wyoming would host a large Japanese population from someplace else. Reactions ranged from racist to xenophobic to apathetic.

Some Wyomingites were practical in thinking that internees could provide agricultural and industrial labor to make up for the shortage created when local men went to fight in the war. However, the consensus was, Japanese internees were not welcome to remain in Wyoming once the war was over.

Members of the Honkawa family were some of the few who remained in Wyoming after the war rather than returning to their homes. Mrs. Honkawa rationalized her camp experience as being a good thing. She ended up moving to Chicago, where she could be out on her own before eventually moving back to California.

The huge local, state, and federal bureaucracies needed to construct, maintain, and operate the Heart Mountain camp, as well as the other nine camps scattered around the United States interior, which kick-started local economies recovering from the Great Depression.

The United States stock market crashed on Black Tuesday, October 29, 1929, and plummeted the world into financial chaos that lasted until the beginning of World War II.

The Heart Mountain Irrigation Project, overseen by the BOR, was a part of the larger Shoshone Project. Because BOR priorities changed to support war efforts, the irrigation system was not completed. In June 1942, the BOR transferred twenty thousand acres to the WRA. The WRA took over the day-to-day operations of the Japanese relocation from the Wartime Civilian Control Administration (WCCA).

The WCCA was established in 1942 to evacuate the Japanese from the West Coast, broken down into Military Area 1 comprising the western halves of California, Oregon, Washington, and southern Arizona, with the remaining parts of these states in Military Area 2. The relocation effort encouraged voluntary compliance to minimize military involvement. Most WCCA administrators were Caucasians who formerly worked for the Work Projects Administration (WPA).

Shortly after his inauguration in 1933, FDR established various agencies as parts of his "New Deal" that employed millions of Americans who lost their jobs during the Great Depression. The projects included road construction and erecting public buildings and made a smooth transition to the war effort.

When the WCCA was phased out, the first WRA director was Milton Eisenhower, a former president of three universities and brother of war hero General Dwight Eisenhower, who would be elected president of the United States for two terms, 1953 through 1961.

Director Eisenhower disapproved of the mass internment. He initially tried to limit the internment to adult men while allowing women and children to remain free. He also unsuccessfully proposed that WRA internment camps be similar to subsistence homesteads in the rural United States established during the Great Depression.

In 1934, one New Deal program recognized the importance of sharing in the community when the Subsistence Homesteads Division was established within the

DOI. The program provided safe housing to the urban poor, who moved onto plots of land where several households would cooperatively grow and sell crops to sustain themselves.

Subsistence homesteads were intentional communities ahead of their time. The effort was marginally successful. If the program were resurrected today, I imagine there would be many takers with the rise in popularity of Community Supported Agriculture (CSA), a system that allows subscribers to share in a farm's harvest.

The five-million-dollar Heart Mountain camp construction began immediately after the land was ceded. The project created local construction jobs and generated more sales for local businesses. Notices in the Powell Tribune said, "If you can drive a nail, you can qualify as a carpenter."

The Department of War—now the Department of Defense—its Army Corps of Engineers, civilian and military labor forces built 468 barracks, 39 communal halls and utility buildings, a 150-bed hospital, schools, and a livestock farm that included pigs and chickens.

Inexperienced workers hastily built shoddy structures unable to withstand Wyoming's cold winter weather. Winds howled into the apartments through poorly installed doors and windows that didn't close and seal tight.

Personal privacy became an issue. Internees strung bed sheets from the ceiling and plugged the cracks with rags and newspaper pages. Conversations carried through the air, and household activity could be viewed through the enormous gaps between wallboards that divided the barracks into apartments.

The first internees arrived at the Heart Mountain camp in August 1942 and were assigned to quarters that varied in size based on the number of family members. Each room was furnished with a stove, a socket with one bulb, and folding cots. Over time, some internees improved their sparse rooms by building furniture from scrap wood.

The barracks lacked running water. Banks of showers and toilets were separated by gender and in communal utility halls that included laundries equipped with washtubs and scrub boards.

An important part of the traditional Japanese diet included fresh food. Internees were served cafeteria-style meals in mess halls. The fare included inexpensive and processed American food like pancakes, macaroni, hotdogs, and pickled vegetables. Camp community gardens provided desired fresh produce.

The camp farms were productive and contributed to the local and state economies. For example, in 1942, the WRA awarded the Big Horn Canning Company in Cowley a contract to can twelve thousand pounds of surplus beans. The hog farm produced forty head per week transported to US Department of Agriculture (USDA) approved slaughter facilities.

An unintended consequence of collective meal service was the breakdown of nuclear family relationships. Young children were no longer reliant on their parents for food preparation. Some older kids dined with their friends rather than with their families. To get enough food, growing kids would often wander to multiple mess halls for extra meals.

Japanese people, including my family, who built lives in places like middle-of-nowhere Wyoming, were deemed little threat to national security.

Both sets of my grandparents came to the United States as typical immigrants. They all arrived from Japan by ships that landed in the Pacific Northwest and eventually made their way to Wyoming.

My parents were both native-born citizens. Dad was born in Kent, Washington, and Mom in Thermopolis, Wyoming, just south of Heart Mountain. My sister and I were born in Cheyenne, where we grew up in the 1950s through the 1970s.

Heart Mountain High School had a first-year enrollment of fifteen hundred students. As a comparison, EHS was one of the largest high schools in the state. My graduating class size was around four hundred and fifty. At Heart Mountain High School, teaching materials were in short supply, but schools provided students an academic routine.

At the Wyoming State Archives, I came across a 1945 Heart Mountain High School yearbook that shows pictures of the band and sports teams that competed against public schools. The high school leadership were white, and they hired Japanese and Caucasians as teachers and teacher aides. WRA pay grades differed by race and favored Caucasians who were paid more.

As I flipped through the yearbook photos, one caught my eye. After further scrutiny, it was a picture of my advanced-biology teacher at EHS, Miss Jean Cooper. Before teaching in Cheyenne, she taught at Heart Mountain High School. Based on the preferential treatment teachers like Miss Cooper received at Heart Mountain, it doesn't surprise me she made no mention to me about her teaching stint there.

Scanning through microfilm copies of the 1990 *Wyoming Tribune Eagle* (WTE), I found a story about an anonymous teacher telling her experiences at Heart Mountain. I'm pretty sure that was Miss Cooper. There was an editorial disclaimer that the source didn't want to use her name because the World War II camp experience was still a sensitive one.

My dad's youngest brother, Jake, recounted his experience growing up in Cheyenne in that 1990 newspaper article. He said the grade school that served the westside neighborhood was naturally integrated. That part of town was where many minority families lived. Uncle Jake said that because of the diverse make-up of Corlett Elementary School, he grew up learning to be accepting of others.

I'm often asked if my family was at the Heart Mountain camp. They are surprised when I mention I was unaware of it until I was well into adulthood. I attribute that to the Wyoming and American history classes I sat through while growing up including nothing about Japanese relocation.

I hear about how educators and mental health professionals think kids are resilient and can deal with or otherwise outgrow life's small and large traumas. That's probably true to a certain extent, but I've always been trying to outgrow my issues around assimilation and imagine what I missed, not being more exposed to Japanese culture.

I was a Model Minority, adopted the American Way, and navigated my way around mainstream society fairly successfully, but I could only rise to a certain level of success. Often, I found myself, and still do, as an Asian in strange places.

SIX: Asians in Strange Places

This was taken at our home at 2213 E. 10th Street. The name of the other kid escapes me.

"Where are you from?" is a question I'm often asked when I meet someone for the first time.

"I was born in Cheyenne, Wyoming," I answer.

"Where are you from," is the follow-up question, which are code words asking about my race and ethnicity. I define my "race" as Japanese and my "ethnicity" as American. This is the plight of the perpetual immigrant.

Even though I'm a third-generation American citizen, the comments I hear through the course of conversation assume that I'm fresh off the boat.

The conversation gets around to their assumption that I was from Hawaii or California. "I'm just a city kid from Wyoming," I reassure them.

It surprises some people that I speak better Spanish and German than basic Japanese salutations.

My paternal grandparents, Toichi "George" and Natsu "Mary" Ohashi, brought their family to Wyoming through Monte Vista, Colorado. Near Tacoma, Washington, George was known for helping farmers maximize their crop yields and developing larger markets for their produce. He brought those skills to arid Colorado to ply his methods in what he was to believe a thriving lettuce growing operation.

When he arrived in Colorado, he was disappointed in what he found and regretted the move. Grandpa was entrepreneurial and started a truck farming business by purchasing vegetables from area farms for resale to restaurants. He also parked his panel van on roadsides and sold his produce to passersby, an early version of the farmer's market.

My maternal grandparents, Jusaburo "Joe" Sakata and Toki Iwasaki, also arrived in Washington State and eventually ended up in Cheyenne through jobs with the Union Pacific Railroad (UP) and eventually in Hot Springs, Natrona, and Converse counties with the Chicago Burlington & Quincy (CB&Q) railroad.

My parents, Frank and Sumiko (Sakata) O'Hashi, married in October 1946 and became very involved in Cheyenne's Japanese-American community. They met at a picnic that happened at Hynds Lodge, west of Cheyenne.

Throughout this story, you'll notice the names O'Hashi, the surname of my dad and his youngest brother Jake, and Ohashi, the name of everyone else in the family. How and why there are two spellings are subjects of family folklore.

One explanation is accidental. In anglicized Japanese, the long ō has a dash over it, a macron, and when the macron was handwritten, if slid over, could have been mistaken for an apostrophe.

In Japanese, ō-hashi means "big bridge" as opposed to hashi, which translates to "chopsticks," with the preceding ō added for grammatical politeness.

Hashi is a Japanese homonym. The kanji characters for bridge and chopsticks, while pronounced the same, are different. Both have strokes that have to do with "wood."

What's the best explanation? My father was born on St. Patrick's Day, and a school principal added the apostrophe in jest. I've had this Japanese-Irish thing following me around since junior high school.

People are often surprised when they see me in person for the first time if we've only talked on the phone or communicated by e-mail.

"Your English is very good," they say.

I'm a Model Minority.

Just married, and before my sister and I were born, my mom was the first secretary of the newly established Skyline Nisei Club in 1950. Local Japanese formed the club in response to the racist backlash towards the Japanese during and after World War II.

Nisei is the term for second-generation Japanese born in the United States, my parent's generation. Their Japanese immigrant parents—my grandparents—are Issei. My generation is Sansei. We're mostly Baby Boomers. The offspring of Sansei are called Yonsei.

When I was young and a frequent denizen of the West 17th Street neighborhood, I took my life hanging around there for granted.

My dad was the production manager for the local Coca-Cola bottling company. He let me tag along on weekends and have breakfast with his guys at Jim's Café on East Lincolnway in the same block as the Buffington's Sinclair station on the Logan Avenue corner. The Buffingtons lived up the street from us on Windmill Road.

After the server cleared our plates, we would go on our separate routes, restocking Coke products around town.

In my opinion, my dad's best stop was the little Buford store, just off the Interstate-80 (I-80) exit to the US Forest Service.

I read that the area of rounded and crystalline rocky outcroppings north of the interstate is named after an anglicized version of the Arapaho word bito'o'wu (earth-born). The 1.4-billion-year-old Sherman Granite site includes a day-use picnic area, an overnight campground, and several popular technical rock-climbing areas.

My dad let us build the EHS class homecoming float in one garage at the Coke plant. Some pals of mine stole one of the water pumps from a Vedauwoo campground that added the final touch to our homecoming float in 1971. The Mighty, Mighty T-Birds played the Sheridan Broncos that year.

The homecoming theme was the title of the movie *They Shoot Horses, Don't They?* (1969) that stars a cast of popular actors, including Jane Fonda and Bruce Dern. The title references a childhood memory of one character who dreams about a horse that breaks its leg and then is shot to put it out of its misery.

We used the water pump as a prop placed next to a horse-watering tank. My mom sewed together a pretty good south end of a northbound bronco that was stuffed with crumpled-up newspapers and spray-painted yellow and blue that draped out of the tank.

When I was a University of Wyoming (UW) graduate student in Laramie, I took a class offered by Rocky Mountaineering, a downtown outdoor equipment store. I learned how to technical rock climb at Vedauwoo. Rocky Mountaineering stayed in business over the years and is now Atmosphere Mountainworks, previously owned by the same guy named Scott.

The sharp nubbins make for great friction climbing. The chimneys between faces also offer challenging off-width crack climbs. Those basic skills were useful when I moved to Gillette, Wyoming, for my first job. I made four ascents up Devil's Tower.

The last time I tried climbing was a couple of years ago at Vedauwoo. I was mostly recovered from a 2013 deathbed illness and had a fantasy about ascending the Grand Teton with a crew lead by a Plein air artist from Laramie named Joe Arnold.

In the mid-Nineteenth century, impressionist artists painted outdoors, Plein in French, to take advantage of natural light. Joe's unique views from mountain summits are the subjects of his work.

After a few steps up the Veedauwoo crack we were climbing, I realized I hadn't regained enough lower body strength after my death-defying illness even after seven years.

Among other things, I'm a movie maker and videographer. My job on that project didn't transpire. I wanted to produce a movie about that ascent. Joe and his son, Jason, ended up finishing the short movie about that climb.

South of I-80, opposite Vedauwoo, is Buford, originally a UP railway section house and later a 1905 one-room school located midway between Cheyenne and Laramie. A railway section house is near or next to a railroad line. During the construction of the Transcontinental Railroad in the 1860s, Buford boomed with a population of around two thousand.

Railroad sections comprised anywhere between six and forty miles of track and maintenance equipment storage areas. Workers lived in section houses from the 1890s to the 1960s.

By the time I began frequenting Buford with my dad, one of the section houses was a quaint neighborhood bar and the area post office. The interior was paneled with varnished knotty pine boards that glistened in the morning sunlight.

It took about thirty minutes to drive from Cheyenne to Buford in my dad's noisy pickup truck. To keep me occupied while he carried the yellow wooden cases of six-and-a-half ounce Cokes, Dad handed me some coins and let me play the arcade bowling game and eat Slim Jim beef jerky sticks, even before lunch.

There was a big jar of pickled eggs sitting on the counter. I hadn't seen a jar like that before. The slightly discolored ovoids were a curiosity that reminded me of a mysterious jar I saw in a creepy Alfred Hitchcock Presents episode called "The Jar" (1964) based on a short story by Ray Bradbury.

"The Jar" is a "must-see" TV show. A farmer buys a jar filled with strange contents at a carnival. It frightens his wife. He refuses to get rid of the jar because he is now locally famous due to the sideshow attention he has brought to himself. The curious come from miles away to ponder what's in the jar. His wife gets creeped out, opens it, and gets rid of the contents.

The enraged farmer kills his wife and refills the jar so all can see the same thing. You're probably way ahead of me on this and can guess whose head was inside.

That story freaked me out when I was a kid. I thought of the TV show when I saw any big jar sitting on counters filled with pickles, pigs' feet, or eggs.

I didn't dare try one of those eggs until I was old enough to know better. That would be when I was away at Hastings College (Nebraska). Instead of drinking Coke and aiming pucks at arcade bowling pins in the Buford Store, I drank beer and slid pucks down the saw-dusted shuffleboard at the Wagon Wheel Bar.

Talk about Asians in strange places. In April 2012, a California-based reality TV show production company contacted me about helping document the auction sale of Buford, with a population of one.

A guy named Don Sammons was the owner of Buford. He served as its mayor, police chief, public works director, and dogcatcher. He bought Buford and its ten acres in 1992 but decided to retire and then put his hamlet up for sale. Buford and Sammons instantly became the subjects of international news stories.

The Buford store had drastically changed since I spent Saturday mornings there as a kid. There were no pickled eggs, for one thing.

I met my TV crew in Cheyenne for a production meeting. The next morning, we formed a caravan to Buford, twenty-eight miles west of Cheyenne on I-80, and halfway to Laramie. We were on location early, scouting and setting up the master shot, then picking up some B-roll from the convenience store.

There were travelers unaware of the impending auction pulling in to gas up, tourists browsing through the close-to-empty shelves and souvenir clothing rack admiring the "BUFORD Population 1" t-shirts emblazoned with a Sammons mug shot.

Soon, a steady stream of cars filled with auction bidders, news media trucks, and the curious rolled into the gravel parking lot.

The auction started at noon. Organizers didn't allow me to record the auction itself but set up a wide shot above the store.

Qualified bidders had to provide evidence of having ready access to at least one hundred thousand dollars, and when the bidding started, many who made the trip to Wyoming hoping to buy the unique hole in the road were left in the dust.

The bidding quickly jumped to the winning nine-hundred-thousand-dollar bid placed by a Vietnamese business executive named Nguyen Dinh Pham, the new proud owner of a house, the store, and gas station on ten acres of land. Rozetta Weston of Al-Roz Auction and Realty in Cheyenne represented him.

Roz is married to Alan Weston, who was a high school classmate of mine. We first met playing Little League Baseball on the AAA Red Sox around 1965. He later worked as a pressman for my uncle Jake at Pioneer Printing on West 19th Street. His mom, Dot, played on a championship softball team with my aunt Elsie.

Legend has it that following his purchase of Buford, Pham now proudly struts his newfound cowboy swagger on the streets of his native Ho Chi Minh City (formerly Saigon) while wearing a Stetson western hat. When I heard that, I couldn't help but picture myself as the "Kimono Cowboy" at Cheyenne Frontier Days (CFD) of yore.

His market development strategy was to rebrand Buford as PhinDeli Town and sell Vietnamese PhinDeli coffee to Americans. Vietnam is one of the largest coffee exporting countries in the world.

Over the years, I'd stop for a cup at the PhinDeli when I found myself between Cheyenne and Laramie. It was pretty good coffee, but it's tough for a business to make a go of it in the middle of nowhere, two dollars at a time.

The point-of-sale wasn't exactly Starbucks. The finger foods available were Lay's potato chips and Hostess Twinkies. The highest value items on the shelves were interesting drip coffee makers from Vietnam.

After the auction, the reporter on my crew wasn't able to talk to Pham, but it didn't matter because the reality TV producers were hoping one of the other American families would be the successful buyer, which they thought would have made a pretty good "fish out of water" story about them moving to Wyoming and all that goes along with that.

After first moving to Windsor, Colorado, Sammons ended up returning and worked with Pham and regained his mayoral status. He eventually hired a formal property manager who, in the long run, could not keep the doors open. The last time I drove by Buford, plywood sheets covered the windows, and the gas pumps were no more.

I had time to visit with Sammons, who was in Vietnam with the US Army, between 1968 to 1970. He said it was ironic that he and Pham were there in the military at the same time. I later heard that Pham had some contact with American culture when he served in the Army of the Republic of Vietnam (ARVN) between 1968 and1969 during "Vietnamization."

As the war in Vietnam became unpopular across America, President Nixon, following his reelection in 1972, began a gradual withdrawal strategy that reduced American involvement in Vietnam by transferring military responsibilities to the ARVN.

Personally, I think if Pham brought his family members from Vietnam to set up shop in Buford, they would have been some even bigger fish out of water and made for a wonderful reality TV show, but potentially with unintended consequences, like Pham characterized as fumbling and bumbling around Laramie trying to fit into an unknown culture.

Given his brief military background, I doubt Pham ever dreamed during his basic training that he'd own a place named for Civil War hero Major General John Buford. He took part in the Gettysburg Campaign that spelled the end of the Civil War in the United States.

Buford is Wyoming's tie to the Gettysburg battle fought between July 1 to 3, 1863. The main Confederate army, commanded by General Robert E. Lee, invaded Pennsylvania. Buford's defensive troop positions holding the high ground south of Gettysburg allowed additional troops to support and better control the field of battle.

The Union won a decisive victory at Gettysburg, with both sides taking heavy casualties. Buford continued to chase the Confederates in Virginia until General Lee eventually abandoned Richmond, the Confederate capitol in Virginia. Unable to reunite his forces, Lee and his twenty-eight thousand troops surrendered on April 9, 1865.

John Buford was well acquainted with the West. Throughout 1860, he was stationed in the western frontier. He and his fellow soldiers heard talk about the secession of the South and the possibility of civil war. That was confirmed when the Pony Express delivered information about Fort Sumter, South Carolina, fired upon in April 1861.

As with many West Pointers, Buford had a tough choice between siding with the North or South. Based on his being a native Kentuckian, son of a slave-owning father, Buford had cultural reasons to join the Confederacy. Several family members, including those of his wife, joined the South.

Buford attended school in the North and graduated from West Point before his deployment to the rugged frontier. He remained loyal to the US Army.

Whenever I drive by Buford, now abandoned, I'm reminded of fond memories as a kid allowed to goof around that bar and store. At eight thousand feet in elevation, Buford is the highest point on I-80. Because of the two-thousand-foot drop in elevation, the uneventful drive back to Cheyenne in my dad's pickup truck in a higher gear was always a little faster.

When we arrived back in downtown Cheyenne, and at the Japanese community, one of our stops was my grandfather's pool hall at 516 W. 17th St., where there was a Coke machine to restock.

My dad didn't allow me to enter for fear I might be exposed to the "libertine men and scarlet women" who frequented pool halls *The Music Man* con artist Professor Harold Hill warned about. After watching *The Music Man* live for the first time with my aunt in Salt Lake City, to date, I've seen six different renditions from dinner theater to community theater to high school productions of what is my favorite musical.

Professor Hill's come-on was convincing the unwitting citizens of River City, Iowa, that to keep boys out of trouble in a pool hall, they needed a town band. His huckster philosophy has served me well over the years.

To keep me pure, I had to wait at the door, but I remember the stale smell of tobacco in the room dimly lit by bluish fluorescent lights glowing above each green felt-covered table and the clatter of billiard balls.

Another downtown stop was at Boyd's Cigar Store at 308 W. 17th St. I couldn't go in there either, but an old "Call for Philip Morris" advertisement that pictured Johnny, the bellhop, on a sepia-tone cardboard sign hung on the wall near the entrance of the store. I still wonder what happened to that poster. It would be a real find today.

Uncle Mooch, my Salt Lake City uncle, was a cluttered kind of guy and took me into other strange places. He was a collector of a variety of things including a wall of old Kodak box cameras stacked neatly next to each other. He amassed them and was going to figure out what they were later. In the 1960s, he was the one who introduced me to organized clutter.

Mooch had all the junk stores scoped out, including the Salvation Army store on the edge of the Japanese community on the corner of Pioneer Avenue and West 17th Street. I started collecting affordable junk, like green and pink Depression-era glass, blue glass canning jars, paper stuff like posters, and baseball cards. As a kid, I knew nothing about the glassware other than it was old and would have value later. The pieces were inexpensive glassware which were premiums in soap and cereal boxes during the Great Depression.

Heirs salvaged leftover junk from family estate sales and hauled it to second-hand stores where it resold for a dime or quarter and, therefore, was affordable for a kid like me. I know Grandma Sakata used her green ice-cream bowls as regular tableware.

Fast forward twenty years, and suddenly, green and pink glassware became actual collectibles once the 1980s rolled around. I still have a couple of boxes filled with plates and serving dishes. Their values have increased by three hundred percent.

The most valuable pieces are known as Vaseline glass. They were made with small amounts of uranium that give them a yellowish iridescent look, like radioactive Vaseline.

My parents supported me in pursuing my junk collecting hobby. My dad enjoyed looking around, too. He always had an eye out for a good deal.

SEVEN: Yes, Nukes

Site of a decommissioned missile launch facility east of Cheyenne. This one was above ground and embedded among farm buildings.

Dad and I spent hours browsing around the Salvation Army, Goodwill, and army surplus stores. I had my eye out for interesting junk. He looked for extra can openers, water containers, tableware, and other sundry items to make life as normal as possible in a ten-by-ten-foot concrete room with no windows.

He led a family project building a fallout shelter in the basement and stocked it with canned food and water. Following a nuclear attack, "fallout" was nuclear dust that remained in the atmosphere and would eventually float down to the earth.

One of the guys who worked for my dad at the Coke plant was Bill Fisher. He was a practical fellow who knew a little about everything. For a kid, that was impressive. My dad hired him to help build the bomb shelter. Bill taught me how to mix up mortar and lay leveled concrete blocks, which is one of those life skills I'm glad I learned.

Our shelter was in the northeast corner of the basement at the bottom of the stairs, making for easy access. There was also a window well that led to the outside. Bill welded an air shaft from a steel pipe that led inside the shelter and vented to the outside.

There was a set of surplus bunk beds, a pantry where Dad stored canned goods and water, along with plates and tableware. The fallout shelter temperature was always the same and was a good place to hang out during hot summer days.

There wasn't a place to cook, but a Sterno camping stove could heat a can of soup in a small space. By this time, we had a roughed-in downstairs bathroom that was probably accessible during a nuclear war, but in the shelter, the backup toilet was a galvanized steel port-a-potty with a sealed cover.

After helping with the bomb shelter project, Bill worked with my dad and finished the basement that included two big recreation rooms, my new bedroom, and a full bathroom. Bill taught me how to solder together a sweat joint that attached two pieces of copper tubing.

While the grandparents were still living, bunches of my cousins came to visit Cheyenne. When my family hosted activities, the bomb shelter was one of the popular places to play. In the hot summer, it was also the coolest place in the house.

The US government became the first and, so far, the only one to deploy nuclear weapons when B-52 bombers dropped atomic bombs over Hiroshima and Nagasaki on August 6 and 9, 1945.

That had an enormous effect on my parents. Their families lived elsewhere in Japan and weren't directly exposed to the blast, but it was sobering to them, nonetheless.

The massive destruction that occurred ended World War II. Flying long distances to deliver bombs was cumbersome, and the US military began research to determine more efficient ways to deploy nuclear weapons on missiles.

In November 1952, the US military developed the much lighter and more powerful hydrogen bomb. The less cumbersome payload enabled missiles to be reduced in weight. Accuracy wasn't as important because the warheads were more powerful. Close only counts in horseshoes and with hydrogen bombs.

Twelve years after Hiroshima and Nagasaki, the Air Force ended up commanding the Atlas and Titan ICBM deployments. The Titan operational base ended up at Lowery Air Force Base in Denver and the Atlas at Warren Air Force Base (AFB) in Cheyenne.

Nuclear weapons began forty-five years of tension during the Cold War between two superpowers. The United States led the Western World, and the Union of Soviet Socialist Republics (USSR) led the eastern European communist countries until 1991.

Even though during World War II, the USSR was a key member of the Allied nations that led to the defeat of the Axis powers of Germany, Japan, and Italy, there was great distrust between the USSR and its allies over the cold-blooded and violent leadership of Joseph Stalin and the subsequent perceived problems that could result from the spread of Communism.

This ideological conflict between the United States and the USSR resulted in an undeclared war fought on nuclear arms and outer space battlefields. The two engaged in proxy wars with each superpower backing opposite sides, for example, in the undeclared wars in Korea and later in Vietnam.

I won't go into the contest to conquer outer space, except to say that when the USSR Sputnik satellite first left the Earth's atmosphere in 1957, that achievement lit a fire under US space program efforts.

The space race intensified when, in 1961, USSR cosmonaut Yuri Gagarin became the first man to leave the Earth's atmosphere and orbit the Earth. Later that year, US astronaut Alan Shepard Jr. was the first American in space, followed by John Glenn, who first orbited the Earth in 1962.

It wasn't until 1989 that the Cold War ended, symbolized by the fall of the Berlin Wall and the 1991 dissolution of the USSR. Russia continues to be at odds with the United States.

The dismantling of the USSR began in Poland in 1989 when the trade union Solidarity won an overwhelming victory in a partially free election in Poland that led to the fall of Communism there. Shortly thereafter, citizen action overthrew governments in Hungary, Bulgaria, Czechoslovakia, Romania, and East Germany.

Nuclear weapon proliferation, however, continues with the US and Russia pitting their best weapons in a war of Mutually Assured Destruction (MAD) with the idea that stockpiled weapons would deter each side from ever initiating an attack on the other.

During the Cold War, Cheyenne became a primary target because of the high concentration of intercontinental ballistic missile (ICBM) sites surrounding the city. The prospects of a nuclear attack were theoretical to me, but the likelihood of an attack was very real for my parents.

In 1960, the US Air Force deployed the first twenty-four Atlas missiles. That boost to the local economy was well-received in Cheyenne, where a military presence has been a constant for three centuries. Besides southeast Wyoming, missiles were scattered on ranches and farmlands across western Nebraska and northeastern Colorado.

By 1963, the Fort Warren AFB controlled around two hundred Minuteman 1b missile silos around southeast Wyoming, western Nebraska, and northeast Colorado.

The nuclear arsenal around Cheyenne normalized the Cold War. When I was in Cub Scouts, my Den made a field trip to visit a missile silo. I remember it to be north of Cheyenne. All the kids were from Fairview Elementary. We loaded up in two Den mothers' cars and drove up to an isolated farmhouse.

The building interior wasn't a farmhouse but a covering for the missile silo control room entrance. An Air Force security guy was there to meet us and account for everyone. We had to give our Social Security numbers. I can't remember if we descended in an elevator or climbed down a ladder, but the guards led our tour to an underground vestibule.

A thick, beveled, round metal door swung open, and we went inside the command room. There were two guys there who explained that it was pretty much impossible for a missile to be launched by mistake since each airman possessed a key that had to be turned simultaneously. I had the impression that the missile was in an underground silo some distance away from the control center.

A friend of mine who restores old train cars bought an abandoned missile site east of Cheyenne. That was a long structure where missiles were stored horizontally above ground and raised upright through a retractable roof.

The Air Force phased out Atlas missiles between 1963 and 1965 and replaced them with Minuteman I missiles, later by Minuteman III, between 1972 and 1975. The US and Russian nuclear stockpiles continue to be irrationally MAD.

There was a heightened time of international tension during October 1962, culminating with the Cuban Missile Crisis, between President John F. Kennedy (JFK) and USSR Premier Nikita Khrushchev.

I remember reading in the Weekly Reader about the USSR missile sites constructed in Cuba, ninety miles away from Florida. I don't know if kids still have access to the Weekly Reader, but it was a four-page tabloid newspaper with age-appropriate news written for elementary school students.

The Weekly Reader could have changed the way I learned.

In the first grade, the reading groups were broken down by the veracity of various birds. The top readers were in the Eagles, and the slow readers that included me were Sparrows.

The classification system was demeaning. Regardless, I saw Mrs. Stogsdill, my first-grade teacher, at the ten-year high school class reunion. I think she appreciated that I thanked her for teaching me how to read.

Had I been allowed to read non-fiction, like the *Weekly Reader*, rather than fiction, I would have become a better reader.

I couldn't relate to the Friends and Neighbors storylines with no character arc about Dick, Jane, Sally, Puff, and Spot, but I digress. To this day, I'm not much of a reader. It turned out I was an auditory and kinetic learner and still am. Not only did we read about the Cold War, but we also experienced it.

The Cold War was on the school agenda. At Fairview Elementary, we had periodic air raid drills. We learned what to do during a nuclear attack by watching Civil Defense filmstrips and movies telling us to duck under our desks and, "Do not look at the fireball." We practiced how to leave the classroom in an orderly fashion and head to the bomb shelter fashioned in the boiler room, ably operated by Mr. Costello, the custodian.

During recess, we boys would cover our heads with the tails of our coats and chase the girls around the playground, yelling "Duck and cover!" The drills were more for peace of mind because the USSR's nuclear missiles pointed at Cheyenne would vaporize everything within at least a one-hundred-mile radius.

When I'm in Cheyenne, I often drive by my old house on Windmill Road. One of these days, I'm going to get up the nerve, ring the doorbell, and ask if I can look around and see if the bomb shelter is still there.

I still roam around second-hand stores and flea markets. Now the big collectibles are mid-century modern artifacts, generally in use during the Baby Boomer Era. I picked up an old cardboard sign from the Cold War era that reads, "Nuclear Fallout Can Reach Your Community." I have it framed.

I've been toting around a set of mid-century modern nested mixing bowls. They are made of milky Pyrex glass painted brown with stalks of wheat silk-screened on the sides. My parents purchased that particular set at Gambles, and they were given to me when I started setting up a household.

They took up too much cabinet space, and I donated them to my cohousing community kitchen. If I need one, I can still put my hands on the big bowl for a batch of potato salad.

EIGHT: Intentional Community

The dorms at Hastings College was one housing configuration that accustomed me to living in intentional and accidental communities. My classmates Karen, Mary, and Debbie are close friends to this day.

Donating that brown mixing bowl set was an insignificant action but is an example of living in harmony with others. Civility includes actions of all sorts, not just political archenemies deciding to get along. It's not that I was hoarding those bowls, but giving something up for the good of the group is sometimes difficult since it means reimagining Superman's American Way.

Civility was a big characteristic of my family's open-door social fabric. That prepared me for my other living situations in the future.

My dad had a huge family, thirteen brothers and sisters. One sister, Mae, died, and the remaining twelve grew up in downtown Cheyenne in a boarding house across from the UP Depot, on West 15th Street, then at 620 W. 18th St.

I'm a user of Ancestry.com and received a hint notification about a boy and girl not mentioned in family lore, and so my research continues.

A new cousin showed up in my paternal family database, too, bringing the cousin total to nineteen. Most of them have families, including my "newest" cousin. I've met very few second-cousins who are children of my first cousins.

My grandparents later moved from downtown to 714 E. 8th St. on the south side, which became the family headquarters. Uncle Rich purchased it in his name since he was a native-born citizen.

We had a huge extended family. I spent quite a bit of time with my dad's brothers and sisters. None of them had kids until later, so I ended up having influences from many adults at an early age. I remember one group activity at 714 around the polio epidemic.

During the early 1950s, polio rates in the United States were above twenty-five thousand annually; in 1952, a domestic outbreak happened with fifty-eight thousand polio cases and thirty-two hundred deaths that year.

According to historical accounts, polio has been around since ancient Egyptian times. A hieroglyph of what appears to be a man with a withered foot dates back to the Fourteenth century BC.

Epidemiologists theorize that polio spread in the industrialized world because improved health conditions left people of all ages susceptible to the virus.

There were a few kids in my schools who had polio. One neighbor kid named Tim wore leg support and a hearing aid. Nobody thought much of it. A leg brace was akin to wearing glasses. Not that many kids wore glasses, either.

The year I was born in 1953, Jonas Salk developed an inactive virus vaccine, which became publicly available two years later, and was delivered to patients by injection.

In 1961, we had a big Ohashi family gathering at my grandparents' house on the south side. We all walked down to the neighborhood fire station, where we stood in a long line waiting to get our sugar cube laced with the attenuated polio vaccine developed by Albert Sabin.

Joining the fight against polio was the patriotic thing to do. It was like taking my first communion when I savored a few drops of grape juice in one of those micro-chalices and washed down a crouton-sized cube of Wonder Bread. It was a badge of honor to say that I had taken my sugar cube.

At school, teachers handed out cardboard coin holders. Every week, the March of Dimes asked kids to donate ten cents. A dime was a lot of money to me and gave me a sense of pride when I slipped the coin into the sleeve.

As I grew older, willingly taking the polio vaccine on sugar cubes, participating in civil defense drills at school, and helping Dad stock the fallout shelter seemed like acts of patriotism.

I inspected Grandma Ohashi's cellar, thinking it would be a bomb shelter of sorts if there was nuclear war and we didn't have time to get home. I don't know how long anyone could stay down there. It was musty but a solid concrete foundation where my grandmother had jars of canned food stored. She was a gardener and put up some of her vegetables, including pickled spicy radishes called takuwan.

Over the years, they added on to the back of the house but didn't encroach on my grandmother's garden.

She had quite the green thumb, and one of the family activities was string bean picking from the vines that wound their way up the laths poked into the fertile earth. After picking, my favorite job was popping off the stems and plinking the pod ends into a pan and the beans into a paper bag. My grandmother rewarded the family harvesters with stir-fried beans and bacon over rice.

There was a revolving door of uncles and aunts who stopped by daily, not to mention frequent formal and informal family gatherings—holidays, birthday parties, random dinners, watching sports on TV, and worm hunting.

The summer was also fishing season. After dark, the cousins helped Uncle Rich catch night crawling earthworms from the backyard. In the cool of the night, the worms wiggled their way out into the grass. Cousin Matthew would be the spotter with a flashlight, and I would grab the slimy creature before it retreated into its hole in the lawn.

The Westside and Southside kids had quite a worm business niche selling them around town, but I figured out that I didn't want to be responsible for any product that had a shelf life.

Both sides of my family were fishers. The summer between my kindergarten and first-grade year, my dad bought bait-cast fishing reels from the Gambles store in the Cole Shopping Center for my sister and me. That's the same Gambles where my mom bought the nested mixing bowl set.

The reason I know when this happened is that we still lived on East 10th Street. Our rods and reels were the same but labeled with our names painted on with red fingernail polish. This was before felt-tipped Magic Markers.

A bait-cast reel mounted on a pole is fishing in its purest form. The fishing line is wrapped around a spool, bait attached to the hook, which is lowered into the water, or lightly cast.

We would make family outings to the lake near the Cheyenne Country Club. There were some pretty good holes near the concrete rickrack made of busted-up street curbing and old sidewalks. We would stop by to see Uncle Rich and pick up a few worms on the way out.

My dad's job was to help bait the hooks. I was never squeamish and was okay with threading the hook through the wriggling critter. Mom's job was untangling the fishing line. The first fishing trip was a successful one. I caught a small perch that was part of our dinner that night. Mom coated it with flour, dipped it in egg, then cornmeal, and pan-fried it.

Of all my dad's brothers, Rich was the most avid sportsman. On the way home, we stopped and showed off the day's catch. He liked to take me along on fishing trips to Crystal and Granite reservoirs a few miles from Cheyenne because he would get to use an extra pole.

My immediate and extended family units were tightly knit. We had disagreements but always overcame them. I remember when I was in kindergarten, having to give up my bedroom when my grandfather moved in with us for a period of time. I complained about it but understood the importance of my dad's role as caretaker since he's the only other local family member who owned a private home.

My grandfather had diabetes, and my grandmother couldn't care for him. After he moved in, it didn't cross my mind to complain about sleeping on a cot in my parents' room or on the couch. Being displaced from my usual sleeping patterns from time to time taught me to sleep anywhere and in any position.

His big insulin syringe that consisted of a glass barrel, stainless steel plunger, and big needle fascinated me. One morning, he showed me how to stab the syringe into his thigh muscle and administer his medication. Maybe that's why I'm okay with being poked by large numbers of acupuncture needles.

Since both sets of grandparents lived in Cheyenne, there were multiple holiday celebrations—two Thanksgiving dinners and two Christmases. My dad always invited Bill Fisher over for Thanksgiving. We were his holiday family. After our family Christmas, while on the way to the grandparents', we always stopped by Bill's place and dropped off baked goodies and a present.

Bill was a hermit, maybe that was Post Traumatic Stress Disorder (PTSD)-related, but he was very smart about science. He worked around the plant sorting bottles, helped on the production line, but his main job was working on the vending machine refrigeration systems.

His place was located across the street from the Coke plant. When I went to work with my dad on Saturdays, I goofed around inside the plant but eventually made my way over to Bill's.

He subscribed to "Things of Science," an educational program launched by the nonprofit news syndicate Science Service in November 1940. A series of science kits, available by subscription, was mailed out each month.

The Science Service packed each kit in a small blue cardboard box, about the size of a portable hard drive, with a yellow address label. Included inside was a simple science project. I remember one being a crystal radio set, and another was a small motor run on electromagnetic current, battery not included.

One Christmas, Bill bought me a subscription. The cost was five dollars for the year. He was a quiet guy and an enormous influence on me. When I was in high school, I put my artistic talent aside to concentrate on the hard sciences that Bill had first nurtured in me.

At college, after living in a high-energy family environment, living in the dorms came naturally to me. Not only did I live in the dorms all four years, but in the exact same room. Altman Hall had a nice lobby and a downstairs with a kitchen and TV room. Altman was also the "co-ed" dorm—men in one wing and women in the opposite side of the lobby but joined by the basement, which had the TV room and a large open recreation area.

I had no yearning to live off-campus, not seeing the utility of living with maybe a couple of other people who may or may not be more irresponsible than me. Most of the kids at Hastings College were from Nebraska and thought living in their own house when they were twenty was a sign of maturity.

My preference was to have many classmates around, share meals in the cafeteria, and play pool or shoot the breeze afterward. Going off to college a day's drive away from Cheyenne was very liberating in my way of thinking.

Soon enough, I got a chance to live with housemates. My first job took me to Gillette, Wyoming, where I chipped in with two other guys. Tom served in Vietnam and used his GI Bill benefits. He qualified for one hundred percent financing, and the three of us purchased a three-bedroom split-level house.

We set up what would now be referred to as a "co-op" house that became known as the "3003 Club," which was our address on Foothills Blvd. We each had a bedroom and added space for another in the basement. We shared the kitchen, living room, and bathroom, prepared common meals, and divided household chores. Our living arrangement was more like a commune because we had a shared economy with each of us owning an undivided third of the property.

After moving for a new job in Lander, my first apartment was downtown above the Ace Hardware store. This was before mixed-use urban living was fashionable.

When commuting from Lander to Boulder, working on a project with Northern Arapaho tribal artists, I did my share of sofa surfing with friends and strangers. Eventually, I lived in what I later learned was an intentional community that had Buddhism as its higher purpose.

Six of us had separate rooms, but decisions were made by consensus, particularly when Richard, the house organizer, invited a new member to live with us. One person we agreed to invite as a housemate was a slob, didn't keep up with his designated chores, and was a short timer.

I'll mention that living around and on top of other people continues to be a way of life for me today. I live in a cohousing intentional community in North Boulder, Colorado.

My cohousing community consists of sixteen privately owned condominiums occupied by around thirty residents who own private homes and have agreed to share a common mission and values about living together while maintaining the common spaces like the courtyard and provide neighborly help to one another.

Because cohousers have a civility agreement among themselves to reimagine Superman's American Way, they are well suited to bridge the massive cultural divides that exist today.

Individual material accumulation characterizes success in America. Bigger and more is better, majority rules, and people viewed as different from the dominant culture are excluded unless they assimilate.

There's nothing inherently wrong with material success and individuals excelling to the best of their abilities, but what rugged individuals achieved Superman's American Way collaboratively?

The basic philosophy behind cohousing is that the good of the group is viewed as more important than self-interested individual wants, smaller and less are better, decisions are by consensus giving a voice to all, including opinions of the few, and there is a recognition that everyone is different, and all are included without assimilation.

Cohousing returns to a community construct when families knew each other because their kids all went to the same neighborhood school. That would be my Baby Boomer socialization.

While the tenets of cohousing are noble, they are easier said than done since Superman's American Way is pounded into our heads from the moment we pop out of the womb.

Based on how I grew up with a strong extended family, living in the dorms, buying into a co-op as my first home as an owner, my transition to cohousing was easy. Getting along by giving and taking has been my way of living.

NINE: Upwardly Mobile Middle Class

The main neighborhood gathering point in the Cole Addition was the community swimming pool.

I lived in Wyoming from my birth in 1953 until 1993 or so. Other than my experiences, I paid little attention to the Japanese community history in Cheyenne until researching this story. It was a cultural renaissance that brought up lots of memories and a bit of angst.

My Wyoming end time is indeterminate since I kept an apartment in Lander. I continued to do work from there, including commuting to Boulder and Bozeman, Montana.

My transition from Lander to Colorado was unsettling. I was a relatively big fish in the small Wyoming pond and didn't prepare myself as well as I should have when I moved pretty much sight-unseen to Colorado. Colorado was a tough crowd.

My work with the Northern Arapaho Tribe initially brought me to Boulder to assist with a cultural exchange project. Ever since then, the Boulder community has placed me in the role of a minority advocate.

I was working for the Northern Arapaho Tribe on the Wind River Indian Reservation. Lander is a border town. Many tribal artists and I were creating a "cultural conduit" between the reservation and Boulder, Colorado, which was the traditional homeland for the Arapaho Tribe.

That was the time I decided to move there.

"You watch out," an Arapaho elder warned me. "You're more like us than them," he said, referring to my skin color. "You know the history of our tribe and the Sand Creek Massacre."

It was a tough move, and he was right. I realized I hadn't experienced any overt racial discrimination in Wyoming as an adult until I moved to Boulder. That was strange since Boulder earned a reputation of being a town of liberals and progressives—The Peoples' Republic of Boulder.

I blended in very well as a model minority. All Asians, regardless of ethnicity, are stereotyped as being hard workers and obedient, which are good characteristics for an outsider wanting to fit in with the American Way. While in Wyoming, I never had to find a job. They always found me.

Looking for work in Colorado was difficult. I did a lot of consulting before the "gig economy" became trendy. While my Wyoming track record ran about a hundred percent success as a fundraiser and grant writer, in my new place, the perspective I met was, "What have you done lately?" Maybe it's because Colorado has more people, but job opportunities passed over me time and time again. I also came to learn that fund development people in Colorado had a certain look that I didn't have.

I thought about moving back to Wyoming since I never had an actual send-off. Many of my Wyoming acquaintances think I still live there.

Wyoming is one of those places where it's tough to make a clean break because there's still a lot of "street cred" around being a Wyoming native. The state is the least populated, with five hundred and seventy-seven thousand people.

There are more than twice as many cattle that graze around Wyoming than humans. Wyomingites characterize our home state as a small town connected by long streets. There's a lot of truth to that.

When I see a random person walking around, pretty much anywhere, wearing a Wyoming-marked garment or a ball cap with the state bucking horse logo, I stop and talk with them. Chances are, we'll have some person in common, or at a minimum, some story about a place or event.

Since 1986, one of my stops in New York City is a bar and restaurant in the Theater District of Manhattan called Sardi's, which has been in business since 1927. The walls are covered with maybe a thousand caricatures of show biz celebrities.

Sardi's is a popular pre- and post-theater gathering spot. A scene in a Mel Brooks movie called *The Producers* (1967) is a satirical look at corruption and the casting couch in the theater business starring Zero Mostel and Gene Wilder. During their musical Springtime for Hitler intermission, the enthusiastic theatergoers flow into a bar, reminiscent of Sardi's.

While I was in Lander, I also was a sportswriter and columnist for the WSJ. The best benefits from being a part of the working news media are press passes. In 1986, I followed the UW basketball team that played in the National Invitational Tournament final four in Madison Square Garden. The Cowboys lost in the title game to Ohio State, 73-63.

A group of Pokes fans who stayed at the Marriot Marquis hotel drank the nearby Sardi's bar out of tequila. I've been going there ever since. The bar snacks are Ritz Crackers and cheese spread with mixed-in port wine. I always have a container of that in the fridge for old time's sake.

A few years later, I visited New Jersey on a project and ended up in New York City in the late 1980s.

An obligatory stop was always Sardi's. My colleague and I tried to get into the bar but were stopped by a tall and wide bouncer. The upstairs was closed for a private post-theater event. Who should walk down the stairs, but US Senator Al Simpson (R-Wyo.) and his wife, Ann. We first met while I was in grad school at UW and as an intern at the Wyoming state legislature when Al represented Park County.

They were in town for a show that opened at the Helen Hayes Theater across the street. It was one of those "What are you doing here?" moments. After some small talk about the event, the bouncer stepped aside and allowed my colleague and me into the private party.

It reminded me of the scene from The Wizard of Oz when Dorothy and her entourage pounded on the door to get in to see the Wizard and were greeted by a mustachioed doorman. "Well bust my buttons, c'mon in!"

Another time, I met my cousin, Milton, from San Francisco in Laramie. We went out to the Buckhorn Bar.

"Hey, I know you," the Buckhorn bouncer said. He and Milton were Galileo High School classmates. Galileo High School also is O.J. Simpson's alma mater.

I'd say any Wyomingite reading this book has a similar "all roads lead through Wyoming" story.

Cheyenne was also very insular and self-contained during my childhood years. My parents moved us to the suburbs of Cheyenne, where living in that cultural environment socialized me to be part of the rising American middle class. They waited until I was out of kindergarten to make the move.

At the end of the Industrial Revolution during the mid-Nineteenth century, Americans improved their standards of living. In the early part of the Twentieth century, the first suburban areas developed, largely because of improvements in mass transportation, and personal automobiles became more available. Americans no longer had to live near where they worked.

Nationwide, during the 1950s and 1960s, suburban residents grew from thirty-five million to eighty-four million, according to the US Census. This alternative to urban living gave a new middle class the chance to separate themselves from other urban-centered economic and racial groups that included our Japanese community.

What happened to all the Japanese?

Between 1900 and 1910, the Wyoming Japanese population increased from 303 to 1,590 persons, surpassing Native Americans as the second largest minority population in the state, according to the US Census. That population increase is generally attributed to work available on the railroads and in agriculture.

The 1940 US Census reports 643 Japanese in Wyoming during the war years. By 2010, the Wyoming Japanese population declined to 485 residents. Suburbanization, coupled with discriminatory land ownership laws in place at the time of World War II, contributed to the demise of the Japanese community.

We lost the Cheyenne Japanese neighborhood's history and all the buildings that were razed over the years. I circled back to my past when I walked around the 400 and 500 blocks of West 17th Street and stared at the asphalt parking lots thinking about my experiences growing up as a kid.

I knew about some of the Japanese-run businesses but was largely detached from the people because I couldn't speak or understand the Japanese language.

TEN: The California Fish Market

Bill Matsuyama and his son, Jim, pose in front of the California Fish Market. They later sold to the Kishiyama family.

When John Dinneen asked me to compile historical information about the Japanese community, that exercise brought up many memories and piqued my curiosity and recalled my recollections of the Japanese community.

The Japanese neighborhood on West 17th Street was once vibrant and active. Some families lived above their businesses, including at the California Fish Market, originally located at 402 and owned by Itsuo and Kamo Hashimoto beginning in 1920.

In the early part of the Twentieth century, with limited transportation, pedestrians were accepting of mixed-use living in homes above businesses. Living and working in the same building was a common configuration throughout downtown Cheyenne, as it was in other urban areas.

Itsuo immigrated to the United States in 1905 and worked in gold mines in California, Nevada, and Arizona. In 1913, he moved to Cheyenne and worked for the UP railroad. He married his "picture-bride," Kamo.

In the early Twentieth century, immigrant workers in the United States, largely from Asian countries, would choose a bride by way of a matchmaker in their home country who paired the bride and groom using photographs and family suggestions as to the best spousal combinations.

Japanese matchmaking is the subject of a movie called *Picture Bride* (1995), about a young Japanese woman who moves to meet her future husband at a Hawaiian pineapple plantation. His "dating" profile didn't quite match up with his current persona, and his bride couldn't afford to move back to Japan.

Kamo operated the fish market while Itsuo continued to work for the railroad. Together, they had six children. Their two sons, Harry and Kaye, had jobs in downtown Cheyenne. Harry was a chef at the UP Depot and the Plains Hotel.

Later, he was well known as the food services manager at UW. Because I lived in both Laramie and Cheyenne, and since all Asians look alike, I was often mistaken for being a Hashimoto.

Kaye was one of the main portrait photographers in Cheyenne. His first studio was downtown at 2300 Carey Ave. He took my high school graduation photo at his studio on East Pershing Boulevard.

Their sister, Grace, was a good friend of my auntie Rose. They both ended up in San Francisco. The two couples lived in adjacent apartments on Webster Street near Japantown. Grace married Toshiaki "Gump" Kubota. Rose married Haruo "Vince" Ichiyasu and reared my California cousins, Carolyn, Milton, Teresa, Leonard, and Walter.

I was contacted out of the blue on Facebook, wondering if I was related to Rose Ohashi. The mysterious person e-mailed me images of a birth certificate for an infant born in Denver who was adopted by a family from Lusk, Wyoming.

I first thought the request was an internet scam. I compared notes with two friends from Lusk. Sue was my cousin's babysitter, and Phil, a retired UW professor, knew Jerry to be a local history buff. After spitting in an Ancestry.com DNA test tube, the stories matched up with the genetics. I learned I had an extra cousin named Jerry (née Gary) and his daughters named Kristi and Roni, my second cousins. Kristi happens to live in Lander.

A freakish industrial accident caused Jerry's death. His non-Japanese father's identity continues to be a mystery.

Grace and Gump had two sons, Warren and Russell. Warren wrote an award-winning play about his Vietnam War-era childhood called *The Webster Street Blues* set in 1972. Knowing Warren, the play narrative is an introspective autobiography based on the Kubota and Ichiyasu families.

The story is about four Sansei friends who hang around Japantown in San Francisco and their angst about living in their Japanese world and also having to exist within the dominant culture. The story ends with the characters grown up and giving in to mainstream society, but not forgetting their roots.

California theater critics didn't understand the story's familial subtexts and largely panned the play. Warren died shortly before the August 1987 premiere in San Francisco. I received permission from his brother, Russell, to produce it. He sent me a draft of the stage play, which I rewrote and produced at the Mercury Café in Denver.

Not being very close to the Denver theater production crowd, it was challenging to find four actors to portray Japanese teenagers. The cast ended up being four pan-Asian twenty-somethings who had no acting experience. The project raised disaster relief funds following the 2011 earthquake that rocked Japan.

In 1931, the Hashimoto family sold the fish market to Masuji and Yoshi Matsuyama. They reinvested the money from the fish market sale and opened the Mikado Cleaners nearby at 1617 Pioneer Ave., which was north of the Dinneen

Garage between 16th and 17th. They operated the business until 1946 when they sold to Tatsu and Marie Takahashi, who renamed the business as Miracle Cleaners in the same location.

During the war, the Japanese community hall was first on the second floor above the Mikado Cleaners and later near the California Fish Market.

ELEVEN: Accidental Disloyalty

My mom's sister Hisako worked at Fort Warren in Cheyenne. She helped organize a big party for the Japanese American soldiers stationed there on December 7, 1941. Nobody was in a very good mood considering the bombing that happened earlier that day.

The Matsuyamas abandoned their farming work near Fort Lupton, Colorado. They moved to Cheyenne, where Masuji worked as a railroad machinist at the UP roundhouse, and Yoshi tended to the fish market. A roundhouse is a huge building into which railroad train locomotives are serviced.

The Matsuyama's oldest son, Bill, took over the fish market in 1932, shortly after his graduation from Cheyenne High School. Things were good for the Matsuyamas until Pearl Harbor was bombed. UP fired Masuji in 1942 because of fears stemming from EO 9066.

Heart Mountain camp internee and author Bill Hosokawa was the editor of *The Sentinel* camp newspaper and a well-known writer at *The Denver Post.* He wrote a book about the Heart Mountain camp experience titled *Nisei: The Quiet Americans* (1969).

Bill was friends with my parents. I think through Auntie Hisako. When out on his book tour, Bill had dinner at our house a time or two. I missed those opportunities and would have liked to know him but wasn't invited.

I likely showed little interest. Local Japanese history was not on my radar screen. I was trying to put what little I knew as far back in my brain as I could shove it, still striving to be the model minority. I should have paid closer attention.

Each of the ten relocation camps published at least one paper. The Sentinel was an eight-page weekly tabloid that the internees published from October 1942 until July 1945. The newspaper kept internees informed about WRA policies and maintained morale with news about internees and camp activities.

Early editions of *The Sentinel* were typewritten offset-printed handouts distributed before the tabloid newspaper format. The newspaper staff named their paper after the geologic Heart Mountain landmark because it watched over the camp like a sentinel. They wanted the newspaper to serve as a guardian for the internees.

According to Hosokawa in his book, *Nisei*, the Japanese were serving in the US military well before the bombing of Pearl Harbor. Several recently inducted Nisei soldiers were stationed at Fort Warren outside of Cheyenne in 1941.

It was an army base where Auntie Hisako worked as secretary to the base chaplain. She arranged to get passes for the Nisei GIs stationed there to attend a dance planned for December 7th at the Japanese community hall.

That day, the Cheyenne Japanese community prepared a spread of traditional food for the soldiers and arranged for a record player, not a common living room item back then, to provide music and accompany some dancing.

Despite all the planning, nobody was in a very good mood to dance to the music and partake in the fancy dinner. All returned to the base and listened to FDR declare war against Japan on the radio the next day.

My aunt's experience after Pearl Harbor reminded me of a family connection to 9/11. That day, the American Airlines (AA) Flight 11 aircraft was a Boeing 767 scheduled to take off from Boston's Logan International Airport (BOS) to the LAX airport in Los Angeles.

One of the crew members that morning was flight attendant Betty Ong. She scheduled herself on AA Flight 11, so she could meet her sister in Los Angeles on their way to Hawaii for a vacation.

The aircraft capacity was 158 passengers, but on September 11th, the flight was only about half full.

After five passengers hijacked the plane, Betty made an Airfone call. Airfone was an air-to-ground telephone signal broadcast over radio frequencies. MCI developed the technology and allowed passengers to make in-flight telephone calls for around four dollars. MCI discontinued the Airfone service in 2006 due to lack of use.

Betty contacted the AA operations center in Raleigh, North Carolina. She told the center supervisor that five bad guys hijacked her aircraft and provided the hijackers' seat assignments, which later led investigators to learn their identities.

Onboard that morning were Mohamed Atta, Abdulaziz al-Omari, and Suqami in business class, while Waleed al-Shehri and Wail al-Shehri sat in first-class seats.

The heroine of AA Flight 11 was Betty Ong, one of the ninety-two passengers who perished that morning, and the fiancé of my San Francisco cousin, Leonard.

By World War II, the fish market was relocated down the block at 422 W. 17th St. Bill Matsuyama, and his wife, Mary Arima, lived in the apartment above the market with their two sons, Brian and Jim. The two boys are much older than me, and I didn't know them, although I received information and old photos from Brian for this story and the companion documentary film.

Mary ended up in Cheyenne by way of Worland after her internment at Tule Lake camp in California, which became the largest and most notorious of the ten camps, with a peak population of close to nineteen thousand internees.

About five hundred Japanese volunteers arrived a month ahead of time to help set up the Tule Lake camp in preparation for the first group of Japanese initially herded into assembly centers at Sacramento, Pinedale, Marysville, Pomona, and Salinas.

After the WCCA sorted and processed the initial thirty-two hundred detainees, they traveled to the Tule Lake camp that formally opened in May 1942. The Tule Lake camp population originated primarily from Sacramento County, California; King County, Washington; and Hood River County, Oregon.

By 1945, the Tule Lake camp developed manufacturing businesses, including a tofu factory, a bakery, furniture factory, a hog farm, and a slaughtering facility. There were also goods and services provided by a shoe repair shop, a beauty shop, a fish market, a funeral home, along with several co-op stores. The Tule Lake camp had eight Buddhist churches, three Christian churches, and four dojos where judo was practiced.

A dojo is a formal training place for the Japanese martial arts ending in "do," which is derived from the Chinese Dao, which means the "way" in the sense of a path or course.

The Tule Lake camp became the most infamous when in February 1943, the WRA and the US Army distributed Statement of US Citizenship of Japanese American Ancestry application forms for leave clearance.

Internees seventeen years old and older in the camp network were required to fill out the questionnaire before they were allowed to exit the camp.

The application form was ill-conceived and resulted in disharmony ranging from refusal to complete the form to outright violence among the internees, resulting in political and bureaucratic nightmares for the WRA.

The Tule Lake camp became known for the largest internee insurrection. News of the Tule Lake "riot" spread quickly and escalated the already high levels of anti-Japanese sentiment.

Two questions intended to separate the "loyal" from the "disloyal" internees sparked the most controversy when respondents gave "no" answers to both. The disloyal became known as the "no-no" boys.

Conversely, those who answered "yes" to both questions were deemed to be "loyal" or "yes-yes" boys.

Question #27: *Are you willing to serve in the armed forces of the United States on combat duty wherever ordered?*

Issei men asked this question were far older than the age allowed to serve in the military, and a "no" answer would be construed as "disloyal." This question caused a split. Some draft-age Nisei were willing to show their loyalty and enlisted, while others, most infamously from the Heart Mountain camp in Wyoming, resisted and were imprisoned.

Question #28: *Will you swear unqualified allegiance to the United States of America and faithfully defend the United States from any or all attack by foreign or domestic forces, and forswear any form of allegiance or obedience to the Japanese emperor, or any other foreign government, power, or organization?*

This question was also problematic to Issei, who were not allowed US citizenship and were asked to renounce allegiance to the only country where they were citizens. The Nisei were reluctant to fill out the questionnaire because answering "yes" to both questions would contradict their Issei parents' responses and would be viewed as disrespectful.

The Tule Lake camp ended up with the largest number of internees who gave clear no-no responses and were deemed disloyal. Those who responded with qualified yes answers by adding comments like "when our family civil rights are restored" were also designated as disloyal.

Of the nearly eleven thousand responses to Question #27 about military service, thirty percent refused to give unqualified yes-yes responses. In their responses to Question #28 about disavowing loyalty to Japan, sixteen percent were considered disloyal because they qualified their yes answers.

Violators could be assessed ten-thousand-dollar fines, sentenced to twenty years in prison, or both. Despite the risks and consequences, authorities locked up Tule Lake camp no-no boys in the Klamath Falls and Alturas County jails.

After that, in July 1943, the WRA changed the camp designation. Tule Lake became a Segregation Center as the camp where no-no Japanese would be corralled. By September, over twelve thousand no-no Japanese were moved from the other nine camps.

The most activist internees lived in one place reminiscent of Stalag Luft III in Germany, which was the German POW camp that imprisoned mostly military officers from the Allied forces and was fictionalized in *The Great Escape* (1963). A movie starring Steve McQueen about how the cunning POWs planned the most daring escape during the war in Europe.

A few months later, thousands of men, women, and children gathered around the Tule Lake camp administrative headquarters, where a meeting was held. The crowd came to support their elected representatives, the Daihyo Sha Kai (negotiating group), that protested food shortages, poor working conditions, and the hospital staff's bedside lack-of-manners.

At the meeting, a story traveled through the crowd about the death of an infant girl who fell into scalding water at the hospital. The attending physician refused to transfer the girl to a fully equipped hospital. The crowd received a report, and a pack of young internees entered the hospital and severely beat the doctor.

In response, the US Army occupied the camp with tanks rolling through the barracks. Soldiers fired tear gas and aimed .50-caliber machine guns at bystanders.

The military moved into Tule Lake. The camp came under maximum-security martial law from November 1943 until January 1944. Internees were subject to a curfew. More barbwire was added to a sixteen-foot-high fence. The camp administrators offered fewer daily recreational activities. The six guard towers surrounding the camp were increased to twenty-eight, and a battalion of an estimated one thousand military police (MP) with armored cars and tanks were deployed.

They pawed through private quarters seeking contraband and searched the entire camp, hunting down the negotiating group leaders.

Tule Lake camp management became more complicated. Two-thirds of the camp population consisted of activist leaders and no-no boys from the other nine camps.

Even though no criminal charges were filed, the Tule Lake camp dissidents were incarcerated, along with hundreds of other disobedient internees from the other relocation camps around the country.

The remaining third of the camp population was considered loyal and did not want to be reassigned to another relocation camp, while other loyals were dispersed to other camps.

While he owned the fish market, Bill Matsuyama became a trusted leader in the Cheyenne Japanese community during the war. He was a liaison with federal and local law enforcement. There were no confrontations or uprisings in Cheyenne.

In 1951, the Matsuyamas sold the fish market to my coattail uncle and aunt Carl and Lucy Kishiyama. Kanekichi "Carl" Kishiyama emigrated from Oredo, Japan, and settled near Scottsbluff, Nebraska. Lucy Shiyomura was born in Lucerne, Colorado, and went to work in Denver to earn additional income to support her family.

Their parents served as matchmakers and arranged for Carl and Lucy to meet. Two days later, they were married.

The newlyweds later farmed near Meridan in eastern Laramie County before moving to Cheyenne. The family lived above the market with their children, Carol Lou, Jeanne, Janice, and Lucy's brother Larry.

Larry was much older than me, and I didn't know him well when I was a kid. When we were both adults, I became reacquainted with Larry after he moved to Boulder, where I live now. He was a martial arts sensei (teacher).

I found out Larry lived in Boulder when we had a random meet-up near Laramie. I made a pit stop at the twelve-foot-tall Abraham Lincoln bust atop a thirty-foot-high granite pedestal monument at the Summit Rest Area and Visitor Center between Cheyenne and Laramie on I-80.

The sculptor, Robert Russin, was an art professor at UW. He originally erected the sculpture in 1959 nearby on Sherman Hill overlooking the old US Highway 30. After I-80 was built, the Wyoming Highway Department moved the monument to its current location.

Russin gained his initial notoriety as a New Deal artist. He has two sculptures at the US Post Office in Evanston, Illinois. I produced a documentary entitled *New Deal Artist Public Art Legacy* (2018) that included Russin and his work that aired on Wyoming Public Broadcasting System (PBS).

Through my Volkswagen Eurovan front windshield, there was Larry walking out of the visitor center. He was cruising around on his motorcycle. We had a brief conversation and agreed to meet up back in Boulder.

We traded services, with me digitizing some of his martial arts video recordings in exchange for carpentry work. Larry passed away before he could get the flower box built.

Jeanne married my uncle Jake, who owned Pioneer Printing for several years at 514 W. 19th St. Pioneer Printing also carried other paper products. Larry's sister, Jeanne, had a presence in Cheyenne's Westside. Carol Lou and Jeanne delivered paper-ware like napkins and cups to area restaurants.

Jake and his partners sold out around the time digital printing took off. The newly configured business moved from downtown but could not catch hold. After 148 years in business, Pioneer Printing closed in 2018.

Jake and Jeanne had two daughters, my cousins, Alison and Leslie. They are the only two members of the original O'Hashi/Ohashi and Sakata families who still live in Cheyenne. Jake and my dad are the only siblings who used the O'Hashi spelling.

Alison is a psychologist, and Leslie operates a Pilates business and the nonprofit Body Lines Dance Studio for which Wyoming Governor Matt Mead presented her an art award in 2017 that honored her work with adaptive dance for mentally and physically less able youth.

Jake was my dad's youngest brother. According to his 1990 newspaper account, Jake recalls their house being searched by the Federal Bureau of Investigation (FBI).

According to the story, agents confiscated the hunting rifles and checked the radio to ensure it didn't have shortwave capabilities.

Jake's taste in music rubbed off on me. Thinking back, the radio station in all the family homes was set to KFBC, which programmed easy listening music, instead of KRAE, which played pop tunes.

He listened to Burt Bacharach. Bacharach was a prolific pop music composer during the 1960s. He collaborated with lyricist Hal David, and the two wrote several hits sung by Dionne Warwick, including "This Guy's in Love with You," which topped the charts in 1968.

I was definitely "planned." My parents were married for seven years before I came along, which explains my taste in music. My peers had parents much younger than mine and listened to rock-and-roll as opposed to my folks, who were more of the Big Band era.

While all my friends were buying rock-and-roll record albums, I was into Herb Alpert, Frank Sinatra, and Andy Williams. When I'm in the car by myself, which is most times, my Bacharach mix is the most played, truth be known.

After the Kishiyamas got out of the seafood business in 1955, the location became Ace Billiards, Dunbar's Recreation, and Geeche's Pawn Shop before being vacant in 1961.

Carl Kishiyama stayed downtown and worked as a custodian at a bank. Lucy was a well-known florist for most of her working life.

TWELVE: Baker's Place: Prohibition and Integration

Tomizo "Bill" Miyamoto poses at Baker's Bar. He was in business with Johnny Baker in what was the only integrated bar in Cheyenne at the time.

According to son Brian, the Matsuyamas lived next to a Cheyenne businessman named John A. "Johnny" Baker near the West 17th Street Japanese community. Brian said Johnny was a good neighbor, but not much else is known about the guy.

Baker was a former Cheyenne police officer and a longtime bar boarding house owner at 416 and 418 W. 17th St. As early as 1922, Aikichi Kake, Sami Yoshimura, Kambe, and Yoshio Nomura occupied the boarding house above 416 that was the Walter Davis Barber Shop. The Cheyenne City Directory first mentions Baker in 1926.

Regardless, all I've been able to find about Baker is his family has a nice headstone in the Lakeview Cemetery, where he, his wife, and mother are buried.

Around 1939, Johnny began a partnership with Tomizo "Bill" Miyamoto. He moved from Denver to Cheyenne to go into business with Baker.

Baker's Bar was reportedly the only integrated establishment in Cheyenne. In response to more Americans owning automobiles and becoming more mobile, *The Negro Motorist Green Book* travel guide was compiled that listed restaurants, bars, lodging, and services where traveling African Americans and other non-Whites, including Japanese, could be safe during the time of racial segregation.

A New York City mailman named Victor Hugo Green authored The Green Book, as it came to be known, which was published annually from 1936 to 1966. Eventually, the book expanded its coverage from the New York City area to continental North America.

If you want to get a feel for what it was like in the world of segregation, there's a 2018 historical movie called The Green Book about an African American concert pianist Dr. Don Shirley (Mahershala Ali), and his racist Caucasian driver Tony Lip (Viggo Mortensen) who negotiates their concert tour through the segregated South.

Through their association, both men learn more about themselves and become more accepting of one another. The movie is based on Tony Lip's memoir.

While other Cheyenne businesses are listed, Baker's Place, curiously, isn't mentioned in any edition of The Green Book. Miyamoto family members say African American enlisted men from Fort Warren, including Private First Class (PFC) Sammy Davis, Jr., regularly patronized the bar during the war.

Typical for the time, Sammy Davis, Jr. experienced high levels of racial prejudice while in the service, and Baker's Place was considered safe. In various TV talk show interviews, Davis, Jr. has fond recollections of one of his sergeants who helped him be a better reader, which later became important as he built a career as an A-list entertainer.

By 1917, the 18th Amendment to the US Constitution prohibited "intoxicating liquors." In 1920, Wyoming was the last state in the Rocky Mountain West to go "dry." By then, the bar's name was without reference to alcohol. It was known as John Baker Billiards in 1932, John Baker Soft Drinks in 1934, and John Baker Beer Parlor in 1938. In 1950, it was simply called Baker's Place.

Elder Bill Miyamoto moved his family into the apartment at 418, where he and his wife, Hatsuye, brought up their three boys, Ted, Bill (Doc), and Tom.

After their father retired, the three sons bought out Baker and operated the business as Tomi's Bar and Lounge. As Cheyenne's downtown began to slow down, Baker's Place was closed, and the brothers transferred the liquor license to the Two-Bar Bowl on the outskirts north of town, and later the Spot Bowl.

Tom Miyamoto was the eldest son who graduated from Manual High School in Denver. He was quite the baseball player at UW, where he also excelled as a wrestler.

Interested teams decided not to risk taking a Japanese player. World War II squelched his chances to play professional baseball. He was a member of the Wyoming Nisei All-Star baseball team that played around Wyoming, Nebraska, and northern Colorado.

Instead, he worked with his father and Johnny Baker, managing the bar business.

Tom eventually married Connie Yashiro from North Platte, Nebraska, but was reared in California when the war started. Her family owned a grocery store that was forced to close when they were sent to the Pomona center. Her destination was the Heart Mountain camp.

Connie was released and moved to Denver, where she met Tom in 1944. Internees could be paroled to a specific location after a "sponsor" was secured. This is how Mrs. Honkawa was released from Heart Mountain to Chicago.

Tom and Connie had three sons, Glenn, and twins Ron and Marty. I met Glenn and Ron for the first time at a recent Miyamoto family reunion. Marty was a popular schoolteacher in Rawlins and later Parker, Colorado, who died in 2008.

In May 1942, the Pomona Assembly Center opened for about four months at the Los Angeles County Fairgrounds about thirty miles east of downtown Los Angeles. That summer, the center population peaked at around fifty-four hundred persons. The detainees originated mostly from Los Angeles, San Francisco, and Santa Clara counties.

Despite only being in operation for three months, three hundred and nine housing barracks were built in eight buildings that included combined bathroom, shower, and laundry facilities. Each building included mess halls and kitchens.

There were thirty-six communal shower and latrine buildings. Detainees wore geta (Japanese clogs) to avoid developing athlete's foot fungus by raising their feet off the concrete floors. Soon, a small geta-making industry thrived.

Since there were no existing buildings, the Pomona center cost more than any of the other fourteen assembly centers, with a price tag totaling a little over a million dollars. The Pomona center was the only assembly center that had a perimeter fence topped with barbwire.

The US Army set a curfew that required detainees to remain indoors from ten thirty p.m. to six a.m. that was later tightened to nine thirty p.m. The WCCA prohibited and confiscated Japanese language publications. Notices written in the Japanese language with an English translation had to be submitted to the camp director for approval before they could be posted.

Detainees could request a pass and be allowed to see visitors in a fenced-off zone at the center's far west end between three p.m. and five p.m. after a pass was approved. Because so many out-of-town visitors were unaware of the procedure, camp administrators issued visitor gate passes. The Pomona center's visitor pass system was one of the most efficient throughout the war relocation industrial complex.

As in all short-term assembly centers, there was a full recreation program that included organized sports leagues and games like bridge tournaments. The detainees were in charge of organizing the various activities.

Classes were offered for ikebana, woodworking, and sewing, as well as band and orchestra instruction. The American Friends Service Committee (the Quakers) donated seventeen hundred books to the Pomona center library.

Detainees showed their patriotism by collecting money from detainees to purchase defense stamps and war bonds to support the war effort. On Veterans Day, internees collected cash donations from the sale of little artificial poppies.

Unlike many other assembly centers, there was no comprehensive school program. A temporary school in two recreation halls held classes after regular hours attended by children aged four to ten was voluntary.

The center director had to approve the use of the Japanese language in church services held initially in two barracks for a Catholic, eight Protestant, and four Buddhist services each week. The amount of space was doubled by June to accommodate twenty-seven hundred detainees.

A small store was opened to serve the center detainees soon after the center was occupied. The inventory included sundry items such as candy, cigarettes, soft drinks, and toiletries.

The detainees ran the mail center operations, which kept them busy while saving the WCCA money. When the center opened, sixteen hundred detainees were given work assignments.

Bill "Doc" Miyamoto finished his optometry degree after he returned from combat. He married Margaret "Marge" Makino while in school in Chicago. They had a daughter, Linda. She was a year ahead of me in high school. Linda also moved to Colorado, where she served a term as the Boulder County Clerk and Recorder. She recently passed away.

Sansei, like Linda and I, went our separate ways. We had more interaction when we were younger, and the Japanese community was more vibrant. During our high school and college years, many of the Issei died. That generation was the glue that bound everyone together.

Marge was sent to the Tule Lake camp. When the camp became an isolation center for dissident internees and was subsequently militarized, she was relocated to Camp Amache in southeastern Colorado.

The third Miyamoto brother, Ted, and his wife, Yoshi Ogata, had two children, Terie and Steve, both older than me.

Terie and I became better acquainted during this writing project. She worked for the phone company through its various name changes and retired in the Denver area.

Yoshi was first relocated to Minidoka Relocation Center in Idaho. She received clearance to move to Minneapolis, where she met Ted.

The Minidoka camp was constructed sixteen miles east of Eden, Idaho, in Jerome County on the Snake River Plain of south-central Idaho, twenty miles northeast of Twin Falls.

In August 1942, internees began moving into the Minidoka camp. They were transported from Oregon, Washington, and Alaska. The camp consisted of forty-four residential blocks and more than six hundred buildings and housed a peak population of a few over seventy-three hundred.

The Minidoka camp was built on BOR property, where the Miller-Gooding and North Side canal systems provided irrigation water to the arid agricultural lands.

The camp configuration differed from the other camps with building layouts that followed the bends in the North Side Canal rather than on a perpendicular grid layout.

The BOR assumed internees would provide an inexpensive labor force to construct irrigation canals and laterals. Most worked in area fields due to labor shortages caused by the war effort. Some area farmers put their prejudice aside when they had to hire internees to help with the harvest.

Like in the other camps, tensions ran high at Minidoka when the WRA required internees to fill out the loyalty questionnaire. Even though civil unrest was relatively low among Minidoka internees compared to some other camps, thirty-eight men were arrested for draft evasion in 1944.

Because of the high level of compliance at Minidoka, there were close to two thousand "yes-yes" Japanese who relocated there from the turbulent Tule Lake camp for their safety.

There were a few other Asian-owned businesses on the 400 block of West 17th Street. In 1922, Takamatsu Matsushima opened a barbershop at 408. He was born in Kumamoto, Japan, in 1887 and died in Cheyenne in 1927. He was married to Kikuyo Matsushima, who kept the barbershop open until 1939. She died in 1944. The family lived across the street at 415 W. 17th St.

In 1942, Wahl's Bicycle and Key shop opened at 408. Wahl's was the local Schwinn dealer. I enjoyed going into Wahl's when my dad needed to copy keys. I browsed around at the bikes. My parents couldn't afford a Schwinn, which was okay with me. Even in the 1960s, the higher quality bikes were older ones.

My first bicycle was a blue one that girls generally rode. It didn't have the top tube. Our across-the-alley neighbor named Danny, who also worked for my dad at the Coke plant, restored the bike. He was several years older than me and in high school.

Unsurprisingly, my friends made fun of me for riding a girl's bike. After being socially derided, I wanted the more masculine Stingray modeled after the chopper-style motorcycles.

Baby Boomer biker movies were very popular, starting with *The Wild One* (1953) with Marlon Brando, who leads one of two rival gangs who terrorize a small town. In *The Wild Angels* (1966), Hell's Angel Bruce Dern has his chopper motorcycle stolen, and Peter Fonda and Nancy Sinatra help track down the thieves.

I wasn't much of a motorcycle guy, but Danny and his friend Verlin were into fast cars and Harleys. They made me a red Stingray. It was the customized foot-pedaled version of a bad-boy motorcycle with the banana seat, high handlebars, and a knobby back tire.

That bike served me well around the neighborhood but wasn't too practical when I rode my bike to junior high school. Although I rode a Cushman scooter in Lander, I didn't get into motorcycles, and I rode an Aprillia Mojito that I recently traded in for an electric scooter.

Wahl's is no longer in business at 408. There have been several retail stores, and currently one that sells antiques and furniture.

Between 1910 and 1920, the Mikado Restaurant occupied 420 W. 17th St. The restaurant was later called the Lee Wung, presumably serving Chinese food through 1938 when it became operated as the Manila Café, likely Filipino. In the 100 block, there was a restaurant called the Shanghai across the street from the Mayflower that later became the Valencia.

I speculate in a short film I produced entitled *On the Trail: Jack Kerouac in Cheyenne* (2010) the Valencia was the Mexican restaurant where Sal Paradise met a Latina food server when he stopped in Cheyenne one night for Wild West Days, aka Cheyenne Frontier Days (CFD).

In 1939, Takematsu Matsushima had his barbershop at 408 for a year. While there is a records gap, Takematsu returned to Japan after the start of World War II, where he died in 1944. From 1939 to 1955, it was the Shamrock Café, Niven's Café, Webb's Café, and Wheel of Fortune before the location was unoccupied.

Other Japanese families lived on West 17th Street to be close to their downtown jobs, including at the railroad yards at West 15th Street and Capitol Avenue.

THIRTEEN: Downtown Railroads

This 1860 campaign token is from Abraham Lincoln's first campaign. While in office, federal land grants and public financing enabled the railroads to expand west.

The railroad played a big part in my mom's family life. My maternal grandfather's family was part of the immigrant workforce, including from Japan, China, and Mexico, that expanded the railroads and sped up westward settlement.

Grandpa Sakata always had work. He transferred around Wyoming and retired in Douglas after forty years, before moving to Cheyenne.

He lived to be a hundred and three and he attributed his longevity to a shot of Old Grand Dad and a Coors beer with dinner. It was quite a life that included the Wright Brothers flying the first airplane and humans setting foot on the moon.

I didn't learn until later that immigrants like my grandfather were paid less than the prevailing wage, particularly during the 1860s.

I remember when he turned eighty-eight, a PR guy from the Burlington Northern Railroad came to the party and presented him with some commemorative pin.

When the transcontinental railroad was completed in 1869, mass transportation made it easier for settlers to seek their fortunes in the western frontiers as the United States population rapidly expanded.

None of my relatives helped build the railroad, but they were part of the crews that maintained it. I doubt my grandfather thought much about the Native Americans killed or displaced because of western expansion.

It's still amazing to me that individuals and families risked trekking thousands of miles on foot and by horses and wagons from points east to Wyoming, seeking better lives.

My maternal grandparents came from Japan as typical immigrants by steamship to the Pacific Northwest. My grandfather, Jusaburo "Joe" Sakata, was born in 1879, ten years after the completion of the transcontinental railroad.

At age twenty-one, he and three of his friends were out chopping and gathering firewood. They engaged in a deep conversation about the merits of moving to the

United States. They had heard that the job prospects were good, as well as the quality of life.

My grandfather was very close to his father. His mother died when he was six. The next day, he left the stability of his family. He departed in January 1900 and stepped onto American soil in Seattle, Washington.

He traveled to Nashua, Montana, to work for the Great Northern Railroad and worked for the Union Pacific (UP) and Southern Pacific throughout Washington, California, and Nevada.

Grandpa found a better and more prosperous life in the United States. Eastern expansion isn't generally associated with "manifest destiny," but there was immigration from Asia that is seldom mentioned. I've wondered what the United States would be like today had West Coast expansion been more prevalent.

The New York *Democratic Review* newspaper editor John O'Sullivan is credited with first dropping the phrase "manifest destiny" in 1845. There was a rift among Americans following the annexation of Texas. Not only did Texas provide more territory into which more settlers could live, but it also meant more non-whites becoming United States citizens.

O'Sullivan urged that the country come together as it expanded westward to meet the needs of an ever-growing population. From 1800 to 1860, the US population expanded from five million to thirty million people. The growth resulted from immigration and high birth rates.

Early American colonists, including Thomas Jefferson, believed that God's plan was to take over the entire continent from coast to coast. His successful effort to purchase Louisiana from France in 1803 nearly doubled the size of America.

Westward expansion began in earnest when President Andrew Jackson signed the Indian Removal Act of 1830 that forced the dispersal of Native American tribal members, particularly those in the southern United States, onto other federal lands in the newly gained territories west of the Mississippi River in exchange for settlement of their ancestral lands.

The forced removal became known as the "Trail of Tears" and included members of the tsalagi (Cherokee), mvskoke (Muscogee), oconee (Seminole), chikashsha (Chickasaw), and chahta (Choctaw) nations.

Subsidies given to the UP by President Abraham Lincoln sped up the US government's expansion philosophy when he signed the Pacific Railway Act on July 1, 1862. The 1862 Act created the subsidized-UP railroad and the existing Central Pacific railroad by granting ten-square-mile sections of land for each mile of track laid.

In 1864, a second Pacific Railroad Act drafted by UP railroad attorneys doubled the land grant to twenty sections for each mile, which created a checkerboard of odd-numbered sections for twenty miles on each side of the line and amounted to over four and a half million acres in the Wyoming Territory, alone. The land grant also gave mineral rights under these lands to the railroad.

In addition, the government loaned the railroads twenty-seven million dollars, amortized over thirty years at six percent interest. That was enough to cover half the cost of construction.

The UP also sold eleven million dollars of stock and thirty million dollars in bonds. Most of the investment came via financiers in New York who sold the stocks and bonds on the East Coast and in Europe. Investors included merchants who earned their fortunes from trade in China, Civil War financiers, and European nobility.

The wars against the indigenous tribes during the 1860s were unintended consequences of manifest destiny. The conflicts involved Native Americans as a new enemy trying to take back their conquered homelands and defending what remained, migrating settlers looking for a new place to live, the railroads enabling easier westward expansion, and the US military protecting the settlers and railroads.

There were many treaties between the US government and Native American tribes, including the Treaty of Fort Laramie, Wyoming, approved in 1851 among the United States and several Plains and northern Rocky Mountain tribes that allowed roads to be built, and military troops stationed along the Oregon Trail generally through Wyoming to protect migrating settlers.

As the rails extended into Utah in early 1869, construction money was running short. There were unexpected obstacles like blowing out more road cuts, feeding mules that graded rights-of-way across rugged terrain, extra costs for loggers chopping down trees for railroad ties, and laborers who spiked rails across the high plains of Wyoming.

The UP route eventually plowed through southern Wyoming. It linked the United States from coast to coast at Promontory, Utah, with the final Golden Spike pounded into the track on May 10, 1869, celebrating the transcontinental railroad's completion.

The railroad project was underfunded. The financial woes delayed the ceremony for a few days. The train transporting UP Vice-President Thomas Durant and his entourage rolled into the tiny western Wyoming town of Piedmont, close to the Utah border. Piedmont was a stop with a roundhouse for train maintenance, a water tank to replenish the steam engines, a telegraph office, and a few businesses to support the railroad crews.

On May 6, over four hundred laid-off tie cutters, who had been waiting three months for their back pay, hijacked the Durant Special. Railway ties in those days were hewn from trees and placed perpendicular to the tracks to keep the rails the same width along the route. The mob greeted Durant and switched his car onto a sidetrack, where they chained his train car to the tracks.

After a futile attempt to gain his freedom, Durant finally relented. The men's pay soon arrived from UP headquarters in New York.

Little remains of Piedmont now, but the town bustled ten miles southwest of Evanston during the railroad boom. In 1868, Mormon pioneer Moses Byrne constructed five beehive-shaped kilns to produce charcoal for Utah steel smelters. Charcoal is near-pure carbon that, when heated, generates the high temperatures necessary to smelt iron ore.

That Utah industry would be tied to the World War II war effort and later, the US Steel Atlantic City iron ore mine south of Lander. When I worked in Lander, that mine was closed, and so was the railroad spur. That closure resulted in a big blow to the Wyoming and Lander economy.

A timber supply from the nearby Uinta Mountains pine forests made Piedmont an ideal place for charcoal processing. To make charcoal, kilns were loaded with wood and fired. Workers sealed the kilns, and the fire slowly smoldered over several days until charcoal is all that remained.

The Piedmont charcoal kilns are now part of the Wyoming state parks system.

The economy was booming further east, in part because of the railroad. By 1908, my grandfather was in California and took off for Wyoming. My grandfather worked for the UP in Hanna, Dana, and various sections through Nebraska and Iowa for the next nine years.

In 1917, he liked the stability of Wyoming and began working for the CB&Q Railroad in Cheyenne. He eventually became the Powder River Section foreman. A section gang led by a section work supervisor maintained each section. The section foreman and his crew kept their section of the railroad in good repair.

He took leave, and Joe returned to Japan and married my grandmother, Toki Iwasaki. After a year away, he and his bride returned to supervise the Thermopolis section in Hot Springs County, Wyoming, where he started his family. They had three children, including my mother, Sumiko, her sister Hisako, and her brother Tokinori (George).

Railroad life was good for my mom's family. Grandfather always had a job, even during the Great Depression. Unlike other railroads that fired their Japanese employees following the bombing of Pearl Harbor, the CB&Q kept my grandfather on the job.

By this time, he was the section foreman at Orpha, across the road from Fort Fetterman in Converse County, Wyoming. He and my grandmother became more settled. Their three children graduated from Converse County High School in Douglas.

Mom's sister, Hisako, was the oldest sibling and first family member who graduated from college. She went to UW and later went to Washington DC, where she worked at the US Department of Health, Education, and Welfare (HEW). She retired from her civil service career as a budget analyst at the Environmental Protection Agency (EPA). After retirement, she returned to Cheyenne, where she was the caretaker of her parents.

Middle brother, George, kept up his family tradition and worked for the Burlington Route that evolved into the Burlington Northern (BN) railroad in Alliance, Nebraska, raising his family there in a converted train boxcar.

It was like a mobile home with all the amenities. I didn't visit them but saw pictures. When I lived in Gillette, I ran into a college friend, Steve, who worked for BN. He lived in a converted boxcar.

The BN came about in 1970 when the CB&Q; the Spokane, Portland, and Seattle Railway; the Great Northern Railway, and the Northern Pacific Railway all merged.

BN acquired the Atchison, Topeka, and Santa Fe Railway in 1996 and formed the Burlington Northern and Santa Fe Railway, which is still in operation as the BNSF, and owned by Warren Buffet's Berkshire Hathaway.

I'm pretty sure Uncle George had undiagnosed PTSD after the war. He chain-smoked menthol cigarettes. He learned during the war from the African-American soldiers to open the bottom of the pack to keep the filter tips clean. My mom described him as being "shell shocked." He was an avid fisher and after returning from World War II, refused to sleep on the ground ever again. He transported a fully equipped camper in the bed of his pickup.

He and Perry had two daughters, Tracy and Tami Jo, and a son, Robert.

When Grandpa Sakata retired and settled in Cheyenne, he and Grandma lived in a very quiet neighborhood a couple of blocks from the state capitol building. Their place was within walking distance of Brannen's grocery store. As long as I knew them, they didn't drive. Otherwise, my mom or dad drove them to other places.

Mayor Bill Nation lived across the street with his big family. Grandpa did some paid gardening work for retired Judge Bloom a block away and landscaped his manicured yard with bonsai-style trees.

My grandmother was quite the seamstress. She had a clothing alteration business in their spare bedroom that led her to travel back to Japan, where she became a master Japanese sakura ningyo doll maker. She designed and sewed her beautiful to-scale doll clothing. My sister ended up with all the dolls. They are museum/art gallery-quality.

One of her steady alteration customers was Wyoming Secretary of State, Thyra Thomson. Over the years, she became a family friend. She and her sons lived a few blocks to the east and south on Warren Avenue.

Thyra and her husband, Keith, were both popular politicians in Wyoming. Keith was a three-term Congressman and was elected to the US Senate in 1960, only to die of a heart attack a month after taking office. Thyra was elected in 1962 to her first of six terms as secretary of state.

When her kids left home, she moved to the Cole Addition and lived a block away from us on Windmill Road. I've since become reacquainted with her son, Bruce, through our mutual connections in the Wyoming arts and culture community.

Grandmother also studied ikebana (flower arranging) and was in a class by herself when it came to winning ribbons at the Laramie County and Wyoming State fairs.

As a kid, I learned some of the basics of ikebana from my grandmother, which was an activity we did together when the Laramie County Fair rolled around. The fair had a men's category for flower arranging. I had the distinction of being the defending men's blue-ribbon winner before I left for college and subsequently for Laramie in 1973.

When it came to other summer activities, their house was a great gathering spot during CFD, when much of the action was downtown. The head of the parade was a short walk to the front of the state capitol building. The shortcut was up the back steps, through the rotunda, and down the front steps.

After Grandpa retired, my grandparents didn't ride the train at all. I was always interested in his railroad life. I inherited two of his railroad lanterns. One is battery-operated, and the other is fueled by kerosene. Working for the railroad wasn't even on my mind, even though I knew it was steady work and paid well.

The UP continued passenger service through Wyoming during my childhood. My family took the train to Salt Lake City. On one trip, my parents allowed my sister and me to ride the train by ourselves. This also was the first time my parents entrusted me with a sum of money greater than my allowance.

The dining car was full service and available to all passengers. It was the first time I read a menu and ordered food. The hamburgers weren't anything special, but there was something about having the steward in a waist coat deliver it to the table.

We made a stop in Rock Springs. I turned around, and my sister was not there. She eventually ended up at the ticketing area, and the railroad attendant reunited us. I don't recall if I got in trouble for that, but it was a heart-stopper.

Passenger rail service boomed, with ninety-eight percent of intercity travelers transported by train in 1916. Before World War II and more competition from airlines, commercial bus services, and automobiles, the railroad market share dropped to 67 percent. That number surged during the War, but in the 1950s, the number of train travelers dropped to thirty-four percent.

By 1971, there was enough rail service demand from the public for the US government to step up and fund what became the National Railroad Passenger Corporation, which comprised twenty of twenty-six railroads that transferred their passenger service to what became known as Amtrak.

FOURTEEN: Enter the US Army

My grandparents' Highway Café was located near to one of Wyoming's first military forts constructed near Crow Creek. The café moved a few blocks north when I-80 expanded.

Wyoming has always been a "pass-through" state marked by the transcontinental railroad bringing business and settlers west, beaten paths where livestock companies drove their cattle herds and flocks of sheep to the north and the subsequent need for the protection provided by the US Army.

Why my family stayed in Wyoming as long as they did, is a mystery to me. When they were first starting, they worked in places with all-Caucasian employees. When the war broke out, my parents were quietly resentful about how they were treated by people, from friends to strangers.

They found solace with their families and the Japanese community in the 400 and 500 blocks of West 17th Street.

When my sister and I came along, we often took quick trips around Cheyenne. One-stop was on Interstate 80 on the way to Laramie, near Buford. It was a state landmark called the Lone Tree. What I learned in fourth grade Wyoming history class is that it was once along the railroad track bed. A pine cone became entrapped in a crack in an enormous boulder and sprouted a sapling.

It's been growing ever since the 1870s. Over the years, railroad workers on the train would pour the day-old coffee onto the plant. The tree has split the rock, and I now tied it into place with a cable.

We took drives to Fort Laramie in east-central Wyoming. It's a National Historic Site where two treaties between the US government and Native American tribes were inked in 1851 and 1868.

When we visited my mom's childhood home in Orpha, there was a stop at Fort Fetterman. Back then, there wasn't anything there except for a sign and imagined scenes of the fort overrun by the likes of Red Cloud.

As we got older, the family took vacations across southern Wyoming, mostly to visit my Salt Lake City relatives in Utah. We took breaks at the rest stops. It turns out, most of them are sites of Army forts.

When the UP stayed north and plotted out its principal route through Cheyenne instead of Denver, that decision transformed Cheyenne from a dusty prairie town into a booming Nineteenth-century metropolis. Denver later paid for a railroad spur to connect with Cheyenne.

With more settlers arriving and business being transacted came a need to protect the railroad route and the towns popping up along the way from attack by the tribes protecting and reclaiming their lands.

The Cheyenne passenger rail service in 1867 lasted until 1983, when Amtrak moved the California Zephyr route through Colorado. Freight continues to be moved across southern Wyoming.

Beginning at the eastern border of Wyoming, the US Army established themselves at Camp O.O. Howard near Pine Bluffs in 1885. It was a temporary military encampment to protect UP laborers.

General Oliver Otis Howard won the Congressional Medal of Honor during the Civil War. He was later deployed to the West, where he was a Native American killer. After the Civil War, he had charge of integrating freedmen (former slaves) into American society.

The Post on Crow Creek was Cheyenne's first military designation. It was constructed in 1867 as the base for the 2nd US Volunteer Cavalry, which included soldiers from Crook, Weston, and Sheridan counties in northeast Wyoming.

When World War II was over, my grandmother Ohashi opened the Highway Café on US Highway 85, also known as the South Greeley Highway. The original building was on the banks of Crow Creek, where my dad and I hiked around the sandstone cliffs above. After World War II, they started that business after my grandmother quit working at the City Café in the Japanese neighborhood on West 17th Street.

The Crow Creek post was renamed Fort David Allen Russell, honoring the Civil War general killed in 1864 during the Battle of Opequon in the Shenandoah Valley of Pennsylvania. In 1867, President Andrew Johnson nominated Russell to be major general, retroactive to his death on the battlefield.

The UP railroad crossed over Crow Creek, a tributary of the South Platte River. The railroad town in the Dakota Territory was renamed "Cheyenne" after the Cheyenne Native American tribe closely allied with the Arapaho.

In March 1868, Dodge put Cheyenne on the map as a key railroad town. He selected the location for the UP-roundhouse maintenance yard for locomotive repair. Cheyenne was eventually the location for a major depot.

Around the time of its founding, Cheyenne quickly had a population of four thousand people. It arose almost by sleight of hand and was nicknamed "The Magic City of the Plains."

Cheyenne boomed. Local businesses provided materials and supplies for the railroad and entertainment for the workers with money to burn but no place to burn it. In 1868, there were brothels, gambling parlors, live theaters, and seventy bars in Cheyenne.

"Hell on Wheels" was a big tent that moved with the boom and set up in Cheyenne. It was an end-of-the-tracks attraction where patrons could down a shot of whiskey, try their hand at poker, hire a prostitute, and get a glass of sarsaparilla to cure venereal disease, all at the same place.

During CFD in the 1960s, the local Junior Chamber of Commerce Club (Jaycees) set up a big Hell on Wheels canvas tent along Crow Creek and later in Holliday Park. The Jaycees is a community service and leadership development organization for men and women between eighteen and forty.

Danny, my across-the-alley neighbor who built my red Stingray bike, was also a Jaycee. During the summer, I went to work at the Coke plant and helped my dad mix up batches of sarsaparilla soda.

Sarsaparilla is a word in Spanish that means "prickly vine with little grapes." Over the years, the beverage evolved into root beer that was originally flavored with sassafras, which is an aromatic deciduous tree that mostly grows in the eastern United States.

That seasonal drink was a big seller at Hell on Wheels. There also was a beer bar set up. I'm pretty sure Dad had no idea sarsaparilla would sell so well. Sarsaparilla was originally a patent medicine that contained the fruit of a spiny vine called Smilex ornata that was claimed to cure syphilis, which explains why it was available in bars during the railroad boom.

Despite the unchecked chicanery in the city, there was a growing need to protect even more settlers and the railroad as expansion continued westward. Cheyenne continued to maintain a military presence.

In 1930, Fort Russell became Fort Francis E. Warren. My Auntie Hisako worked there as the secretary to the base chaplain. The Air Force took over the base in 1948. Francis E. Warren was awarded the Medal of Honor as a soldier in the Civil War. He served as Wyoming's first territorial governor in 1885 and was elected as the state's first governor in 1890. He resigned as governor when he was elected to the US Senate.

South of Laramie and east of the Laramie River, Fort John Buford was built in 1886 to protect railroad workers and settlers trekking west on the Overland Trail. The Fort was different from the Buford railroad section stop between Laramie and Cheyenne but named after the same guy. It was later renamed Fort Sanders, and now the Cavalryman restaurant.

The ruins of a stone guardhouse and magazine remain and were marked by a monument placed by the Daughters of the American Revolution in 1914. It is said that frontierswoman Martha "Calamity Jane" Cannary was stationed there in 1872 as a scout during the Indian Wars.

Staying true to the boom-and-bust cycle, in February 1868, as the end-of-the-tracks moved west, Cheyenne lost population to fast-growing Laramie.

By spring 1868, crews laid rails to Laramie, but not before extending them over Sherman Hill. At an elevation of eighty-two hundred feet above sea level, the rail line over the Sherman summit in the Laramie Range became the highest railroad in the world when it was completed during the spring of 1869 before descending into the Laramie Basin.

A bridge one hundred and twenty-five feet high and fourteen hundred feet in length was required to span Dale Creek, just west of the summit. That trestle became the highest along the UP route west of the Missouri River.

The boom time in Laramie did not differ from those in other rail camp towns. Railroad work attracted men earning too much money and no place to spend it. There was trouble waiting to happen among single men, prostitutes, gamblers, and thieves who scrounged the money trickling out of the pockets of drunken rail workers.

Between Laramie and Rawlins, Fort Fred Steele was built in 1868 to protect the railroad and settlers heading north to Montana on the Bozeman Trail. Fort Steele was a key settlement that protected the railroad bridge across the North Platte.

The fort guarded a shipping point for lumber and railroad ties cut from Medicine Bow National Forest timber that floated down the North Platte to the railroad loading dock.

Frederick Steele served in the US Army as a Major General during the Civil War. He was assigned to the Army of Arkansas and credited for taking Little Rock and returning Arkansas to the Union.

After the fort was abandoned in 1886, more businesses opened, and settlers took up residence. The site was restored by the state of Wyoming and is now a part of Seminoe State Park.

Next along the route, Fort Rawlins was originally sited in 1868 at Rawlins Spring, north of the current city of Rawlins, to protect railroad workers. It was named after Civil War General John Aaron Rawlins, a longtime advisor to President Ulysses S. Grant.

The fort was later relocated to the north bank of the Timpanogos River, two miles east of Provo, Utah, in 1870 to quell growing Mormon insurrections there.

President Grant appointed Rawlins to be the Secretary of War. In 1869, Grant dispatched Rawlins to the Utah Territory, thinking the dry climate would be good for the secretary's tuberculosis, which took his life a few months later.

His primary orders were to observe Mormon life, mostly monitoring men marrying multiple women. When Rawlins returned to Washington DC, he convinced Grant to adopt a hardline policy against the Mormons, particularly their polygamy doctrine.

On the west edge of Wyoming is Fort Bridger, established in 1843 by Jim Bridger and Louis Vasquez. It was a trading post for westward travelers, the Pony Express, the transcontinental railroad, and the Lincoln Highway. The fort was also where Native American tribes could trade.

Jim Bridger migrated west from Virginia. He was a well-known scout and led many excursions throughout the western frontier. Bridger gained a reputation for mediating conflicts between Native Americans and settlers.

Luis Vasquez was based in St. Louis. He descended from a Spanish father and a French-Canadian mother and became a successful guide in his own right before partnering up with Jim Bridger.

Fort Bridger consisted of two log cabins about forty feet long with a fence to tie up horses and became a military outpost in the late 1850s and is now part of the State of Wyoming parks and historic sites system.

While the railroad no longer transports passengers along the southern Wyoming passage, I-80 and US Highway 30 (the Lincoln Highway) continue to be important east-west routes. All the forts evolved into state parks, or historic sites where travelers can stop and stretch their legs, and constant reminders of Wyoming's role during early westward expansion and as a pass-through state.

FIFTEEN: Exclusion and Uncivil Unions

Marriages between Asians and Caucasians were against the law in Wyoming. Uncle Tom and Auntie Joan were married in Colorado.

Poet Emma Lazarus wrote a sonnet in 1883 that she donated to an art and literary works auction to raise money to construct the Statue of Liberty pedestal on Ellis Island. The last stanza reads:

"Keep, ancient lands, your storied pomp!" cries she
With silent lips. "Give me your tired, your poor,
Your huddled masses yearning to breathe free,
The wretched refuse of your teeming shore.
Send these, the homeless, tempest-tost to me,
I lift my lamp beside the golden door!"
— "The New Colossus," by Emma Lazarus (1883)

Her sonnet rings true if a European immigrant agrees to Superman's American Way, but an émigré from Asia after 1924 was not allowed entry into the United States.

Before 1924, the West 17th Street neighborhood attracted a host of Japanese. When the national Immigration Act of 1924 was signed into law, the subtext was to preserve the Caucasian racial and ethnic homogeneity of the United States and decrease entry of a cheap labor force that would compete with existing American workers.

Both sets of my grandparents made it into the United States, but their immigration added to the perceived problem of too many people entering from Asia.

The 1924 Act excluded immigrants from anywhere in Asia and limited the quota of other immigrants, particularly southern and eastern Europeans who could enter the United States through a quota system based on a person's national origin.

The quota provided visas to two percent of the number of immigrants of each nationality currently in the United States, based on the 1890 census.

As background, the US Congress enacted the first widely restrictive Immigration Act of 1917 in the name of national security during World War I. The 1917 Act required immigrants over sixteen years of age to prove basic reading comprehension in their native language.

The immigration tax paid upon arrival was increased. Immigration officials were given more discretion to determine who to include or exclude.

The 1917 Act excluded anyone born in a defined "Asiatic Barred Zone" except for Japanese and Filipinos. This is because the Japanese government voluntarily limited Japanese immigration to the United States. The Philippines was a US colony, so its citizens were US nationals.

Following the Transcontinental Railroad completion, the Chinese Exclusion Act of 1882, signed into law by President Chester Arthur, denied any additional Chinese visas for ten years.

During this moratorium, the UP re-deployed their Chinese labor force to work in the company mines along the railway rights-of-way.

There was an anti-Chinese movement that arose among the mainstream labor force largely because the UP hired Chinese because they would work for lower wages. Labor-related racial tensions reached their peak in September 1885 when the Rock Springs Massacre in Wyoming resulted in the deaths of twenty-eight Chinese miners and destruction of seventy-eight homes of Chinese miners.

One of the key topics of the 1924 immigration debate was the deeply engrained quota system. While there were some who wanted to increase the number of immigrants allowed, the agreed-upon plan lowered the quota from three to two percent of new foreign-born residents based on the 1890 census, rather than the 1910 census, to further restrict the number of immigrants.

The 1924 Act meant that Asians, including Japanese, would no longer be admitted into the United States. The new provision ran contrary to Japan's voluntary immigration limits that had been observed since 1917.

That change created tension between the US government and that of Japan. The US Congress determined that preserving the racial homogeneity of the United States was more important than good relations with Japan. That tension would flavor US foreign policy over the next couple of decades.

On top of it all, further westward expansion coupled with a more diverse citizenry from Africa, the Middle East, Latin America, and Asia, would mean the new citizens would have the right to representation in state and territorial legislatures, and the US Congress.

This would be problematic, based on the desire for racial homogeneity and maintaining systemic oppression of the new racially and ethnically diverse population.

It wasn't until the bombing of Pearl Harbor in 1941 that the 1924 Act became more relevant.

Near the end of the 1943 Wyoming state legislative session, Senate Joint Resolution Number 1 was approved, and declared, "the people of the great State of Wyoming to join in a program of unity, to the end that all differences be laid aside in a spirit of mutual coordination of our efforts toward the one thing we all seek at this time—victory in the present war."

Despite the resolution of civility, the legislature passed that same week and Governor Nels Smith signed Senate File 24 into law that prohibited land ownership by "aliens ineligible to citizenship."

Two state senators representing people near the Heart Mountain camp sponsored the Wyoming Alien Land Act. Republican George Burke of Powell and Democrat JA Farlein of Worland, wanted to prevent West Coast Japanese relocated to the Heart Mountain camp from acquiring real estate in Wyoming. The bill excluded Chinese from the law's provisions. The penalties included a five thousand dollar fine or five years in prison or both.

The 1924 Act and the Wyoming Alien Land Act explain why no property on West 17th Street was under Japanese ownership. The 1943 law remained on the books until February 2001, when the legislature repealed it during the Governor James Geringer administration. State Representative Keith Goodenough from Casper introduced the legislation to repeal Wyoming Alien Land Act.

The Immigration and Nationality Act of 1965, signed into law by President Lyndon Johnson, abolished the National Origins Formula, that decreased de facto exclusion of Asians, southern and eastern European immigrants willing to work for lower wages.

The 1965 Act resulted in a change in immigrant demographics to include more migration from Mexico, Africa, and Asia. Congress intended to create a more democratic immigration system by doing away with the National Origin Formula. American society hasn't yet caught up. After 1965 to the present, there continues to be animosity stemming from discrimination toward immigrants from Asia, Africa, and Latin America.

There were other systemic constraints. In 1955, interracial marriages were against the law in Wyoming, which forced Auntie Joan and Uncle Tom Lee to be married in Greeley, Colorado.

Joan was the youngest in my dad's family. I really didn't know her that well growing up, mostly because she and Tom were in Colorado. I didn't know Tom at all, but at first glance he was a James Dean, *Rebel Without a Cause* (1955) kind of guy. That movie was about a troublemaker who moves to a new town, but learns, no matter where you go, there you are.

At one point, Joan and Tom were involved in a serious car crash. I know Joan broke her back in that accident. She wore an upper torso body cast. I don't think she ever fully recovered from that accident.

I knew Tom as a stock car racer. He parked his car in the garage on my grandfather's ranchette south of Cheyenne near the racetrack. I'm not sure of how Grandfather purchased the split-level home built into the side of a hill.

I don't know why he had it, but I think Tom and Joan stayed there off and on. It was sparsely furnished with Western-style oak chairs and tables. Grandpa raised a few pigs and chickens.

Grandma Ohashi and my parents took my sister and me there to tend the chickens. It wasn't until much later that I viewed the outing as a rite of passage.

One visit, the mission was to slaughter chickens. I won't go into the gory details, but it was the first and only time that I'd seen a chicken running around with its head chopped off. It should have dawned on me that animals have no chance against humans.

When Uncle Tom was racing, my dad took my sister and me to the stock car track in the summer. We parked at my grandfather's place and walked down to the backstretch of the track. There was a double chain-link fence that had obviously been slammed into by more than a few racecars.

Thinking back, it wasn't the safest place to watch, but I liked being near the dust flying and the banging sounds of metal-on-metal, despite the risk.

Why did Tom and Joan end up in Colorado? The Wyoming law banning interracial marriage was adopted in 1913. Wyoming was one of a dozen states that banned marriage between Asian variations (Mongolians and Malays) and Caucasians.

My cousin, Jerry, born of Auntie Rose happened in Denver because mixed-race relationships between Caucasians and Japanese, including births, were unlawful in Wyoming. Larry Kishiyama and his Caucasian wife also were married in Colorado.

Uncle George and Auntie Perry were married in Kansas, never to return to Wyoming.

In Wyoming, interracial couples found guilty of the misdemeanor could be fined between one hundred and one thousand dollars and sent to prison for up to ten years. Historically, laws banning mixed-race marriage go back to 1661 when the first law banning interracial marriages was passed in Maryland.

It wasn't until 1965 that the Wyoming miscegenation law was repealed. However, interracial marriage in the United States has been legal since the 1967 US Supreme Court (SCOTUS) decision in *Loving v. Virginia.*

I didn't date at all during high school or in college, mostly because there was a lack of young Japanese women. While interracial dating occurred, my adolescence was but three or four years removed from when the miscegenation laws were repealed. My perception, though, was that interracial dating was not yet socially acceptable.

It wasn't just the public sector that institutionalized racism in the wake of the nationwide anti-Japanese sentiment. The American Bowling Congress (ABC) kicked my parents out during World War II.

They were part of a league that included other Nisei bowlers. I don't know why, but the league was allowed in Cheyenne despite the long-standing ABC "White men only" policy in place since 1916 that happened to coincide with the timing of the 1917 Act.

Not only were all teams in ABC-approved city leagues restricted to Caucasian men, but also the ABC could disallow matches at any bowling alley that sponsored tournaments for mixed-gender or non-White teams. ABC had the power to restrict the number of bowling lanes available to non-Whites.

Following the war and after being released from the relocation camps, Nisei bowlers scattered across the country where they formed teams in their new communities. By 1947, the Japanese American Citizen League (JACL) estimated that over four hundred Japanese-American bowling teams formed around the continental United States and Hawaii.

In March 1946, the JACL began efforts to reverse the ABC exclusion rule by picketing tournaments around the country. The protests grew into a coalition that included the National Association for the Advancement of Colored People (NAACP), the JACL, and labor organizations like the Congress of Industrial Organizations (CIO).

Despite grassroots pressure, the ABC continued to discriminate when selecting members. The ABC disregarded legal actions in Illinois, Wisconsin, New York, and Ohio. ABC Secretary Elmer Baumgarten said that if the ABC lost its right to select members, the American way of life would be lost.

In the spring of 1950, an Illinois judge found the ABC abused its corporate franchise to do business in the state and ordered the organization to drop its discriminatory policy and pay a hefty fine or have its state corporate charter revoked.

At the ABC annual meeting in May 1950, a resolution was introduced to overturn the national exclusion policy. The resolution was adopted quickly on a voice vote. Shortly thereafter, the JACL issued a statement hailing the move.

The first integrated tournament was held in Minneapolis in 1951. My parents were reinstated and my dad's team won the ABC Cheyenne city league 1953–1954 tournament, and I have the patch to prove it.

The news wasn't all positive. To ensure enough votes to support the change, there was an exception made that allowed ABC chapters in southern "Jim Crow" states to use race to determine membership.

Jim Crow describes segregation and discrimination that was lawful particularly in the South until the Civil Rights Act of 1964.

Jim Crow isn't a real Southerner.

A Caucasian actor named Thomas Dartmouth Rice, based in New York City, began performing in blackface, wore shabby clothing, and emoted the stereotypical slow-moving demeanor of lazy slaves he claimed to have observed. His racist song and dance act was called, "Jump, Jim Crow."

His act was popular in New York, where blackface minstrel shows became a common form of musical theater. Jim Crow became associated with legalized racial segregation.

The Cheyenne Japanese community was a Jim Crow neighborhood. It may have seemed normal, but following the issuance of EO 9066 by FDR, travel restrictions were placed on at least some Japanese because Fort Warren, west of Cheyenne, was considered a likely strategic military target, but not as important as any on the West Coast.

FIFTEEN: Civil Disobedience and Reparations

EO 9066 authorized the secretary of war, Harry Stimson, and any military commander designated by him to prescribe military areas from which any or all persons may be excluded.

I'm unaware that my parents or other relatives had to report their whereabouts, but Carol Lou Kishiyama Hough showed me a fistful of letters. Her family had to notify the US Attorney in Cheyenne about their travel over five miles from their home. They had family in Colorado. One of the forms was filled out by my dad. I recognized his handwriting. A Japanese person could be arrested if travel occurred without approval.

Back then, my parents likely didn't have any place to travel outside of Cheyenne, mostly because their families were in town. When life was simpler, most small towns, like Cheyenne, were more self-sustaining. For example, Coke and Pepsi were both bottled in town. There was a third plant that made Cliquot Club. Cheyenne had two dairies, Plains and Dairy Gold, that were supplied by local dairy farmers. In the food stores, produce was seasonal tomatoes, and they weren't available all the time.

Following the bombing of Pearl Harbor, the Cheyenne Japanese community quickly came together. While I never talked to her about this, Auntie Hisako was likely one of the community organizers. She was later active with the JACL in Washington DC, and related national politics.

For various birthdays and Christmases, she nurtured my campaign button hobby and gifted me political memorabilia, including from US Congressional Representative Bob Kastenmeier (D-Wisc). His buttons are now part of my Watergate pin collection.

The JACL was formed in 1929 in reaction to the Immigration Act of 1924. Several already-established Nisei organizations merged, including the American Loyalty League in Fresno, the Seattle Progressive Citizens League, and New American Citizens League based in San Francisco. The JACL held its first national conference in Seattle in 1930.

During its early beginnings, the JACL began work expanding citizenship rights of Japanese and other Asian Americans, who were ineligible for citizenship.

A group of Cheyenne Japanese worked with local leaders, including Mayor Ed Warren, Governor Nels Smith, news media owners, and law enforcement officers. They published a resolution signed by several Cheyenne Japanese in the *Wyoming Eagle* and *Wyoming State Tribune* newspapers. They later merged into the WTE.

While civility among local Japanese was the rule, the federal district court in downtown Cheyenne was the venue for a high-profile case involving draft resisters from the Heart Mountain camp.

In 1944, a group of draft-eligible men formed the Heart Mountain Fair Play Committee that attracted sixty-three draft resisters. The committee did not wish to be perceived as disloyal to the United States or as a pacifist, and established criteria for membership: A man needed to be a US citizen who was loyal to the United States; willing to serve in the US Army if his legal rights were first restored; and pay a two-dollar membership fee.

Beginning in February 1944, the committee organized evening meetings in the camp mess halls. As more and more men received orders to report for pre-induction, meeting attendance grew.

Through March, the resisters who refused to report for their physicals went about their lives behind the barbwire. The committee ignored the WRA that prohibited organized meetings. At the end of the month, US Marshals stormed the camp, arrested offenders, and charged them with draft evasion, eventually imprisoning them in the city of Cheyenne and Laramie County jails.

The sixty-three men were tried in the largest federal district court mass trial in Cheyenne before Judge T. Blake Kennedy. After a quick trial, the judge sentenced the sixty-three defendants to three years in prison.

The younger men served their time at the McNeil Island Federal Penitentiary near Tacoma, Washington, and the older Issei men at the Leavenworth Federal Penitentiary in Kansas.

On appeal, the US 10th Circuit Court in Denver affirmed their convictions and sentences. The defendants served out their jail terms and didn't return home until after the war in 1946.

The draft evasion prosecution didn't include the committee leadership. Because of their ages, the Issei men didn't receive draft notices. They were later charged with conspiracy to abet others to evade the draft.

In October 1944, a federal district court jury convicted them. A few months later, the Federal Court of Appeals in Denver overturned their convictions on a technicality.

The military draft resistance efforts at the Heart Mountain camp created a divide between the Japanese who were patriotic and those who supported civil disobedience.

After the war, President Harry Truman pardoned the sixty-three draft resisters and recognized the injustice of the WRA and the unjust treatment of Japanese Americans.

The buck didn't stop with Truman.

President Ronald Reagan signed the Civil Liberties Act in 1988. US Representative Norm Mineta (D-Calif.), who was an internee as a child at the Heart Mountain camp, and US Senator Alan Simpson, who, as a Boy Scout from nearby

Cody, met Mineta while visiting the camp originally sponsored the act. The two continue to be friends.

In 1988, it was estimated that sixty thousand internees were still living. The legislation had its roots in a 1979 National Council for Japanese American Redress class-action lawsuit against the federal government on behalf of former relocation camp internees.

A year later, US Senator Daniel Inouye (D-Hawaii) Representatives Robert Matsui (D-Calif.), Spark Matsunaga (D-Hawaii), and Mineta, successfully urged Congress to appoint a committee to study the effects of the incarceration and recommend potential reparations.

The Commission on Wartime Relocation and Internment of Civilians held hearings around the country. The commission heard testimony from over seven hundred former internees who recounted their experiences in camp and discrimination after the war.

In 1983, the commission reported its findings in a publication called Personal Justice Denied, writing that the displacement of Japanese Americans during the war resulted from "race prejudice, war hysteria, and a failure of political leadership," and recommended monetary reparations be made to former internees.

The bill to issue a formal apology and appropriate twenty thousand dollars in reparation funds to each internment camp survivor was introduced in 1987. Despite resistance from President Ronald Reagan and Senate Republicans opposed to increased federal spending, the bill was signed into law in August 1988.

The approval of reparations and apologies to former Japanese relocation camp internees generated more public interest in the camps themselves. Heart Mountain would be a location for one of my first movies. Following a circuitous path that wound me back to Wyoming and my cultural roots as a filmmaker.

SIXTEEN: A Little Bit of Discipline

My second short movie production was A Little Bit of Discipline which forced me to examine my suppressed Japanese roots.

In 1996, the Heart Mountain Wyoming Foundation, dedicated to the historic preservation of Heart Mountain camp, was established. The foundation received National Historic Landmark status for the Heart Mountain camp. Visitors to the Heart Mountain camp can walk through the permanent and temporary exhibits at the interpretive learning center.

After my first visit to Heart Mountain, I didn't return for another twenty years. When I made my second stop at the historic site, it would be the location for my second short movie production that I made in 2005 about the relocation camp experience.

When I moved from Lander to Colorado in 1993, it was a difficult transition. It took me several years to establish myself. When the economy tanked following 9/11, I was laid off twice. I was the development director for two nonprofit organizations. It was a tough time for a guy charged with raising money, particularly because the charities associated with 9/11 received proportionately more funds as donors changed their giving priorities.

Meanwhile, I was in graduate school again, this time at the University of Colorado-Denver, earning a master's in public administration (MPA) in domestic violence (DV) prevention. The MPA has been of some use to me around writing grants to fund my creative projects. I continue to be part of the DV industrial complex as a volunteer working with my colleague, Randy, documenting his DV and sexual assault survivor panel presentations.

After my second layoff, I reinvented myself as a moviemaker. My friends counseled me to try something I've always wanted to do, but haven't done it because I shackled myself to a job. I didn't really "follow my dreams" but the fresh path allowed me to get better at the two things I was great at, which are fundraising and writing.

I'm proud to be a starving artist.

Throughout grade school and college, I'd written for the school newspaper and eventually plied my vast stores of general knowledge writing sports, obituaries, weddings, news, and sundry columns for the twice-weekly WSJ in Lander. After moving to Colorado, I abandoned any news or creative writing.

I collected unemployment insurance payments, food stamps, and leveraged my student loans. In exchange for the monthly stipends, I was required to look for work, get retrained to do something else, or both. I enrolled in some TV production classes at the Boulder public access TV station and tried my hand at screenwriting.

My friend, Clay, dragged me along to his screenwriting class sponsored by Lighthouse Writers Workshop in Denver. A fantastic writer named Alexander taught the class. I eventually figured out story structure after traveling to New York City for a story seminar by renowned script doctor Robert McKee. That had a tremendous impact on me, I think in three-act structure.

In case you don't know Robert McKee, his gruff and cussing character is portrayed in a movie called *Adaptation* (2002) starring Nicholas Cage and Meryl Streep. It's a story about screenwriting, writer's block, and orchids. Beyond that, you'll have to look it up yourself and watch the movie.

I was active with the Boulder Asian Pacific Alliance (BAPA) that sponsored an annual film festival. As part of the festival, I organized a screenplay contest around any Asian theme.

What was the prize? The festival would produce the winning story. In 2005, a writer from Powell, Dennis Goldberg, won the contest with a screenplay called *A Little Bit of Discipline*. I made some edits to make it more Japanese-esque.

It was difficult to find Japanese actors to be in the movie. Peter Park, who was Korean, played the part of a former Issei camp internee, Uncle Seito. He remained in the rural community near the camp where he was interned and faces his struggles with the continuing prejudice towards the Japanese by the townspeople.

That is complicated by his reluctant acceptance of his Nisei nephew, Kenji (Phil Chung), and his modern ways that include accepting Diana, Kenji's Caucasian girlfriend (Robin Litt).

Also in the movie was Aya Medrud, who was interned at the Minidoka camp as a child. Aya was honored at a Martin Luther King Day celebration a few years ago. I made a short tribute documentary about her.

Following the war, she was working as a librarian in occupied Japan and met Nelder "Med" Medrud. He was a scientist stationed in Japan, where he monitored the weather. Aya and Med married and because they were a mixed-race couple, they could only move to certain places, stateside. They eventually came to Boulder.

She recalled her World War II experiences. When EO 9066 was ordered, Aya said the FBI came calling and arrested her father.

"The FBI came shortly after that and ransacked the house. I remember being a neat and tidy child and saying to the guy who was dumping the stuff out of my dresser drawers onto the floor, 'You going to put it back, aren't you?' My dad just didn't say anything. He put his hand on my shoulder and said in Japanese, 'Shut up,'" Aya recounted in my Voices of Change tribute to her.

The establishing scenes for *A Little Bit of Discipline* were shot on location at the former Heart Mountain camp in Wyoming. A story ran in the *Powell Tribune* seeking background actors to walk around the camp remains. We were unprepared for the casting call response. There were well over thirty would-be actors from all over Wyoming and Montana. Some were serious actors who brought a headshot and resume.

Every extra was placed, and I'm pretty sure there hadn't been that many people at the Heart Mountain camp since World War II.

After the shoot, I stopped for a beer at the Union Bar in Hudson, a town between Lander and Riverton. There was a segment on the Casper TV news about the *A Little Bit of Discipline* production at Heart Mountain. There's nothing like unanticipated earned media.

Hudson was one of my haunts when I lived in Fremont County during the 1980s and the 1990s. The town has a population of around four hundred people. Hudson was initially incorporated as a "company town" that primarily served two Poposia Mining Company coalmines. At one time, the boomtown was said to have had as many as ten thousand miners who resided there.

For a small town, it was best known for two steak houses, The Club El Toro owned by the Vinich family, and Svilar's, owned by the Svilar family. The Union Bar was largely a hangout for Democrats when the Vinich family owned it.

The family matriarch, Mabel Vinich, was mayor of Hudson for many years. I got to know her through city government circles. Son John Vinich, who was a state senator, managed the bar. I taught his sister Michelle's daughter violin lessons.

I didn't get to know their father, Mike, until later. He was a behind-the-scenes guy. At the time of his death, he and I were planning a documentary about his time in the navy and the friendship he had with future president John F. Kennedy. They served together in the South Pacific.

I had a steep learning curve to get ready for *A Little Bit of Discipline.* It was the first time I'd taken any ownership of the World War II relocation camp experience. I wouldn't learn until later that my grandfather Ohashi and Uncle George were detained in a California assembly center for a few months.

After the war in 1945, the internees left the Heart Mountain camp, and most returned to where they originated on the West Coast, but some remained, like Uncle Seito in my movie, but most returned to their original homes.

Returning Caucasian veterans could set up homesteads on the former camp, and some acquired barracks repurposed into starter homes for one dollar each. The WRA auctioned the camp farm equipment to area farmers and ranchers.

After the war, one of the barracks buildings was sold to the town of Greybull, Wyoming, sixty miles from the Heart Mountain camp. Later, the structure was acquired by Iowa State University and moved fifteen miles east of Greybull to Shell, where it was converted into a geology field station.

In 2015, Iowa State donated the building to the Heart Mountain Foundation and paid the hundred- and forty-thousand-dollar relocation and historic preservation refurbishment costs. It is now a part of the Heart Mountain Interpretive Center collection.

A few months later, *A Little Bit of Discipline* screened at the Rosebud Film Series at Northwest College in Powell. Much to everyone's surprise, following the pre-screening socializing, the movie was disrupted before it started when the projectionist discovered that the digital versatile disc (DVD) was stolen out of the player.

I learned later that the culprits were from a small sect of young, local racists. I had another DVD in the car and was able to play the movie.

A month or so later, I received the disc back in the mail. At least the troublemakers were honest.

At one level, I'm glad the movie got some notice, but on the other hand, it was an eye-opener that some people still reacted negatively about the Japanese World War II experience, even in the Twenty-first century.

SEVENTEEN: Out of Sight, Out of Mind

A Little Bit of Discipline, like all my work, has a social change component. As long as I'm telling a story, it may as well have some higher purpose. I attribute that to my childhood and maturation in Wyoming, particularly in the aftermath of World War II and the subsequent Cold War and my pushing back from the model minority stereotype.

As Cheyenne boomed in the 1960s during the Cold War, there was general urban flight. Cheyenne boomed when the railroad came through, followed by a network of US Army forts to protect the expanding West.

Pre-territorial Fort Warren would again play a role in the national defense because of Wyoming's geographic isolation and sparse population. Cheyenne boomed a hundred years later with workers moving into town to construct the highest concentration of Atlas nuclear missile sites in the country during the 1960s.

Coincidentally, when the Fairview Elementary school boundaries changed, before I entered first grade, my parents moved to the suburbs so that my sister and I would be closer walking distance and stay in the same school.

Housing developments sprouted up in the Buffalo Ridge, Cole, and Sun Valley additions on the north and eastern outskirts of Cheyenne to meet the growing need for places to house the construction workers and employees from accompanying support businesses.

During the nuclear boom times, Cheyenne's emerging middle class migrated from outside the state and into tract developments that consisted of single-family, ranch-style homes, and continue to be occupied today.

Shopping centers popped up around town to serve the expanding population in the 1960s. On the east side, Wyo Plaza opened and served the Cole and Sun Valley additions. The anchor business was a department store called Tempo. Cousin Leslie currently has her Pilates practice and Body Lines Dance studio located in that strip mall.

It was a quick bike ride up Windmill Road and across Nationway, named after long-time Mayor Bill Nation. The Nations lived across the street from my grandparents Sakata on Capitol Avenue. Even they made the move to the north and east side of town.

My grandparents Sakata sold their place on Capitol Avenue to the adjacent First Christian Church that was expanding. They moved closer to us on Converse Avenue and East 16th Street.

They had a downstairs apartment, which eventually became quarters for Auntie Hisako, who retired from the EPA and moved from DC to Cheyenne to take care of her mom and dad—my grandparents.

On the north side, the Melton Shopping Center (later renamed Indian Hills) opened near the Miyamoto's Two-Bar-Bowl, holding the Baker's Place liquor license, and was more convenient to the Buffalo Ridge subdivision.

Cheyenne's south side was literally on the wrong side of the tracks. There was no significant suburban development. Town & Country shopping center, where Uncle Roy worked at the liquor store that served the south side. That end of town now has a high concentration of discount "dollar" stores and several payday loan businesses.

When the indoor Cheyenne Frontier Mall opened in 1981 on the north edge of town, businesses fled downtown, including mainstays JC Penney on West 17th Street. JC Penney first went into business in Kemmerer, Wyoming, in the far western part of the state. The first storefront in downtown Kemmerer is a tourist attraction.

The historic Cheyenne Opera House was torn down during the urban renewal craze in the 1960s to make way for the brand-new Penney store and Cheyenne's first escalator.

Fowler's, a longtime local department store in the Carey Building on the corner of Carey Avenue and West 17th Street, opened a second location at the Frontier Mall, but eventually could not compete with large chain department stores and closed its downtown and mall locations in the early 1990s.

After Fowler's went out, the Carey Building storefront was then occupied by Z's Furniture that was owned by EHS classmates Dave and Kim (Stogsdill) Zwonitzer. Their store eventually moved to the northeast side of town. Kim is also the daughter of my first-grade teacher, Mrs. Stogsdill. Remember, she's the one who taught me how to read.

The Carey Building fell into disrepair under absentee ownership. The Cheyenne city government recently razed the historic structure in favor of new construction of an expanded municipal court building.

My family bought into the suburban lifestyle, largely to blend as model minorities. Even though all suburbanites have unique experiences, on the surface, my outward family life was no different from that of my neighbors.

When it came to birthdays in the suburbs, we had the family who came from miles around with the Japanese version of the birthday party with lots of favorite Japanese food, like maki sushi, teriyaki chicken, and fresh mochi (rice pounded into a glutinous paste and shaped into sweet delicacies).

Mochi is traditionally made during a New Year's ceremony called mochitsuki. It's a big community activity. A mortar is hollowed out from a large diameter tree section. Hot rice is placed in the vessel, and mochi pounders take turns mashing the rice into a paste with a big two-fisted mallet.

The women in my family didn't do the rice pounding, but smooshed up hot rice in a suribachi (ceramic mortar) and kneaded with a surikoji (wooden pestle). It was definitely a team sport.

Then we had the neighborhood All American version of the same birthday party for schoolmates. On my eighth birthday, I remember giving out packs of 1961 Topps baseball cards as party favors. I wish I had those back. We noshed on plenty of hot dogs from the charcoal grill and washed them down with Coca-Cola.

In Cole Addition, within a four-block area, all the kids knew each other since we all went to the same nearby school, Fairview Elementary.

We knew each other so well, sometimes a childhood disease epidemic would spread through the school. Parents talked amongst themselves about illnesses going around and planned play days with kids with mumps or measles so we could self-infect ourselves to develop future immunity.

It was community building through communicable diseases.

The downtown activity also waned because of in-fill urban sprawl like at Grand Central Plaza that was constructed next to Eastridge Elementary school—now part of Carey Junior High School—on East Pershing Blvd and Concord Road. Montgomery Ward moved there from its downtown location on East 17th Street and Central Avenue.

Grand Central department store was the Target of the 1960s and the only place in town that carried my mom's favorite perfume, Desert Flower, which I bought her most Christmases.

Fairview Elementary was a feeder school for Carey Junior High. The Grand Central turned out to be a big after-school hangout at the snack counter. A bag of piping hot French fries right out of the deep fryer for a dime was my go-to after-school snack.

Much earlier, in 1953, Frank Cole plopped down the Cole Shopping Center at Pershing Blvd. and Converse Avenue in east Cheyenne. At that time, it was on the edge of town. Over the years, it became surrounded by a residential neighborhood and was an oasis on the way to and from Carey Junior High.

There was a Ben Franklin five-and-ten-cent store that overflowed with kids making their way home from school. The Garber's had a dry cleaner. The Gambles hardware store expanded from the south side. That's where my parents bought that brown Pyrex bowl set.

I recall a place where Sperry & Hutchinson (S&H) Green Stamps could be redeemed. The business was founded in 1896 and was very popular during the 1960s.

Green Stamps were rewards given to shoppers in a variety of businesses like grocery stores and gas stations in exchange for spending a certain amount of money, similar to the "points" reward programs used by coffee shops and airlines to promote customer loyalty.

One of my family jobs was to lick the glue on the back of the stamps and place them in the books that kept track of the stamp quantity. The trade value was based on the number of books.

It was fun to browse around the store. We accumulated enough stamps to trade for knick-knack items like sets of drinking glasses, games, and toys. I don't know why this sticks in my mind, but we had two aluminum plaques with bas-relief pilgrims that hung on the wall.

One of the anchor businesses was Garvalia Music that eventually gave way to Blockbuster video rental. Garvalia sold pianos and other band instruments. It was where my piano teacher, Miss Hess, sent her students to buy sheet music and lesson books.

I must have had an identity crisis when I was young. I never showed an aptitude for music, but I was pretty much forced to take piano lessons. I'm thinking I wasn't crazy about performing and the possibility of screwing up.

Music certainly didn't come naturally to me. I didn't feel the music but had to memorize it. That's why I took to the Suzuki violin teaching method. Miss Hess lived less than a block away from us and not being able to commute to lessons was not a viable excuse for skipping. During the holidays, she put up a silver artificial tree flocked with that spray-on snow and decorated with the same silvery and shiny glass Christmas tree balls.

I didn't like to practice. We had an old upright piano that was in my sister's room. There are tales that I flogged the piano with a chain from one of the swings from the backyard swing set.

The last piece of music I was playing when I quit lessons was from Opus 68, the Album Für die Jugend (Album for the Young) No. 10, *The Happy Farmer* by Robert Schumann. He composed forty-three short works in 1848 for his three daughters.

I quit piano in favor of baseball, which was a disappointment for my mom. As it turned out, I wasn't that great at baseball and later pursued music, at least teaching music as an avocation.

Mr. and Mrs. Garvalia were the "older" couple that lived two doors down from us on Windmill Road. They didn't have kids and weren't crazy about us careening down the hill on our skateboards.

Remember my grandfather's ranchette on the South Greeley Highway? One of the oak end tables from the living room had broken. In my junior high woodshop class, I fashioned a skateboard from one of the table slats and mounted wheels repurposed from a pair of Uncle George Sakata's roller skates. He was a competitive figure roller skater.

The last place to turn before gaining too much speed was into the Garvalia's driveway or bailing out onto their front yard. Sometimes a smooth turn was made, but other times the landings weren't so graceful.

When they heard the clatter of skate wheels hitting the sidewalk cracks, their front drapes were pulled open to give us threatening scowls when we crashed on our skateboards on their perfectly manicured lawn.

On the opposite side of the shopping center was the other anchor, the Cole Store, which sold clothing. We pretty much quit shopping at Fowler's downtown since Cole's was so much more convenient and biking distance with lots of parking.

We could still make multiple shopping stops, like at the Safeway and Roedel's Rexall drugstore, not to mention buying Candy Buttons at the Ben Franklin's store. Roedel's also had a downtown location. It was a West 17th Street mainstay that opened a second store in the suburbs.

My mom and sister liked another clothing store, Cooksey's. That was the place where I could consistently buy dress shoes since they stocked narrow sizes.

The little kids' knock-around shoe store was Dick's Bootery that specialized in brands like Buster Brown and Golden Goose. I bought my sneakers there, a pair of Posture Foundation (PF) Flyers that made me "run faster and jump higher."

Thinking back, I first chose PF Flyers because Boston Celtics star Bob Cousy endorsed and wore them on the Boston Garden parquet floor during the 1960s.

My dad played hoops in the city basketball league and sported plain-colored canvas Converse All-Star Chuck Taylor high tops. Because Celtics center, Bill Russell, wore them, I later opted for Converse black oxfords and wore them through high school.

Somewhere along the way, I picked up a pair of PF Flyers that I wear when I shoot baskets, which happens on rare occasions these days.

There also was a small branch library that opened up. That also meant way fewer visits to the main Carnegie Library in downtown Cheyenne.

A credit union recently purchased the Cole Shopping Center property and will soon begin constructing a new campus.

Post-war suburban development happened on undeveloped land where the economies of scale were more desirable. Members of Cheyenne's Japanese community, including my family, chose to blend in with the American Way, followed suit, and moved to the suburbs.

The Japanese neighborhood gentrified into parking lots and government buildings. Not only was the physical landscape altered forever, but the history was gone, too, until the Dinneen's Nishigawa townhouse development rekindled some sense of the past.

EIGHTEEN: Cupid's: The Last Building Standing

After gaining city government approval, the Dinneens knocked to the ground the last building standing in the once vibrant Japanese community at 509 and 511 W. 17th St. and made way for the new Lotus townhouses in the Nishigawa neighborhood.

When the contractor demolished the structure, souvenir scroungers salvaged some of the building materials like the tin ceiling tiles and the storefront's leaded glass windows. I suggested the Dinneens save some of the red bricks and repurpose them into the base for a sign to be erected summarizing the neighborhood history.

One of the first denizens in the neighborhood was Mrs. Yoshio Shuto. She came to Cheyenne through Colorado and Nebraska. Her first business venture was a rooming house above the Cheyenne Tent and Awning at 509 W. 17th St. Her Japanese boarders, including Kanbe Nomura, Kenji Sakuma, Minor and Tomo Sakuma, lived there through the 1930s.

When the city gave the Dinneens permission to raze, as an homage to the Japanese history of the area, they changed the name of their housing development to Nishigawa, which means "Westside neighborhood" in Japanese.

Between 1945 and 1974, the storefronts between 509 and 511 continued to have boarders living upstairs. Light industrial uses downstairs included Cheyenne Tent and Awning from 1928 to 1982 and Wortham Machinery from 1950 to 1982.

When Cheyenne Tent and Awning vacated 509, the Salvation Army, Jet Ink Sports, and Westside Thrift Store occupied the property.

My dad had a large green canvas that was used as a lean-to for campouts that developed a big rip which my dad had patched at Cheyenne Tent and Awning. I fondly remember the aroma of oiled canvases. It was noisy there, too, with the clanking of big sewing machine feet striking the bobbin cover plate.

We didn't have any camping equipment. Our first family camp out was a car camping excursion in the Medicine Bow National Forest. Dad fashioned a tent with that canvas. He borrowed sleeping bags from Uncle Rich. He was an avid outdoorsman. His sleeping bag was one of those heavy ones with the inner flannel lining stuffed with cotton.

I'm cold-blooded and because the late summer night air was cold, I didn't sleep much. Maybe it wasn't the chill that kept me awake, but the musty odor that smelled like Grandma Ohashi's basement.

After that first camping experience, I saved up enough money and split the cost with my dad for an army-issued down-filled bag from Sargent Surplus. My TV heroes were Sgt. Saunders and Lt. Hanley on the TV show *Combat!* (1962–1967) starring Rick Jason and Vic Morrow. The show was about the lives of US GIs as they fought the Germans in France. The stories had good plot arcs with World War II as the backdrop. I had it strapped to my surplus backpack for effect more than survival.

We didn't make any more family camping trips after that first one. Our outdoor life moved to tents set up in the backyard. The nylon down bag became bedding in the fallout shelter.

The Presbyterian Skyline Church Camp would be where I spent most of my childhood summer camping time.

When Wortham moved, new tenants included the House of Upholstery, Upholstery Unlimited, and Old Gold Antiques. The upstairs boarding house rooms were vacant beginning in 1988.

Probably the most controversial occupant was Cupid's adult entertainment store, which opened in 1989. John Dinneen took me on a tour of the structure before he reduced the building to rubble. There was evidence of peep show booths and a marijuana growing room.

Mrs. Shuto provided tasty meals to her boarding house tenants until around 1945.

NINETEEN: The City Café

Tommy Shuto managed the City Café along with his aunt Yoshio.

Across the street from her boarding house at 509, Mrs. Shuto turned her cooking skills into her most successful business venture, the City Café, which epitomized the mishmash culture of America.

There's a musical called *Flower Drum Song* that opened on Broadway in 1958. The EHS theater department produced the Richard Rodgers and Oscar Hammerstein II stage play that's about the conflicts between the older immigrants from China and their children. The American Way in the form of exotic dancer Linda Low (Nancy Kwan) lures Wang Ta (James Shigeta) to abandon his cultural past.

My sister was cast and played one of Ta's younger siblings and I drove her to rehearsal. I lingered to watch. She was the only Asian on the stage.

One of the big production numbers is a song about how living in America is like chop suey. The Americanized Chinese food dish is a metaphor of contrasting cultural iconography ranging from Hula Hoops to nuclear war, and Dr. Salk of polio vaccine fame to sexy Hungarian-born screen siren Zsa Zsa Gabor.

The City Café would become the allegory for my life. Chop suey was a staple on the menu, as was any connection I would have with the Japanese culture.

In 1926, the first place to open at 514 was the Tokio Café. Through 1934, several restaurateurs operated the business but didn't thrive. The last owner worked out an arrangement with Mrs. Shuto. She acquired the café and operated it with Seiyo "Johnny" Saiki (aka Saiki San). She changed the name to the City Café.

The City Café layout was segregated in reverse. The non-white patrons sat in the front and Caucasians walked through the kitchen and sat around large tables in the back.

The place became known for its Americanized, pan-Asian short orders but with a Japanese touch: teriyaki steak, egg foo yung, chop suey, and chop suey with the crunchy noodles also known as chow mein were among the favorites.

When my family went out to dinner, we always went to the City Café. I always ordered the same thing, the pork noodle bowl.

The broth was from meat and bones other than chicken, thick udon (noodles), a slice of pork cutlet, napa cabbage, maybe thinly sliced carrot for color, and when available sliced up kamaboko (fish sausage, for lack of a better descriptor.)

Pork noodles continue to be my preferred choice, even though fancy ramen is now a trendy Japanese dish. Ramen noodles are said to have originated in China and are made of wheat flour. When I order beef noodles at a Chinese restaurant, the noodles are ramen.

Thinking back, most of the other restaurants downtown were more upscale, like at the Plains Hotel. The City Café had a more integrated customer base.

Locals considered the west side to be the rough part of Cheyenne. Regardless, patrons came from all over for the cooking of Mrs. Shuto, Saiki San, Haruyo Tani, and my grandma Ohashi. There was also a big takeout business, for those who thought the neighborhood was a little too seedy.

During the 1950s and 1960s, the City Café after hours became the gathering place for the Skyline Nisei Club and many of their indoor Japanese community events. It was also a safe place for the Issei generation to hang around.

On the weekends, the club screened silent samurai movies in the front dining area for women and kids. I liked the stories about the Japanese warrior class that thrived in pre-modern Japan from the Seventeenth through the Nineteenth centuries.

One of my favorites is *Yojimbo* (1961) that was directed by Akira Kurosawa starring Toshiro Mifune as an unattached samurai ronin who comes into a town where two competing bad guys want to hire him as their bodyguard. MGM and director Sergio Leone remade the plot as a western called *Fist Full of Dollars* (1964) with Clint Eastwood.

They reserved the back of the café for drinking scotch whiskey and rousing Hanafuda (flower) card games, which is like gin rummy, but with pictures of flowers on thick cardboard tiles that made a clatter when slammed on the table.

The club meetings attracted Japanese from all over town. The City Café was a destination. The club later rented a separate hall in the 400 block of West 17th Street near the California Fish Market and Baker's Place.

In 1958, Mrs. Shuto invited her nephew, Takeshi "Tommy" Takeda (Shuto), from Japan to help her run the café. Mrs. Shuto returned to Japan in 1964, where she became ill and unable to return to Cheyenne. She eventually died in Japan.

Tommy and his family operated the café for a few more years until around 1970 when they built a new building on a piece of land owned by Johnny Baker at West 19th Street and O'Neil Avenue, where it still stands as a pan-Asian restaurant.

The City Café closure displaced the Tani family that boarded there. They moved to a place on West 27th Street.

Jitsuzu Tani came to the United States in 1916. His soon-to-be wife, Haruyo Tsukichi, arrived a couple of years later with her mother. The two eventually married in Colorado and farmed until 1926 before moving to Cheyenne. They lived in a room above the City Café.

Jitsuzu went to work at UP and Haruyo managed the City Café rooming house. Residents included the Tanis, Kanji Nagata, and Mrs. Shuto. Haruyo also worked at the City Café until 1941. When the war broke out, Jitsuzu was laid off from the railroad. They both worked odd jobs until 1960 when they retired.

Grandfather Sakata was fortunate to keep his railroad job. His CB&Q supervisors were sympathetic and allowed him to keep working.

My observation is that he was a work supervisor in the interior of Wyoming. Finding a replacement for him would be more trouble than risking cultural backlash. The UP was more of a strategic route that spanned from coast to coast.

When the City Café closed, that was the last hurrah for the West 17th Street Japanese community that held on for a few more years, but it was largely uninhabited by the mid-1970s. It reopened two blocks away, but it wasn't the same.

TWENTY: Japanese Diaspora

My parents' first home was on East 10th Street. When the Fairview School boundary changed, we moved to the suburbs.

The Japanese scattered away from downtown Cheyenne for a couple of reasons. In my view, the foremost rationale was the cultural upheaval caused by assimilation following World War II. That included the passing of the Issei generation, and the Nisei and their families were no longer obligated for their parents to be the center of the family.

Second, there was a general slowdown in downtown activity resulting from consequences of the American Way, including urban sprawl, and Nihon-Jin Crow discriminatory and exclusionary real estate practices that followed World War II. A nihon jin is a Japanese person.

The middle-class American suburban lifestyle was an idyllic way of living. No matter what our perceived social class might have been, the American Way stereotyped the admirable middle class as consisting of members with personal resiliency and hard workers.

Had the wider Cheyenne citizenry exercised more civility and collaboration with the Japanese after the war, would the West 17th Street neighborhood continue to exist?

In hindsight, probably so. In my ideal world, Nisei would have purchased land and started new businesses that would serve the wider community. Maybe my grandmother would have stayed at the City Café and eventually taken it over rather than opening the Highway Café on the south side. The Stop 'n Shop store might still be in business, or my grandfather could have opened a small grocery store filling a retail niche that is empty today.

Based on the Japanese community experience on two blocks in Cheyenne, the residents who lived there identified with and had a sense of belonging to the neighborhood where they lived and worked. When those feelings of community dissipated, with little support from the greater Cheyenne, the sense of community was lost.

Indicative of this, after getting out of the fish market business, the Kishiyama family moved from downtown. The California Fish Market didn't reopen. After they purchased a home with some acreage south of Cheyenne, Carl taught judo classes from a Quonset building. When I was in high school, I took a few lessons from him, thinking it would help me modify some wrestling moves, but martial arts have a very different skill set.

The Miyamoto brothers moved the Baker's Place liquor license to the Two-Bar Bowl on the north edge of town. That was the new growth area where the Frontier Mall would eventually be built.

Grandparents Ohashi moved from their downtown home on West 18th Street and opened the Highway Café closer to their new and more spacious place on East 8th Street.

The July 4th Japanese community met outside the city limits at the Kishiyamas. Before the big day, after my family moved to the Cole Addition, while not legal, we shot a few off in the backyard, mostly bottle rockets.

I remember a Roman candle standoff between Mr. Murray and Mr. St. Clair, with the green, red, and white balls of fire launched from the cardboard candlesticks flying across Cactus Hill Drive. The Murrays and St. Clairs lived across the street from each other.

My dad had a bunch of young guys working for him at the Coke plant. As near as I can figure, they made a fireworks run to Nebraska where big firecrackers like cherry bombs and M-80s were legal.

When my dad was finishing our basement, there were short lengths of half-inch copper water line left over from the bathroom installation. That was another Bill Fisher handyman project. He taught me how to work with copper tubing. I dug out the special tool used to cut through copper and buffed off the sharp edges. My friend Tad and I fashioned rocket launchers from the tubes that were the barrels. We had wars at his uncle and aunt's home on the Preston Ranch west of Cheyenne.

I do remember one of my errant rockets side-winding its way into Tad's cache of fireworks that set off quite a series of explosions. I'm surprised we didn't shoot our eyes out.

Around the 4th of July, the neighbor kids—mostly boys—rode our bikes to the fireworks stand. The city limits ended close to the Cole Addition boundary. The one and a half inch Zebra firecrackers were the largest allowed in Wyoming, and not large enough.

One of my projects was to mount a variety of firework display items like various kinds of pinwheels and bigger rockets on a piece of plywood and set off my own grand finale at the Kishiyamas. It was spectacular but in a dangerous sort of way. I didn't put out anyone's eyes during the festivities.

My pals and I unraveled firecrackers for the gunpowder and made small bombs out of my uncle George's cigar tubes. There was no Internet in those days, so we had to design our improvised explosive devices (IED) on our own.

An episode of *Combat!* about a bombing entitled "Cry from the Ruins" (1965) is a favorite of mine with an anti-war theme. It's about a distraught mother who searches for her baby buried in a cellar following an air raid. The American troops encounter a squad of Germans who begin shooting at each other.

The woman disrupts the skirmish and implores the two sides to put down their weapons and help find her baby. Turns out, the woman imagines her baby crying in the ruins after the bombing stops.

The story was a poignant cultural cue during the Cold War. Germans and Americans part peacefully realizing that killing each other is pointless.

The Goepferts had a color TV and their living room was a popular gathering point to watch *Combat!* in its final 1967 season, which was in color. There was something about previous seasons being black and white. Actual World War II footage was effectively inter-cut with the TV story.

Cole Addition was on the edge of town and there were plenty of vacant lots where we played World War II. We put on our *Combat!* gear, dug foxholes, and set our explosives to blow the treads off imaginary tanks that would rumble across the fields.

During the summer, day or night, the Cole Addition boys grabbed our *Combat!* toy guns and took our war strategies into the neighborhood.

My hero was Sgt. Saunders. He wore a helmet covered with a camouflaged fabric and carried a Thompson submachine gun. His commanding officer was Lt. Hanley. They communicated by walkie-talkies.

"Checkmate King-2, this is White Rook, over." Code words would be barked into the bulky two-way radios.

One of my prized possessions during my World War II phase was a Tommy gun toy made by Mattel. Since it was the Vietnam War era, my submachine gun was molded out of olive drab-colored plastic. I also had a spring-loaded toy bazooka that shot plastic projectiles.

We blew stuff up in the nearby vacant lots and shot each other during our war games. Between firecracker bomb explosions and walking alone to and from school, I don't know how I made it through childhood alive.

When I was born in May 1953, the Skyline Nisei Club minutes congratulate my parents. Mom and Dad cut back on their volunteer work in the community to set up a household. My sister came along two years later.

We lived in a one thousand square foot home at 2213 E. 10th Street at Logan Avenue, which extended over the railroad viaduct to the south side.

There were places in Cheyenne where people with high financial risk purchased homes on the west and south sides. These "pockets of poverty" came about because of "red-lining."

In the 1960s, a sociologist named John McKnight created geographic boundaries where banks could avoid making investments based on community demographics. Banks that charged loan applicants who lived in red-lined areas higher interest or required higher down payments based on these maps turned out to be a discriminatory practice.

The Federal Housing Administration (FHA) was formed as a part of the National Housing Act of 1934. New Deal FHA policies that were intended to provide banks with criteria to guide safe lending practices ended up speeding up inner-city decay in areas inhabited by lower-income minority households.

In 1935, the Federal Home Loan Bank Board through the Home Owners Loan Corporation evaluated 239 cities and designated areas on "residential security maps" to show the real-estate investment risk levels:

* Type A "Newer" Green-line areas in the desirable suburbs
* Type B "Desirable" Blue-line neighborhoods
* Type C "Declining" Yellow-line older areas
* Type D "Risky" Red-line poor investment areas

Based on these risk assumptions, an externality that arose was an increase in racial segregation and urban decline. While red lining is not prevalent today, its legacy is one of decaying urban areas in need of revitalization or redevelopment.

Right after the war, my parents married and purchased their first home in 1946 on East 10th Street, which was at the gateway to the south side.

Mom and Dad were natural-born American citizens and allowed to own real estate. It was a good place for early childhood. There wasn't much street traffic. We knew the neighbors on our side of the street, not so much on the other side. Fairview Elementary was a half-mile walk straight up the street. Quite a hike for a three-foot-tall kid.

When the Fairview Elementary boundaries changed, my parents moved to the Cole Addition suburb on the east side of Cheyenne. The alternative was Alta Vista School, which was closer, but in my mother's view, was more urban and a rough and tumble school compared to Fairview. Ironically, the school district rebuilt Alta Vista, which is now in a newer structure. Fairview is still the same and, like me, a mid-century modern 1950s relic.

In the suburbs, there was a sense of homogeneity in the Cole Addition. Kids all went to the same neighborhood school, meaning kids all knew each other, which meant parents got to know each other because hordes of kids traipsed through every house on the block.

There were neighborhood parties, lots of pick-up football games at the nearby Triangle Park, and half-court basketball games in the Goepfert's driveway. They had a double car garage and the widest, flattest slab of concrete in a two-block radius. Our driveway was narrower and at more of a slant that threw off my shot at the Goepfert's.

Later, because of the Japanese diaspora from downtown, Paul Kubota, who became a dentist but was still single, moved with his aging parents a block from us on Windmill Road. The Kubota family sold my grandfather their pool hall at 516.

He eventually married his wife, Mary, and both continued to live with Paul's folks until they died. The only time I saw my dad with a lingering hangover was after Paul Kubota's bachelor party.

He had a place on the floor where he took his afternoon nap, but on this after-party Sunday, it was an all-day nap.

Because of their West 17th Street connection, the Kubotas were an excellent support system for my parents. Paul and Mary didn't have any kids, but maintained a connection with some of the other Japanese families still in Cheyenne, particularly among the mushroom hunters, who we didn't associate with much.

Civil rights for Japanese people began to be restored around the time I was born. My parents got their bowling league cards reinstated.

The home front advocacy by groups such as the Skyline Nisei Club helped provide a safe place for Cheyenne Japanese, considering a few years before, Japanese, even in Wyoming, had to report their whereabouts to law enforcement.

Even though Grandfather Ohashi was self-employed in the safe haven of Wyoming, he was the one who was in the wrong place at the wrong time.

TWENTY-ONE: Wrong Place, Wrong Time

Auntie Elsie worked with federal and state authorities to get her father and brother released from the Tulare Detention Center in California.

Before the war, my grandfather Ohashi and his oldest son—my uncle George—operated a truck-farming business. Grandpa was an award-winning farmer in Washington State and helped other farmers find new markets for their crops.

He and his family arrived in Wyoming by way of Colorado and opened the Western Growers Exchange at 1619 Pioneer Ave., just north of the Dinneen Garage. They later moved nearby to 304 W. 15th St., across from the UP-railroad yard.

During the summer of 1942, Grandfather and Uncle George were buying vegetables in California for their customers in Wyoming and Colorado, when FDR issued EO 9066.

I don't know if they voluntarily turned themselves in or not, but the US military detained the two. According to family accounts, they lived for several months at the Tulare center, halfway between Fresno and Bakersfield, California, where authorities confiscated their truck.

My family mentioned little about this experience to me. Discussions about World War II weren't encouraged or volunteered. It wasn't until my Auntie Elsie was in hospice at a continuous care facility in Cheyenne that I learned any details about this story.

It's not like I didn't have time to visit, and I should have kept in better touch with my uncles and aunts. Upon Elsie's death, I'm the unofficial keeper of family history and I inherited a box of her old photos. I've been sorting through them and trying to identify people the best I can, but with little luck.

If you've lost touch with any of your relatives, call them, write a letter, go visit them. Ask for help to identify people in photos.

It's too bad it took me so long to hear family stories. Don't make the same mistake I did. I was very young when I hung around with my grandpa and Uncle George at the Café. Even if I knew about World War II, hearing about EO 9066 would have flown over my head. I might have been less oblivious if those stories were told to me when I was in high school and college.

I would have appreciated hearing about this family history and the circumstances around their experience being two out of ninety-two thousand Japanese forced into one of the fifteen assembly centers established by the US Army.

The US Army herded Grandpa Ohashi and Uncle George into the Tulare Assembly Center where they spent several months awaiting transfer to one of the ten permanent war relocation camps constructed in the interior of the United States. A third of the total number of internees not sent to assembly centers went directly to one of the ten relocation camps.

The primary purpose for the hastily established assembly centers was to immediately detain West Coast Japanese before they traveled elsewhere domestically or returned to Japan.

Beginning in 1942, the Tulare Assembly Center was set up on the Tulare County fairgrounds outside of Tulare, California.

The fairground site began around 1917 as a livestock sales ring and became one of California's most important county fairs. The US Army leased the site in March 1942 and renovated the fairgrounds to accommodate approximately forty-eight hundred Japanese who mostly lived north of Los Angeles in Ventura, Santa Barbara, Guadalupe, Santa Maria, Arroyo Grande, Pasadena, Torrance, and Gardena.

The Tulare center was about half a mile long and a quarter-mile wide. In April 1942, the Army Corps of Engineers turned the project over to the WCCA. The WCCA completed the retrofit construction project a month later at a cost of five hundred thousand dollars.

The Army Corps renovated nineteen horse stalls and built barracks and communal halls for housing, food services, and sanitary facilities. The barracks were twenty by one hundred feet and had eight-foot-high plywood partitions dividing the long and narrow structures into family apartments.

Auntie Elsie told me she worked with Cheyenne law enforcement agencies, the US Attorney's office, and the WCCA. They agreed to release her brother and father back to Wyoming.

She played down the incident, saying that everything worked out okay. This was just before Christmas 2015. I planned to stop by again in January but didn't make the trip. She died in February and I didn't get to hear the full story.

Had she been unsuccessful, they would have been transferred to the Rivers Relocation Center in Arizona. The camp, informally known as "Gila River," was unique because it was on an Indian reservation.

Over the objections of the Arizona governor, the Rivers camp was on the Gila River Indian Reservation, also home to the akimel o'odham (Pima) and the pee-posh (Maricopa) tribes. The camp was named after Jim Rivers, who was the first Akimel O'odham tribal member killed in World War I.

During the war, the Gila River camp interned over thirteen hundred Japanese, mostly from California. The camp was divided into two smaller camps, the Canal sub-camp, which had the fire station, and the Butte sub-camp, which was the hospital site. Both camps had elementary and high schools.

The Bureau of Indian Affairs (BIA) commissioner, John Collier proposed that the DOI be authorized to work with the Japanese who would provide labor for the BIA and the BOR on irrigation and agricultural projects. The BIA manages land held in trust by the US government on behalf of recognized Indian tribes.

Besides the Gila River Indian Community, the US War Department chose the Colorado River Indian Community, home to the nüw (Chemehuevi), the aha makhav (Mohave), hisatsinom (Hopi), and Dine (Navajo) tribes, also in Arizona, for the Poston Relocation Center.

The BIA asked to manage both camps but approved to administer only the Gila River camp. The WRA took over the Poston camp after a disagreement with the BIA over lands that should be farmed. The BIA was formed in 1824, originally under the Department of War, and later transferred to the DOI in 1849.

Unlike other camps around the country, residents who were Gila River Indian Community tribal members had low priority to be hired for jobs during construction and working inside the camp in favor of area Caucasian residents.

Internees first arrived at the Canal sub-camp during July 1942 to finish setting up the Gila River camp before others arrived from assembly centers or directly from restricted areas.

Initially, the ten thousand internees who came to the Canal sub-camp were double the capacity. There were tight quarters by the time the Butte sub-camp opened a month later.

The Gila River camp opened at the height of Arizona summer heat, with forty-eight days over a hundred degrees in July and August 1942. The barracks were not insulated. Some internees fashioned homemade swamp coolers to lower the temperature.

There was also widespread dissension around the loyalty questionnaire. About thirteen hundred internees were ruled as disloyal no-no boys relocated to the Tule Lake camp.

To keep their families intact, four hundred and fifty no-no internees at Gila River were sent to the Crystal City camp in Texas, where families could stay united or reunite. Some families were split up at assembly centers or when the FBI barged into homes.

Former Minidoka camp internee Aya Medrud told me about the time when she was a child and the FBI came into their home in Washington State and took her father away, believing he may be a Japanese spy. She didn't find out about his whereabouts for three weeks.

The Gila River camp operated a dehydration center to preserve vegetables and later set up a canning operation. The internees learned how to grow crops in the dry and hot conditions of central Arizona.

The climate was much different than that in central California. Their efforts resulted in shipping over four million pounds of produce to eight of the other WRA camps in 1944.

Life at Gila River was like other camps. Activities included Boy and Girl Scouting, women's clubs, theater groups, and sports teams. Internees attended Buddhist and Christian services in the camp. Students attended elementary and high schools at the Gila River camp and Butte sub-camp.

My grandfather and uncle dodged the full relocation camp experience, even though living in a detention center sounded similar. They returned to Cheyenne, only to find their storefront closed and business at a standstill, with no produce to peddle.

To make ends meet, Grandpa took jobs on West 17th Street as a custodian at Stockgrowers National Bank and washed dishes at the Mayflower Café. Mrs. Shuto hired my grandmother to cook at the City Café.

TWENTY-TWO: Rack 'Em Up

Grandpa Ohashi purchased the pool hall from the Kubota family. He was quite the shark and liked showing me his trick shots.

My grandfather was entrepreneurial. While Grandma had a steady job at the City Café, he ended up buying the pool hall at 516 from the Kubota family. There were several businesses there before it became a pool hall and my grandfather took over.

In 1922, Taigo and Nao Suzuki operated a Japanese goods store at 516 W. 17th St. and also lived there from 1926. The Suzukis sold their market to Kazuma and Ume Mikawa. Kazuma initially worked for the UP railroad.

Ume, recently widowed, married Kazuma in 1924, and two years later, they bought the grocery where they made and sold tofu. The store was closed when they moved to Colorado in 1932.

It was next to the David Cantor Meat shop that sold kosher food to the local Jewish community, which had a prominent presence in downtown Cheyenne.

Masaka Hosokawa originally came to Cheyenne in 1930. He was a machinist with the UP and roomed with Takematsu Matsushima in his barbershop apartment at number 408.

Masaka converted the meat shop into a pool hall in 1939 and three years later, sold the pool hall to Gontaro and Kiyo (Sato) Kubota. After selling out, Masaka worked odd jobs and continued to live in the west side of Cheyenne, including above the City Café.

Gontaro Kubota came to the United States in 1906. He moved to Wyoming in 1915 and worked for the UP as the Sherman Hill section supervisor east of Laramie. In 1921, he returned to Japan and married his wife, Kiyo.

The two returned to Wyoming and stayed their first night in Mrs. Shuto's boarding house at 509 W. 17th St. The UP rehired Gontaro and they returned to the Sherman Hill section where the couple started a family and later moved with the railroad to the Buford section between Cheyenne and Laramie.

After the bombing of Pearl Harbor, the railroad fired Gontaro, and he moved his family to Cheyenne, which is when he bought the Hosokawa Pool Hall. The Kubotas operated the pool hall until 1957 when they sold to my grandfather Ohashi.

It was taboo for me to go into my grandfather's business. When I was on the weekend Coke route with my dad, I had to wait outside. To find out what I missed, while researching this story, I posted on facebook asking for any recollections about the West 17th Street business district.

Henry responded. He worked for my grandfather, racking billiard balls for tips. He was paid fifty cents a table to remove the covers and brush them off. He befriended a "fat Anglo," who was the bouncer and held the side bets for all the tables.

Grandpa Ohashi owned the pool hall until his death in 1966. I inherited one of his old Brunswick tables. The heavy oak rails and pedestal that supported two flat slate table pieces literally weighed a ton. I hauled it around to Lander and later donated it to the Northern Arapaho senior citizen center in Ethete on the Wind River Indian Reservation.

I kept the 9-ball, and many memories of that table, particularly when my dad and I assembled it in the basement next to my new bedroom in our home on Windmill Road. I had plenty of time to practice by setting up shots and developed a pretty good eye.

Since I wasn't allowed into the pool hall as a kid, when I was old enough to know better, I spent plenty of time shooting pool when I worked the late shift at the Bellevue House student center at Hastings College. I didn't shoot much eight-ball but learned how to play on a much bigger snooker table with small pockets.

In Lander, I was a member of the One Shot Lounge Valley 8-Ball team. Those tables were small, with large pockets. Accuracy wasn't as important, and the games moved along quickly. Considering the legacy of my grandfather, winning two trophies and many a 9-ball game were rites of passage for me.

Grandpa Ohashi was a gambling man. He came to the United States in 1898 and worked mostly in farming around Tacoma, Washington, before moving to Ketchikan, Alaska.

In 1970, I was a high school junior and part of a Presbyterian Church summer work crew at Sheldon Jackson College in Sitka, Alaska. Our group took a ferryboat field trip to Ketchikan. While walking around on the boardwalk, I saw a wooden sign that read, "OHASHI Candy and Tobacco."

My eventual Hastings College roommate Sam and I went in and found out the store was owned by my grandfather's brother. I have relatives who live in the Pacific Northwest. In a past life when I was building affordable housing, I attended a Habitat for Humanity conference in Seattle and ran into a distant cousin.

As a teenager, Grandpa was a cook at an Alaskan mining camp and learned the hard ways of the world at a young age shooting pool. He learned to say all the best cuss words in English.

In 1911, he returned to Japan and married Natsu Yonago. While in Washington, they had seven children. The others were born later in Colorado.

In 1925, my grandfather got a lead from a friend about a place in Monte Vista, Colorado, that was good lettuce-growing country. He regretted that move because the land wasn't as productive as his friend led him to believe.

Making the best of the decision, he ended up in Brighton, through Denver and Ft. Lupton, where he opened a produce store selling vegetables from area farmers.

In 1934, he expanded his business into Cheyenne, where he and his family eventually settled. According to Auntie Elsie, their first home was in a boarding house across from the UP-rail yard.

On the other side of West 17th Street at 515, Tsunesaboro "Tsune" Ogasawara had a cigar store. Tsune had the business from 1920 to 1936. He died shortly in 1937 and was buried in the Cheyenne Lakeview Cemetery.

According to Arlene Ogasawara, Tsune is distantly related to her well-known Ogasawara family that initially settled in Sweetwater County and eventually ended up in Cheyenne.

Shiro Ogasawara immigrated to Reliance, Wyoming, in Sweetwater County in 1922, where he operated a boarding house for miners. He married Chizo Futa, who was born in Cheyenne.

In 1941, they were living in Stockton, California, and were sent to the Rowher Relocation Center in Arkansas. Rohwer was the easternmost of the WRA camps, and along with the Jerome camp, the only ones in the Jim Crow South.

Arkansas Governor Homer Adkins opposed the Rowher camp being in his state. He agreed only after being assured that white soldiers would hold the internees under armed guard and that the WRA would transport the Japanese out of Arkansas after the war.

Rohwer is in Desha County, twelve miles northeast of McGehee and a hundred and ten miles southeast of Little Rock in forested and swampy lowland in the Mississippi River floodplain. The Jerome camp was twenty-seven miles away.

During the Great Depression, the newly established Farm Security Administration (FSA) purchased unproductive farmland, including Arkansas swampy areas, from struggling farmers and resettled them onto group farms that were more productive. The FSA preceded what is now the Farmer's Home Administration in the USDA.

The WRA purchased the ten thousand acres from the FSA in 1942 and the Army Corps of Engineers built the camp.

As at other camps, a large percentage of the population was school-age children. Kindergarten through high school enrollments totaled over two thousand students taught by close to ninety instructors. WRA wanted to hire white teachers from the local community.

The federal wage scale for teachers was more than double the average salary of Arkansas teachers. The WRA didn't want to hire away too many local teachers for jobs at Rowher and agreed to a quota system that allowed the hire of one or two teachers from any single school district.

Spectator sports like softball, baseball, basketball, and football leagues were popular activities among Rowher internees. The camp's thirty-two softball teams drew up to two thousand fans.

The biggest events were camp variety shows produced by the Issei Recreation Department that attracted audiences of five thousand show-goers. The traveling revue visited different blocks over several days.

I don't know this for sure, but I imagine the camp entertainment included audience participation in the Obon Festival bon odori folk dancing. The Japanese-American version evolved from odori nembutsu dancing, which was a popular Buddhist chant and dance dating back to the Eighth century.

Bon odori is a circle dance with participants of all ages moving to the music and the rhythmic beat of daiko (drum) drumming. There are various sizes of daiko. Players play the daiko with various sized bachi (sticks). A yagura stand supported the daiko perched atop.

A unique activity in the Rohwer camp was creating kobu (natural wood sculptures). Rowher was in a swampy area. The wet terrain was an excellent source for hardwood tree limbs like oak, hickory, elm, and cypress. Interesting natural wood pieces were polished and mounted for display.

After the war, Chizu and Shiro moved to the Cheyenne south side where they live today.

At 517 West 17th Street, a businessman named Mr. M.S. Jow opened the Continental Supply Company specializing in imported food and sundries from Japan. He was also part-owner of the Bon Ton Café at 531 West 16th Street along with Mr. T.S. Okana.

Across the street, Wortham Machine eventually took over the building at 515 and 517, which was torn down years ago. The Dinneens purchased the lots and they are now part of their Nishigawa Neighborhood townhouse development.

At the end of the block to 520 were apartments occupied by Tetsu Takahashi, the Kubota family, and Fred Futa. Fred was the son of Chizu Futa and Shiro Ogasawara and was a member of the Cheyenne Nisei baseball team.

All that remains where the City Café once stood to the end of the 500 block is a parking lot. The Cheyenne Historic Preservation Board required the Dinneens to erect an information sign about the Japanese community that once thrived there.

TWENTY-THREE: The Highway Café

My grandparents Ohashi moved out of downtown and opened the Highway Café.

After the war, life became a little more stabilized for my family. Grandma quit cooking at the City Café in 1951. My grandparents Ohashi and Uncle George moved from downtown Cheyenne and opened the Highway Café on the south Greeley Highway.

In the summer, Uncle George continued the truck farming aspect of the business. He set up a vegetable and fruit stand next to the café. It was an early version of a farm-to-table restaurant.

I helped George organize the point-of-sale by constructing some rudimentary aisles from the makeshift tables and displaying the produce with price signs. The stand was in the sun, and I helped build a shelter from the green tarp that my family used on that camping trip to Lake Marie in the Medicine Bow National Forest.

Uncle George let me help "tend the store." He let me use a knife. When a customer wanted a watermelon, my uncle allowed me to "plug the melon." That entailed cutting a trapezoidal wedge through the rind and removing it to show the patron.

It was obvious when the melon was ripe or not. If the customer rejected it, I replaced the plug for the next curious buyer. If we did not sell the plugged melon by the end of the day, it would go from the fruit stand to the restaurant table.

I was a shy kid. That experience gave me more confidence, particularly when it came to sales and developing my entrepreneurial tendencies.

The café was originally farther south but was forced to move a few blocks north when I-80 came through. That was a good move because the café was then in the heart of the south side motel district, where many CFD rodeo cowboys stayed.

Working in the family business was my first summer job. My sister and I weren't old enough to do actual work, but she waited tables and I washed dishes. My sister may have kept tips, but George compensated me with candy.

One of the occasional jobs I did for my grandmother was to write the daily specials on a blackboard that hung next to the counter. I scrawled with a stick of chalk the menu items that included short order favorites like hamburger steaks, a meatloaf served with a scoop of canned green beans or corn, and a mound of mashed potatoes or rice. I don't know what happened, but my handwriting has gone downhill since.

The only place I've found that came close to the City Café or my grandmother's pork noodles was the 20th Street Café across from Sakura Square in Lower Downtown Denver.

Whenever I was in Denver, I stopped for lunch. The wooden chairs pushed up to tables covered with light-greenish vinyl covers, a throwback to my childhood at the Highway 85 Café.

The Okuno family ran the business for two generations. The current Sansei owners, Rod and Karen Okuno, closed their restaurant for good during the Corona Virus 19 (COVID-19) pandemic.

The patrons were all friendly. They enjoyed the novelty of being served by kids. The Café was on the south side, and the clientele was diverse. There was a Filipino fellow named Carl who came in every night. I think he worked at the Plains Hotel that is still on Central Avenue, north over the railroad viaduct. The Plains hired a lot of Filipino guys who were bellhops and worked in the restaurant. He always had a half order of the daily special.

A big Japanese guy named Frank Omoto used to come in and sit at the far end of the counter. I learned later he was a mechanic at Halladay Motors. Hank was a jolly sort, always had a big smile on his face. I think that's because he was such a successful fisher. He was Uncle Rich's fishing buddy.

Hank would sometimes bring in part of his catch, and Grandma would cook it up for him. Hank also was the first president of the Skyline Nisei Club.

I don't know how much work we did, but there was plenty of time to play around with the neighbor kids. Directly across the highway was the Corral Motel, and a few blocks to the north was the Lariat Motel owned by Marvin Goldhammer and his family.

One of his sons, Randy, was around my age. We spent quite a bit of time hanging around together at the café, mostly because my uncle was freewheeling when it came to giving candy to kids.

During CFD, the Highway Café was hopping, particularly for breakfast. One job I had when I wasn't goofing around was grating potatoes for hash browns. After his day job was over at the Coke plant, my dad went in and flipped steaks until closing.

When my grandmother slowed down, and Uncle George went to work at Laramie County Community College, my dad wasn't interested in taking over the business when it closed in 1966, after my grandfather died. The café has since transformed into several businesses, including a tobacco store and now a doughnut shop.

My dad worked there in the evenings after his day job. He didn't have the entrepreneurial spirit like his dad. He had an opportunity to keep the business open. My guess is that he had a steady job and family obligations. Mom likely would have had to go to work, which would have been disruptive.

I've often wondered what may have happened if he decided to take over the restaurant. My life would have taken a big turn. Having inherited the entrepreneurial gene, I would have gladly taken the challenge to own and operate it.

My experiences being around the Highway Café would serve me a few years later in life. If I had a resumé back then, having "no queasiness around dirty dishes" was a valuable job skill that would serve me when I landed my first summer job.

TWENTY-FOUR: Summer Jobs and Jerks

One of my Carey Junior High School teachers, who was also a neighbor, Sam Contos, lived on the corner of Windmill and Old Trail roads along with his wife, Stella, son John, and daughter Marti, who got me a job at the Hitching Post Inn as a busboy. Stella still lives there, probably one of the few "original" members of my old neighborhood.

He must have had a conversation with my dad about getting me out of the house. That job was an eye-opener. My blinders were taken off when I found myself exposed to people who were way different from my family members and neighbors.

I gained an appreciation for jerks at an early age at the Hitching Post. Occasionally, I felt openly discriminated against. I later figured out that the remarks by out-of-towners of all types—rednecks to big city folk—during the day shifts were made based on their privilege and entitlement.

Me working in a menial job placed me in the perpetual immigrant stereotype.

"Hop Sing, bring me more coffee," some scrawny guy with a bad mustache and a Texas-like drawl hollered at me in reference to Ben Cartwright's Chinese servant (Victor Sen Yung) on the TV show *Bonanza* (1959 to 1973). Sen Yung's role was primarily that of the family cook. Producers paid him considerably less than others in the cast with similar supporting roles.

The show was about a three-time widower, Ben Cartwright (Lorne Greene), and his three sons, each born from a different wife. The eldest was Adam (Pernell Roberts). He was an engineer and designed the stately Ponderosa ranch house. Hoss (Dan Blocker) was six-foot-four and three hundred and twenty pounds, worthy of his nickname. The youngest was Little Joe (Michael Landon).

I didn't have a snappy answer to his obnoxious request. Coming up with clever responses is a skill I've had to develop over the years. Mad Magazine had a recurring department called "Snappy Answers to Stupid Questions."

When I first moved to Boulder and was shopping at the local camera store, a woman approached me at the display counter and asked, "Can you read this," while pointing to one of the language versions of a camera operation manual.

"No, I don't know Spanish," was my answer.

Another time on an airplane, I was sitting in one of the emergency exit row seats, you know, the ones with extra legroom.

"Can-you-speak-English?" the flight attended loudly annunciated at me while also staring at me, being sure I could see her lips move.

"I'm Japanese, not deaf," was my retort.

The Hitching Post was a big hotel and convention center on the west edge of Cheyenne but had humble beginnings. In 1921, Petter and Nathan Smith, who emigrated from Russia, and nephew Harry joined the American Way when they were granted Homestead Act land twenty miles west of Cheyenne.

Their original idea was to raise potatoes on the dusty prairie, but they ended up selling the property and used the money to buy land on the west end of Cheyenne, where the brothers built the Lincoln Court along the Lincoln Highway in 1927.

Western expansion continued as the American citizenry became more mobile. As car ownership became more affordable, motor hotels like Lincoln Court popped up all along main highways, including the transcontinental US Highway 30 and Route 66 from Chicago to Los Angeles.

Lincoln Court evolved into the Hitching Post Inn that became a regional resort that hosted movie stars, politicians, and was the unofficial headquarters of the Wyoming State Legislature. When I worked there, Harry Smith and his wife Harriet were the owners of the Hitching Post Inn managed by their son, Paul.

I knew the popular spot as the "Hitch," the "Post," and "HP."

The Hitch was my home away from home for two summers, sometimes fifty or sixty hours per week, mostly at night. As a new busboy, they trained me during the breakfast and lunch shifts in the coffee shop. There was a pecking order.

I remember clearing a table in the coffee shop during the lunch rush and being approached by a frantic mom. Her son left his dental retainer on the paper placemat and wondered if I remembered clearing it from the table. Being a braces wearer myself, I identified with the kid's angst.

After going back to the dishwashing area, I dug through the paper trash and, sure enough, found his retainer. That mom better be paying that favor forward, which could explain the good luck I've had over the years.

As I became more experienced, tips during the dinner hours in the two dining rooms—the Beefeater and Patio rooms—from four p.m. to midnight were much better.

The CFD day shifts were like other days, except way more people. Things died down in the afternoon when the crowds were at the rodeo.

My favorite shift was the ten p.m. to six a.m. late shift during CFD. I ran booze and glassware from the bar to the Coach Rooms in the conference center, where there were big shows. I could have sneaked in for a closer view, but I was not allowed into the big parties.

There was a fairly well-known lounge singer named Jody Miller who played the Hitching Post. She won the Best Female Country Vocal Performance Grammy award in 1966 for "Queen of the House" that climbed to number twelve on the Billboard Hot 100 and number five on the country singles chart. The song was her answer to Roger Miller's "King of the Road" and was sung to the same tune.

She was the most well-known person I met at that job. I took room service to her from time to time. She wasn't much of a tipper. Maybe she left tips when she checked out, but the cashier didn't hand them over to me.

The only other celeb who showed up on one of my shifts was a movie actor named Victor Jory. He sported a jungle field jacket and sat at the end of the coffee shop counter having breakfast. How people can eat and smoke a cigarette at the same time was a mystery to me.

His roles include that of Injun Joe in the movie version of *The Adventures of Tom Sawyer* (1938), by Mark Twain. Jory played the part of slave master Jonas Wilkerson at the Tara plantation in *Gone with the Wind* (1939).

He co-starred with cowboy actor Hopalong Cassidy in seven films between 1941 and 1943. I didn't know who he was, but the waitresses were gaga over him. He graciously signed a few autographs before digging back into his eggs.

The Hitching Post job was also the first time I'd gotten to know adults other than those in my immediate family environment. The service staff members were all older than me. I hit it off with a funny guy named Mark Samansky.

He went to Central High School and was four or five years older than me. I was a seventh-grader at Carey Junior High. We both preferred the late CFD shifts. I wasn't old enough to drive, and he drove me home if my dad couldn't come to get me.

Mark introduced me to what is now my favorite lunch or dinner meal, two sliced chicken sandwiches with mayo and lettuce on white bread. There was something about the food at the Hitch that tasted better than other places. Smoking was allowed in restaurants back then. Maybe that was the difference.

When Mark and I began or ended our shifts together, we would relax in the coffee shop under a fake tree protruding from the center of the staff break area, eating that meal.

The big Coach Rooms in the conference center could have the inner walls pulled back to make one gigantic space. One night during CFD 1968, after a big show, Mark climbed behind a drum kit and played the drum solo from "Inna Gadda Da Vida," by the acid rock band Iron Butterfly.

Our boss, Paul Smith, called Mark and me into his office about that. He didn't fire either of us. "Nice drum solo," Paul said, as a reminder that even though nobody saw, the walls had ears.

I was in and out of that big-night show in the Coach Room busing tables, bringing in fresh glasses to the bar, and hauling up boxes of booze from under the main bar. Some popular acts played the Hitching Post during CFD, including the Sons of the Pioneers. That night I didn't know the band, but then again, I wasn't paying attention.

CFD or not, the Hitching Post was the go-to place for other celebrities who came to town. A movie premiere for *Cheyenne Autumn* screened at the Lincoln Theater on October 3, 1964. That was well before I worked at the Hitching Post, but it was the place where star Carroll Baker disembarked from her train right in front of the hotel.

The actual premiere was in London, but former Mayor Bill Nation arranged the press premiere. He was a photographer and had an eye for the public relations benefit of screening *Cheyenne Autumn* in downtown Cheyenne.

TWENTY-FIVE: Hitching Post Inn and RFK

The Hitching Post was the place for movie stars and prominent politicians who came to Cheyenne. On April 26 and 27 in 1968, US Senator Robert Kennedy (D-NY) (RFK) was running for President. He came through Cheyenne on a whistle-stop tour. The local Democratic Party held a reception for him at the Hitching Post in the afternoon before a speech he was to deliver at the Pavilion in Lions Park later that evening.

My first taste of up-close retail politics greatly influenced me and resulted in my continuing relationship with the Hitching Post Inn.

Wyoming was politically purple back then, and presidential candidates from both major parties regularly stumped for votes in the Equality State.

For me, it was mostly about the symbols of politics. Campaign 1968 marked the beginning of my political memorabilia collection. My mission for that election cycle was to collect a bumper sticker and button from each candidate.

There was no internet. I mailed handwritten letters to the campaigns to collect their campaign materials. Since then, I've scrounged buttons for each major party nominee and their running mate starting in 1896.

Campaign 1968 was the first presidential election that interested me. I was old enough to know about the election in 1964 but not old enough to take any personal interest.

"Accordingly, I shall not seek, and I will not accept, the nomination of my party for another term as your president," President Johnson declared. Even though LBJ won the 1964 general election by a landslide, because of his withdrawal, the 1968 race was wide open with huge Republican and Democratic fields.

My Carey Jr. High School pal, named Mike, was big into Democratic Party politics, mostly because of his parents. His mom, Janet, was Laramie County Clerk, and his dad, Ed, was a state legislator. He served in the Wyoming State Legislature with Ellen Crowley, Tosh Sueymatsu's wife, also an attorney.

Cheyenne was the first stop on a long train trip through Nebraska, which ended in Omaha just before the Nebraska primary in mid-May. Nebraska was a key state for RFK.

Mike and I decided to see him. We taped six pieces of poster board together and stapled them onto two sticks of lathe. I scrawled "Kennedy Is Our Man" on the sign with Magic Marker, a new writing medium back in those days. I was the cartoonist for the school paper, *The Tumbleweed*, and drew a pretty good caricature of RFK on the bottom of the sign. We rolled it up and hauled it on foot four miles from my house in the Cole Addition to the Pavilion in Frontier Park.

Saturday afternoon, there was a reception for RFK and his entourage at the Hitching Post before his speech that night. I wasn't on the schedule that day in favor of attending the rally. Working in the banquet room where the local Democratic Party held the reception would have been fun.

I came to realize that this is what old-fashioned politics was about. A *Wyoming Eagle* story estimated two thousand supporters, and the curious packed the place. RFK was there with his family members, his wife Ethel, and maybe some of his kids. He was a rock star. I couldn't hear anything he said because of the crowd noise.

Afterward, RFK noticed our sign. He came over, shook our hands, and autographed a "Join Now" campaign card I picked up at the door, which I still have.

I also learned at that rally how accessible politicians could be at any level of government. I didn't realize it then, but this was my first taste of federalism, the relationships between the national, state, and local governments.

I ended up studying political science in college and graduate school, which grew into a public service career in my first past life. That experience has stuck with me to this day, not to mention my fascination with autographs and political buttons.

RFK won the Nebraska primary.

A few weeks later, on June 6th, my clock radio turned on early in the morning to a live broadcast from Los Angeles about RFK's murder. A bad guy named Sirhan Sirhan shot him at close range.

TWENTY-SIX: Naïve in the Deep South

It was turbulent during the spring of 1968. Prior to RFK getting murdered, James Earl Ray assassinated Martin Luther King, Jr. (MLK) in Memphis on April 4th. He was standing on the Lorraine Motel balcony.

His death didn't affect me much at the time. I'm thinking that my world in Wyoming was very insular. Civil rights, generally, weren't talked about at all in my home. I don't recall any conversations at school.

I was oblivious. Maybe that was because the rest of the state played it down. The headline in the April 5th CST had nothing to do with the assassination. It read, "President Calls Leaders to Deal with Tensions."

Compare that to the June 6th CST headline "Sen. Kennedy Dies—Victim of an Assassin's Bullet." The difference to me was having shaken RFK's hand in Cheyenne made his death more real.

As for race relations, I knew there were problems around civil rights issues, but they were distant from me. It wouldn't be until a road trip through the deep South that new experiences would open my eyes.

The mainstream news media covered the Kennedy family. I don't recall hearing anything about MLK except negative spins around marches and protests that erupted into violence.

In 1989, one of my friends in Lander, Raymond, and I decided to go on a Cheech and Chong college football bowl-athon. Ray is Latino, and we both had roots in Laramie. I worked with Ray's brother, Don, at the Laramie Coke plant. We met in Laramie and drove to Denver, then flew into New Orleans on Christmas Day.

When the hotel clerk noticed two brown guys checking in together, the first room we were assigned wasn't made up. We stayed in what turned out to be one of those "rent-by-the-hour" hotels.

Two years earlier, Cheech and Chong took a road trip to San Diego and watched our alma mater, UW Cowboys, lose to Iowa 20-19 in the Holiday Bowl that included an interesting night in Tijuana, Baja California, Mexico.

It was my first time south of the border. Raymond knew his way around. He showed me everywhere there were no tourists. The attractions included a dark and dingy bar where women sat on benches around a sunken floor. Patrons would pay a few pesos to dance.

A decade later, being in that under-belly would be useful when I lived off-and-on for six years in Sombrerete, Zacatecas. When I traveled to Mexico, my mother warned me to be careful. She didn't want to get a phone call from the police that thieves left me abandoned in a dingy hotel with one less kidney.

After a night of gunshots in the streets, the next morning, we headed out for Memphis. We had to be there by December 28th for the Liberty Bowl game between Ole Miss and the Air Force Academy.

Raymond had the itinerary mapped out that included an Elvis Presley tour. I was mostly unaware of Elvis and rock 'n' roll music. My parents didn't play it around the house. They set the radio to KFBC, easy listening. My dad was an early adopter and one day brought home a record player with stereophonic sound.

When I was a kid, the records we had around the house were the likes of Frank Sinatra and Tony Bennett. I owned a Beatles 45 rpm with "She Loves You" and "I Wanna Hold Your Hand."

I became an Elvis fan because Raymond was an Elvis fan. He insisted we stop at the King's childhood home in Tupelo, Mississippi, and his mansion in Memphis. It seemed like anything he touched, or clothes he wore were interspersed among his Grammy Awards and Gold Records in the display cases. I knew Elvis was famous, but I didn't know he was that famous.

Raymond was also more aware of diverse cultures than I was. He experienced more blatant racial discrimination and was well aware of Martin Luther King Jr.

As long as we were in Memphis, he wanted to find the Lorraine Motel where MLK was assassinated. By 1989, the Lorraine was closed and cordoned off. It was being converted into the National Civil Rights Museum.

We met a woman named Jacqueline Smith who lived in a makeshift blue tarp tent on the sidewalk outside the chain-link fence blocking off the motel from the public. She lived at the Lorraine until she was evicted two years before.

A judge ordered her to move in 1990. She believed Martin Luther King, Jr. would have rather seen the motel converted into housing for homeless people rather than repurposed into a multi-million-dollar museum that opened the next year on July 4th.

Raymond was much more in tune with the civil rights movement. He was a high school teacher and filed an internal civil rights complaint against one of his colleagues for making disparaging racial remarks to him.

I thought and felt my upbringing was very safe growing up in the suburbs of east Cheyenne until I made that extended road trip.

Talk about being out of my comfort zone. Raymond took me to some different places. While in Memphis, I learned that there is a wet barbecue and dry rub barbecue. We caught the Blues at Lou's. I was an obvious Yankee when I asked for sauce. Memphis is definitely dry rub BBQ territory. I have since adopted the dry rub style for my cooking.

The Liberty Bowl game was anti-climactic compared to the adventures of the two days in Memphis. Our next stop was Jacksonville, Florida, by way of Orlando. BTW, Ole Miss defeated Air Force 13-0.

Raymond also was a Menudo eater. Menudo is a soup with tripe (cow stomach). Until this trip, I had never heard of it. Being a connoisseur of animal inerds, he wanted to find a place to try some chitterlings (chitlins). That's soul food in the South made from hog intestines.

There are Japanese versions of chitlins, but nobody offered them to me.

This was before Yelp, Trip Advisor, and Google, so we had to ask around. Some local person directed us to a small café in Orlando. I don't remember the name, but it was one of those places with a white wooden screen door that slammed behind you.

They didn't have chitlins that day, but hog maw made with a pig's exterior stomach wall. We ordered fried hog maw and eggs. It was crunchy and not appetizing. From what I have learned since then, these may not have been seasoned very well.

Our next stop was the Gator Bowl in Jacksonville. The Clemson Tigers defeated the Mountaineers of West Virginia 27-7 on our way to Miami.

The UW Cowboys didn't play in a 1989 game. Raymond and I chose our bowl-athon largely because of the probability of two undefeated teams playing for the national championship in the Orange Bowl on January 1, 1990.

Colorado would finish the season with an 11-0 record. Notre Dame was unblemished until the last week of the regular season and lost to the Miami Hurricanes. That loss deflated the hype.

The game wasn't that exciting. The Fighting Irish prevailed in the Orange Bowl 21-6 over the Buffalos. Rather than stick around for some post-game reveling, we decided to drive towards New Orleans after the game.

I was driving and pulled over at a rest stop to catch some shuteye. It was dawn's early light when a rap on the window awakened me. It was one of Alabama's finest who rousted us up. I didn't know what to expect after being caught "parking while brown." I only had the stereotype of a redneck sheriff dancing in my head. The officer ordered us to get back on the road. We dropped off the car and made it back to Denver without incident.

Before that road trip, I had been to Florida, but not around racial diversity. My senior year in college, I took an interim class about the ecology of the Southeast. It was the inaugural road trip for my graduation present, a brand-new base model 1974 pea-green Ford Pinto station wagon. I didn't have much luck with the Pinto, which was the tiny cousin to the Mustang.

I drove to Denver and picked up Brooke at her parents' house. We drove to pick up Lynn from his place in Nebraska and headed south through Kansas and probably should have waited overnight. I drove into a white-out blizzard and ended up sliding off the road. It was dark, and we camped out in a ditch on US Highway 20. The next morning a nice fellow pulled us out with his pickup truck. This would be the first harrowing incident that car and I would experience.

Arriving in the Florida Keys was a nice change from winter in the Midwest. Spending extended time in the deep South opened my eyes to racial injustice and civil rights. Maybe my friends didn't notice, but the stares made me uneasy.

Wyoming wasn't immune to civil rights unrest. I was in high school when UW football coach Lloyd Eaton kicked fourteen black players off the team in 1969 for protesting racial discrimination at Brigham Young University (BYU).

Diversity wasn't my experience growing up in homogenous Wyoming, even though I didn't meet an African-American person until 1964 going to a baseball game. My limited exposure to diverse people during college and as an early adult meant I was a late bloomer.

TWENTY-SEVEN: Sports and Race

I met my first African-American guy at the Fix 'n Mix in 1964. That bar and liquor store was on the western gateway to the Japanese neighborhood on the corner of O'Neil Avenue and West 17th Street in the 600 block. The companion Stop 'n Shop grocery store where Uncle Rich worked as a meat cutter was located just to the north.

When I say "met," we sat next to each other and talked. He was a nice guy and knew lots about baseball. We were on the way to a game in Denver. The AAA Denver Bears played in the American Association and was one of the farm teams for the New York Yankees over the years.

I'm a third-generation Yankees fan and thought everyone was a fan since they were on TV all the time.

The Yankees had five consecutive World Series appearances. After losing to the Pirates in 1960, Casey Stengel was fired, and Ralph Houk was promoted to team manager.

The Yankees won the World Series in 1961. They were in a race to break Babe Ruth's regular-season home run record. That was the year Roger Maris was in a friendly competition with teammate Mickey Mantle. Maris won the contest in game 161 with an end-of-the-season blast off Boston Red Sox rookie pitcher Tracy Stallard.

That would be his 61st home run of the season, surpassing Babe Ruth's longstanding record of 60. Major League Baseball (MLB) marked Maris's record with an asterisk since his feat happened in 161 games, while Ruth played in 154 games during his record-setting season.

Former Yankee Bud Daley lived in Lander after retiring. He pitched the winning fifth game in the 1961 series. He was quite the golfer, and he ran a landscaping business. My colleague from the newspaper, John, and I opened up a sports card store in Riverton called "Pine Riders."

For the grand opening, we invited Bud to stop by and sign autographs. Another major leaguer, Woody Held, mostly known for playing for the Cleveland Indians, was also a special guest. He lived nearby in Dubois. Both knew each other during their playing days. Bud wore one of his World Series rings.

The last time I chatted with Bud was in front of a slot machine at the Northern Arapaho Tribe's Wind River Casino. He was with another baseball guy named Joe Lanham. Joe was a tall, lanky pitcher who played semi-pro ball in Georgia.

When I worked in Lander, he brought me back a Mason jar filled with moonshine. Over a few sips of "white lightning," Joe told a story about a time he was pitching. After the catcher returned the ball to him, he heaved a white object into the stands. The runner on third, a little confused, took off for home. Joe threw out the guy at the plate.

It was his version of the hidden ball trick, except that the thing he threw into the stands was a peeled potato.

The Yankees won again in 1962 but lost back-to-back, first to the Los Angeles Dodgers in 1963 and then to the St. Louis Cardinals in 1964.

In the 1963 off-season, catcher Yogi Berra was the new manager, and Houk was the new general manager. Elston Howard took over the full-time catching duties.

In my later baseball and softball years, I became a catcher and an Elston Howard fan. Howard was the first African American player on the Yankees who joined the team in 1955.

The Yankees were the next-to-last non-expansion team to integrate. The Red Sox put it off until 1960, when they added Pumpsie Green.

The Yankees signed Howard on July 19, 1950, and assigned him to their Central League farm team, the Muskegon Clippers. He served in the US Army and missed the 1951 and 1952 seasons.

After his discharge, Howard played for the Class AAA Kansas City Blues of the American Association. The following season, the Yankees invited Howard to spring training in Florida.

Watching the Yankees play in the World Series was on my list of things to do. I met that challenge when I traveled to New York City in October 2001 and saw two World Series games. MLB rescheduled the post-season championship match-up between the Yankees and the Arizona Diamondbacks because of the 9/11 attacks.

Terrorists reduced the World Trade Center to rubble, and that freaked out the traveling public. Airplane fares were cheap. I picked up tickets on eBay to games 3 and 4 in Yankee Stadium that I had mailed to my favorite Midtown Manhattan dive, the Hotel Pennsylvania, where rooms were plentiful.

This was before counterfeit tickets became a growth industry. The hotel's phone number was made famous by the Glenn Miller Orchestra rendition of "Pennsylvania 6-5000."

After the Diamondbacks dominated the first two games in Phoenix, play resumed in the Big Apple, with the Yankees winning three games in dramatic fashion. Derek Jeter hit a home run in the early morning hours of November 1st, adding to the sweep and taking a 3-2 game advantage back to Arizona.

During those three days in New York City, every baseball fan in the world was a Yankees fan. The Yankees playing in the 2001 World Series was a rallying event that unified Americans.

There was a high level of civility. Suddenly race, ethnicity, and social class didn't matter. The feeling I had in the ballpark was one of solidarity with everyone around me.

If I ever felt like a patriotic American, it was when the stars and stripes that flew over the World Trade Center fluttered in the centerfield fall breeze with Lee

Greenwood in the house who sang "I'm Proud to Be an American" as President George W. Bush threw out the first pitch.

It was emotional and electric even though the Diamondbacks won the Series in seven games on a blooper hit into shallow center by Luis Gonzalez off Yankees closer Mariano Rivera scoring Craig Counsell to end game 7.

Visiting New York to watch the Yankees was exciting, but being around the aftermath of the terrorist attack was sobering even a month later. To this day, when I visit New York City, I make a quick train ride downtown to the 9/11 "Ground Zero" site.

Those feelings of civility waned, and there was a dark side. According to FBI statistics, the five years before the 9/11 attacks, hate crimes against Muslims numbered fewer than thirty. That number jumped to 481 in 2001. Since then, Muslim hate crimes have averaged 139 through 2014.

The 9/11 attack wouldn't be the only experiences tied to my baseball life. My dream job was to play shortstop with the Yankees in the World Series, but the job was always taken. During the hey-days, it was Tony Kubek (1961-1962), Bucky Dent (1977-1978), and Derek Jeter (1996, 1998, 2000, 2009).

After Jeter retired, the Yankees have had a revolving door at shortstop. The scouts passed over me again. I should have kept up with piano lessons instead of Little League.

I might have had a better chance banging out "Take Me Out to the Ball Game" on the Yankee Stadium organ than diving for hot ground balls up the gap.

Grandpa Sakata traveled around, including visiting his daughter, Hisako, in Washington DC. One trip, he brought me back a Washington Senators cap with the red W emblazoned across the front.

That must have been around 1960 before the Senators became the Minnesota Twins. While I appreciated his gesture, my mom helped me embroider a replacement Yankees NY on that cap.

The 1960 World Series was my first to see on TV, making my Yankee fanaticism more real, at least in two dimensions. One of the low points of my baseball fan life was watching Bill Mazeroski's walk-off homer at Forbe's Field to win game seven and the series.

I'm still not much of a Pirates fan today, and don't get me started about Mazeroski being in the Hall of Fame, but I digress. I have a 1960 Roberto Clemente card that I'll trade you for anything.

Mr. St. Clair and his family lived across the alley. He organized the neighbor kids and took us on field trips to places like Plains Dairy. There are pictures of me wearing that makeshift NY hat.

The exhibition game in Denver between the Bronx Bombers and the AAA Denver Bears is a life highlight. It was my first professional baseball game. The Bears were a Yankees farm team off and on over the years. Minor league game or not, didn't matter. It was the Yankees.

The Cheyenne Little League sponsored an annual pancake breakfast each summer as a fund-raising event. The League tasked players with selling tickets, and the team that sold the most got to attend the game between the Yankees and the Bears. The second-place team won tickets to a regular-season Bears game.

I had a good network of potential pancake eaters. My dad took some and sold them at his work. My neighborhood wasn't a very good market since all my friends played on other Little League teams.

The gold mine was Uncle George at the Highway Café. He kept them in the cash register drawer, and instead of change, he gave out my tickets.

When the League revealed the final ticket tally, my team took second place. That was a big disappointment. I don't know if he arranged it on my account, but my dad and a bunch of his guys at the Coke plant bought tickets to the Bears v. Yankees game and invited me along.

If anything cemented my relationship with my dad, it was that gesture taking me to watch the Yankees. We bonded around baseball. He bought me my first baseball glove. I played with that one until I signed up for Little League.

One summer, I was playing catch with one of the older neighbor kids. He burned one to me. My glove didn't have a very deep pocket, and the ball ricocheted off and bonked me on the cheek. It was the first time I was knocked out. After that, I was on the lookout for a different glove. I couldn't afford a new, higher-quality one.

I found my second glove at one of my mom's church activities. The churchwomen's club had a big rummage sale in the fall. My mom was a member of the women's circle, and I liked to help sort out the piles of clothes and sundries. Mostly I looked through all the merchandise and picked out a thing or two before the doors opened.

At the 1963 sale set for Saturday, November 23rd, I dug out a Rawlings baseball glove from a box in the inventory room. Wally Moon of the Los Angeles Dodgers endorsed it.

He was the National League Rookie of the Year in 1954. Moon played on three Los Angeles Dodgers World Series championship teams in 1959, 1963, and 1965.

The glove fit my tiny hand perfectly. For a dime, I used it throughout Little League and Babe Ruth baseball.

The reason I remember this, the Friday before, on November 22nd, JFK was assassinated in Dallas. There was quite a bit of chatter about the incident among the women.

"It served him right," one of the women's club members growled, apparently a Nixon supporter. She stormed into the church kitchen, disgusted about the assassination conversation as the others in the room stood aghast and quiet. The disdainful woman in my mom's church group was one of our neighbors in the Cole Addition.

Shortly before he was assassinated in 1963, JFK made Wyoming stops in Cheyenne, Laramie, and Jackson. Local newspaper mogul Tracy McCracken arranged his visit.

There's an often-used TV news clip of McCracken barking out the Wyoming delegation votes that put JFK over the top and secured the nomination for president. That moment played on a hotel room TV in the 2016 movie *LBJ* with Woody Harrelson.

I was one of the Cheyenne students let out of school to see JFK at the Cheyenne airport, where he gave a brief speech before heading over Sherman Hill to speak to a capacity crowd in the Field House on the UW campus. My mom took my sister and me, but we arrived a little late and watched from behind the perimeter fence.

That mitt I bought at the Presbyterian Church rummage sale held more memories created that day in November than those around the Little League baseball field.

I brought my Wally Moon glove to Denver, hoping to catch a home run ball hit by Mickey Mantle.

We carpooled down to the game played at Mile High Stadium, where the Bears and the American Football League Broncos also played.

One of the Coke truck drivers was Tony Rizzuto from New York. He was a relative of former Yankees shortstop Phil Rizzuto. On the way out of town, we pulled up to the front of the turquoise-painted concrete block Fix 'n Mix bar to pick up Tony's friend, who was an African American airman stationed at FE Warren Air Force Base.

I assume the two befriended each other because Tony had the airbase Coke route. The airman was another big Yankees fan deployed from New York City to Wyoming. I thought it odd that we met him at a liquor store.

I had seen African American people before, but it was always from a distance, and all were sports figures. My dad graduated from Cheyenne High, now Central, where he played basketball. At five-foot-eleven he was tall for a Japanese guy and had a pretty good left- and right-handed hook shot.

Once in a while, Dad took my sister and me to watch his high school alma mater play at Storey Gym. In 1964, my favorite Central player was Barry West. What I remember about him most, not only was he a great all-around athlete, but he also was a musician a great vocalist, along with teammate Percy Johnson.

I recently befriended Barry's brother, Grant, on social media and learned that Barry had passed and Percy is a minister in Illinois. He also mentioned that his grandmother owned the restaurant at 408 W. 17th Street.

We would occasionally drive over to Laramie and watch UW basketball games. In 1964, the Cowboys' best player was Flynn Robinson, who eventually played in the NBA for the Cincinnati Royals and the Milwaukee Bucks.

He missed out on winning the NBA championship with the Bucks in 1970-71 when Milwaukee traded him back to the Royals for guard Oscar Robertson.

Robinson would play on the great Lakers team that won the championship in 1972, with Jerry West, Elgin Baylor, and Wilt Chamberlain.

I met Flynn when the UW Athletic Department inducted him into the Hall of Fame. I was on the field taking photos. He autographed a basketball card for me.

Also, on that Wyoming team was center Leon Clark. He was a great rebounder and scorer. For a small forward, he dominated the boards at six-foot-six. It was because of Leon Clark that I became a Boston Celtics fan.

The Celtics were always dominant. They had one of the last picks in the NBA draft. The Celtics selected the best of the leftover players, who were from smaller conferences like the Western Athletic, including Leon Clark. Sports pundits touted Clark as the next Bill Russell, but he was too small and faded after a couple of seasons in Boston and finished his career playing in Europe.

Later, the Celtics drafted Charles Bradley from UW and Danny Ainge and Greg Kite from rival BYU. I witnessed, in my opinion, the best basketball game between the Cowboys and BYU on February 26, 1981, in the UW Fieldhouse.

I made the drive over to Laramie from Cheyenne with a friend and colleague named Barry. We were there lobbying the state legislature on behalf of the Wyoming Association of Municipalities.

The Memorial Fieldhouse, known as the "Barn," was a big home-court advantage for Wyoming because mulch-like woodchips covered the surface. It was the perfect substrate for mushrooms to grow.

The UW rodeo team competed indoors there, too. The basketball floor was in sections and assembled over the mulch. Visiting teams had to play at seventy-two hundred feet in elevation and breath the moist, musty, and thick Fieldhouse air.

I had forgotten the details of the game, but here's the play-by-play from UW Sports Information Director Kevin McKinney. BYU led 68-64 with 1:28 to play in regulation.

Mike Jackson hit a jumper followed by a monster slam-dunk to tie it 68-68. BYU guard Danny Ainge missed a one-and-one, then missed a jumper at the buzzer, which sent the game to overtime (OT).

BYU led 76-72 in the first OT, before Bill Garnett and Mike Jackson each hit two three throws to send it to the second OT. Garnett was a picked fourth overall in the first round of the 1982 NBA draft by the Dallas Mavericks. Jackson was a fourth-rounder a year later and selected by the Kansas City Kings.

In the second OT, with BYU trailing 85-81, Ainge got a three-point play with nineteen seconds left. It was 85-84. BYU fouled Charles Bradley. He made the first free throw and missed the second, and the Pokes extend their lead by one point 86-84. BYU grabbed the rebound, and Ainge had a last-second shot, but he missed. Bradley got the rebound, and the game was over.

The stands emptied. Screaming fans stormed the floor and tromped past Danny Ainge, who crumpled to the floor after missing the last shot of the game.

After graduation, Ainge played baseball and signed with the Toronto Blue Jays, where he had a so-so career before being drafted by the Celtics. Bradley was the last pick in the first round of the 1981 NBA draft by the Celtics.

They were all part of the Celtics 1980s dynasty teams with teammates Robert Parrish, Larry Bird, Kevin McHale, and Dennis Johnson. Charles Bradley lasted only one season and became a college coach.

UW and BYU were also big football rivals. Games between the two teams were heated, not to mention the "despicable" UW Cowboy fans, as BYU basketball coach Frank Arnold dubbed us.

Wyoming's negative relationship with Mormons went beyond sports. My earliest memory of the rivalry goes back to 1967 that led to the infamous "Black 14" incident. There's plenty of information on the Internet if you Google it.

In 1967, I had a big interest in Wyoming football. The Cowboy gridders were the only undefeated team in the nation, going 10-0 during the regular season and they were ranked fifth in the nation.

The Pokes lost 20-13 to unranked Louisiana State University (LSU) in the Sugar Bowl played in Baton Rouge. One of the first stories I wrote for the Carey Jr. High School Tumbleweed newspaper was about the UW Sugar Bowl appearance.

My eighth grade PE student teacher was Paul Toscano, who was the quarterback on that team. He showed off his Sugar Bowl watch. He was drafted by the Houston Oilers but opted to coach high school football and basketball.

The 1968 season brought high hopes for the Pokes, but the team went 7-3 while winning their third consecutive Western Athletic Conference (WAC) championship.

Racially charged unrest plagued the country following the assassinations of Bobby Kennedy and Martin Luther King, Jr. The political upheaval of those events slopped over into Wyoming.

The team began the 1969 season strong with four straight wins and being ranked sixteenth in the nation. Before the BYU home game, the campus Black Student Alliance (BSA) met with the African American football team members just before the game, asking the fourteen players to wear black armbands to protest BYU's religious ties to the LDS church. The LDS church didn't allow African Americans to join the priesthood.

Governor Stan Hathaway mobilized the National Guard to move into Laramie as a show of force. The story made it into the November 3rd edition of *Sports Illustrated* but was buried inside on page 26. The headline read, "No Defeats, Loads of Trouble."

The players agreed with the BSA. After a team meeting, coach Lloyd Eaton booted the fourteen players off the team. Short-handed Wyoming soundly defeated their rivals 40-7. The Cowboys lost four out of five of the remaining games and in 1970 lost nine out of ten games.

I was in high school and intellectually got the controversy but didn't emotionally understand it until years later.

To commemorate the 50th anniversary of the Black 14, UW issued an apology to the former students. Wyoming's football program has never fully recovered from the controversy.

The civil rights and anti-Vietnam War movements affected professional boxing. Hanging around with Grandpa Ohashi, one activity we did together was watching boxing on TV. That was during the time of the great heavyweight fighters.

I was a big Cassius Clay fan, aka Muhammad Ali. He was flamboyant and had a cool name. He was on TV and the sports pages often. Clay won the Gold Medal in the 1960 Olympics in Rome.

I remember in 1964 huddled around my parents' clock radio in their bedroom, listening to a bout between Clay and Sonny Liston that took place in Miami. Clay was the underdog and knocked out the Denver boxer in six rounds.

A year later, Liston booked a rematch, this time in Lewiston, Maine. My dad, sister Lorinda, and I lay on my parents' bed and settled in for a night of boxing.

By this time, Clay changed his name to Muhammad Ali. We were disappointed when Ali stopped the Big Bear in the first round. Hard-core boxing fans have questioned the win. Sports pundits think the "fix was in," and Liston took a dive.

Ali converted to the Muslim religion. He evaded the draft and lost his heavyweight championship belt, and was thrown in jail. He didn't want to fight in a war where young black men were killing other dark-skinned people.

"I ain't got no quarrel with them, Viet Cong . . . Why should they ask me to put on a uniform and go ten thousand miles from home and drop bombs and bullets on brown people in Vietnam while so-called Negro people in Louisville are treated like dogs and denied simple human rights?" Ali mused.

I've always admired him for giving up his boxing title and sitting in jail. There were rumors the leaders of his faith coerced him to make the statements that he did. His actions validated my views.

Professional boxing was one of the family activities. My dad often dropped me off to watch TV with Grandpa Ohashi. He couldn't see very well because of diabetes but could distinguish the contrasting black and white trunks on the B&W TV.

"Kuronbo," he called them in Japanese. It was an African American racial slur in Japanese. I laughed because it was a funny-sounding word. I thought it was Japanese for a boxer.

At the dinner table one night, I asked my dad what it was. It was common terminology among the men in my dad's family. I had heard Uncle George say it as well as Uncle Rich. My mother was quick to chime in and forbade me from using the word.

Visiting my Grandpa Ohashi's place was more like a clubhouse than my grandparents Sakata's house, which was more staid and polite.

I think Uncle George subscribed to the magazines that were on the Highway Café tables. Salespeople came around selling subscriptions. When new issues arrived, the old sports magazines found a space on my grandfather's end table. I liked to go over to his house to flip through *Ring* magazine and find out the latest heavyweight rankings.

Uncle Rich kept *Field and Stream* in the stacks that would sate my interest in nightcrawler wrangling for our fishing trips. There were also back issues of *Baseball* magazine that had loads of pictures of Yankee players.

When our party arrived at Mile High Stadium, we sat together in the right-field bleachers by the foul pole. The airman who came to the Yankees v. Bears game with us was the only black guy I would personally meet until much later. I sat between him and my dad. The main attraction for me was watching Roger Maris (9) in right and Mickey Mantle (7) in center.

I thought about my grandfather's disparaging kuronbo moniker. That was when I realized for the first time, I was out of my comfort zone. I was a kid hanging out with a bunch of adult men, which was different. On top of that, I didn't have any preconceived notions about the airman except that he was a Yankees fan.

Later, I thought I was assigned to sit next to the airman because the others were uncomfortable about that in public even though they were friendly to one another.

Mantle and Maris only played about half the game, but to this day, seeing 9 and 7 play is a big highlight of my life. A close second was sitting in Yankee Stadium for the 2001 World Series games.

By 1964, the Yankees had traded Moose Skowron to the Dodgers, and Joe Pepitone was the everyday first baseman. After the game, Joe walked across the outfield.

"Hey, Joe, how ya doin'?" my baseball pal yelled out as if he knew him, and maybe he did. Pepitone was from Brooklyn. Joe waved back at us.

It makes perfect sense to me now. Baker's Place was no longer in business. Fix 'n Mix, on the west side and near the airbase, was probably a safe, integrated bar.

There were a few west side businesses listed in The Green Book editions in the 1950s and 1960s. The Barbeque Inn at 622 W. 20th St. and the Minnehaha Motel, now the Firebird, on East Lincolnway at Logan Avenue, were listed as safe hotels, but not Fix 'n Mix.

Advertisements and subscriptions supported The Green Book. According to a note in the front of the publication, editors compiled many of the listings from word of mouth, and nobody told the book about Baker's Place or Fix 'n Mix.

There were two listings in The Green Book for hotels and two tourist homes in Cheyenne. A tourist home was like a bed-and-breakfast. Families would have a spare room or apartment in their private home where travelers could stay.

Mrs. L. Randall at 612 and Mrs. M. Hermann at 621 W. 18th St. offered tourist home lodging. My father's childhood home was in the same block at 620 W. 18th St. and is now a vacant lot.

It was a late night, and we stopped at the Fix 'n Mix and dropped my new baseball friend off. I never saw him again.

Living on the east side of Cheyenne limited my exposure to diverse people, which is why, I think, my parents made a move away from our East 10th Street place when the school boundaries changed after my kindergarten year at the newly constructed Fairview Elementary School.

My parents invested in some land on the east side of Cheyenne. They sold that and kept their East 10th Street house as a rental. We moved to the Cole Addition at 1115 Windmill Rd. to stay within the Fairview School boundary.

Fairview was a feeder school for Carey Junior High School. When I was on the Carey wrestling team, I met a black kid named Willie who went to McCormick Junior High. Not in the cafeteria but on the wrestling mat.

Wrestling opponents get pretty close to each other. I don't know about others in the sport, but the first time I went up against Willie, his skin felt different, his hair, too. I wondered how he experienced me.

TWENTY-EIGHT: Aimless Academics

I didn't have much academic guidance in high school. I followed along mostly oblivious about my future. This was a summer school history class I took along with kids from Central. Meeting kids from the other side of town was a worthwhile experience.

When I was in junior high school, sports rivalries were friendly. My junior high wrestling opponent, Willie, and I would occasionally meet each other when Carey played a basketball road-game at McCormick. I still wonder about him. At my fiftieth high school class reunion, I asked some of the Central kids if they knew about Willie's whereabouts. So far, no reports. The west side kids seldom came to games at Carey. We infrequently ran into each other when I was in high school. Maybe his dad was in the air force, and he transferred out or just moved someplace. It wouldn't have surprised me if I saw him in the East High School hallways.

In 1970, when I was a junior, we had many new kids in school, mostly from Johnson Junior High, maybe some from McCormick. During this time, school districts desegregated students by voluntarily busing minority kids into predominantly white schools. According to a classmate, the school boundaries changed that year.

The SCOTUS in 1971 ruled in *Swann v. Charlotte-Mecklenburg Board of Education* for school districts to achieve racial balance even if it meant busing students or redefining boundaries.

Forced or not, there were many fresh faces at EHS. The odd thing was, the kids were white students but from another part of town. It worked out okay for EHS. After adding the new students, East won the state football championship, and the wrestling team did pretty well.

The EHS student body was racially homogeneous. Like most other schools, there was an informal caste system. During my high school years, not counting myself and my sister Lorinda, there were maybe three other Japanese kids who all lived in the east Cheyenne suburbs.

One was Linda Miyamoto, whose family had Baker's Place on West 17th Street. Bill Shiba and his sister Marilyn were my neighbors in the Cole Addition. Their brother Bob was younger and went to school with my sister. Mary Tsumagari, whose father was a doctor also was in my class.

I identified with a TV show called *The Many Loves of Dobie Gillis* (1959–1963) that starred Dwayne Hickman. It was about a high school kid who always had some crisis with the women he dated. His sidekick was Maynard G. Krebs. He was a bongo drum-pounding collector of tin foil who shunned authority.

Like Maynard G. Krebs, I did not focus my attention much on the future. Upon high school graduation in 1971, I didn't know what I wanted to do other than go to college, particularly since the only contact I had with a guidance counselor was to be informed that I had enough credits to graduate. Nonetheless, my academic path was a circuitous one that landed me back at the Hitching Post Inn.

My parents didn't give me any guidance, either. Neither of them went to college and they didn't have career paths based on academic study. Had anyone pushed me in one direction or another, I would have majored in something more useful than political systems analysis and ecological sciences.

Ever since grade school, my primary interests were in the arts and telling stories with my art. I was a cartoonist for my school papers from junior high through college. I became more committed to biology after the student exchange trip to St. Louis Park, Minnesota.

I had to raise funds to pay for that trip. That became a family effort and a chance for me to know Uncle Roy a little better.

By the 1970s, a growing middle class fled to the suburbs, along with its mass consumerism. One externality of the "throwaway society" was aluminum-can recycling.

Uncle Roy was a night owl and the janitor at Town & Country Liquor on the south side. He suggested saving aluminum cans from the bar that I could sell at the metal salvage place.

"Free money," he said. "I'm getting paid to bag them up. I either put them in the dumpster, or I give them to you. You'll need to get them ready to sell back."

I picked up the bags of cans at his place. He never married and lived in a very cool trailer house in a mobile home park behind the Highway Café that had changed little from when I was in elementary school.

When I was at the Café, I walked over to his place and pounded on the door with a porthole window near the front of the two-toned silver and blue aluminum outer skin. I hadn't been up close to an airplane but thought that's what one would be like.

A smoldering briar pipe dangled from his mouth as he swung the door open. He always chuckled and waved me in like the Land of Oz gatekeeper.

Stale cherry-flavored Sir Walter Raleigh tobacco smoke wafted out of his dimly lit digs. I considered it to be a pleasant aroma.

Uncle Roy had little food around to share since he took meals at the Café or his mom's place but offered his menagerie of birds and fish to admire. He took care of colorful parakeets and little finches in cages.

The tweet, tweet, tweet from warbling birdies and gurgling bubbles from the submerged fish tank aerators filled his front room, which was also the kitchen.

There were aquariums with all kinds of smallish exotic fish—sunfish, Dory clownfish, guppies. My favorites were the suckerfish that cleaned the insides of the glass and vacuumed up the fish poop dropped by the others on the bottom of the tank. It was the first time I realized my life was also self-contained in a bowl and I was a bottom feeder.

He loaned out his parakeets. My parents allowed me to keep one at a time only if I learned to take care of them. Not that I'm the over-nurturing type, but I enjoyed replacing the newspaper on the bottom of the cage and picking out food from the Petland store on the east edge of town.

I outgrew the Hitching Post job when I was in high school. My dad hired me during the summer of 1970. The wages I was making at Coca-Cola were triple what the Hitch paid me clearing tables, and I didn't have to wear a uniform. I also learned about mass production and efficient workflow. My dad took pride in his work, adding value to water, sugar, and some flavoring.

Working for my dad was an enjoyable and useful experience. I learned how to drive a forklift, which was a good life skill, and could still unload a truck if called upon. It was tedious stacking pallets of bottles so they wouldn't topple over.

In the early 1970s, Coke adapted to industrial progress that included cutting overhead to make more profit. Our little bottling plant was no exception and joined the convenient throwaway society to cut costs.

We stopped filling returnable glass bottles. That meant making my job easier. I no longer had to fish cigarette butts out of the bottles with a hooked wire before loading them into the soaker and washing machine.

Corrugated cardboard boxes of disposable bottles arrived on pallets shrink-wrapped in plastic. My job was to unload them. One day, the delivery truck didn't park on the crown of the street but on the downslope. After inserting the forks and lifting the pallet, I maneuvered the forklift to a flatter grade, but the top-heavy load slowly collapsed to the pavement.

Around that time, we no longer sweetened our soft drinks with granulated sugar but with high fructose corn syrup. Sugar was sugar with no worries about whether one was healthier than the other.

That change also eliminated one of my jobs. Before each bottling run, I lifted fifty-pound bags of sugar, poured the contents into a stainless-steel vat, added a graduated amount of Cheyenne tap water, and stirred it up with a big stainless-steel paddle while adding the top-secret Coca-Cola flavoring. The concoction was gravity-fed into the bottling line.

Premixed high fructose corn syrup eliminated much of my job. I opened a big valve that released the new sweetener into the production system that flowed into the flavoring.

It was also the first time I'd seen my dad around other men besides neighbors and relatives. He could cuss and talk trash with the best of them.

Regardless, the guys liked and respected him. He brought in doughnuts for coffee breaks and let them off to see their kids during the workday or run errands.

He was a team player and filled in to perform any of the jobs if there was an illness or emergency. His horizontal management style was ahead of its time. Out of twelve brothers and sisters, he was one of the middle kids. Herd management skills were a part of his upbringing.

In my past "real job" life and to this day, I learn everyone's jobs and make it a point to at least allow everyone to learn one another's jobs.

After working for my dad at the Coke plant and cashing in aluminum cans, I paid for my first jet airplane ride flying from Cheyenne on Western Airlines to Minneapolis, and a suburb called St. Louis Park just before graduation in 1971. John Dinneen was on that trip, too.

The school administration let St. Louis Park High out on April 22nd for Earth Day. Attending Earth Day for the first time in a progressive community influenced my late-blooming interest in biology and politics.

I ended up taking more science classes and, for someone who wasn't that great at math, did pretty well in the courses I took—including advanced biology taught by Miss Cooper, the science teacher at the Heart Mountain camp high school. I became a science major in college.

One of my wrestling coaches took me on a recruitment trip to Colorado State University (CSU) in Fort Collins. I was an okay wrestler, but not great. My role on the team would have been the "other guy" for the first-stringer to toss around the mat during practice, and that would have been it.

Later, I knew the rules of baseball and soccer well enough to coach youth sports. Occasionally, an exceptional athlete would come along.

"Go where you can play" was always my advice when we talked about future plans.

A kid on one of my Lander teams, Aaron Elling, went on to be the placekicker for the UW Cowboys football team and later the Minnesota Vikings in the National Football League (NFL). I like to think I had something to do with his development as a player, but he was physically gifted and had a supportive family, which were the primary factors.

I enjoyed coaching youth sports. I had a knack for facilitating people to do their best and be team players. That's a throwback to when I was on the Fairview Elementary basketball team.

I was small but had pretty good skills. Back then, the school district required students to attend schools in their neighborhoods. I ended up going to elementary school with the same kids, including two of the star athletes, Bobby and Husty.

Fairview had an away-game at Eastridge Elementary, across the street from the Grand Central store that sold the ten-cent French fries. Coach Goff picked me to be part of the traveling team. Maybe everyone got to go, but it didn't matter, I was elated to see my name on the roster posted on the corkboard outside the gym. When we loaded up on a school Yellow Dog, that was my first time on a school bus.

We disembarked and entered the dank and dark gym. Our footsteps echoed as they hit the gymnasium floor. It was reminiscent of the Oscar-winning movie *Hoosiers* (1986) when the awestruck players from a small high school basketball team enter the gigantic arena where a washed-up coach (Gene Hackman) inspires them to win the state championship against the heavily favored big city team from Indianapolis.

Bobby and Husty didn't have their best outing. Coach Goff substituted me for one of them. I finally got to play in an actual game. I stole the ball a couple of times and scored four points on easy layups.

"That O'Hashi had a pretty good game yesterday," Coach Goff said the next day at practice. Ever since then, I always give people a chance. I've hired people on their word and haven't had any disappointments from my random vetting process. Nobody has let me down.

Out of the hundreds of kids who went through his basketball program, I doubt Mr. Goff knew what a positive influence his words had on me. I recognized then how important it is to always be on the top of my game. I don't know who I will have an influence upon.

When I coached kids, it wasn't until later that I realized I may have been the first brown-skinned person who they and their parents got to know, which was even more important that I always kept a positive mental attitude.

In several seasons of coaching, I only had one father who pulled his kid from one of my soccer teams. He said it was because I didn't coach like the other men by being boisterous. The team and I hadn't been doing as well as in the past. The week after his kid left the team, we won our first game.

In the end, I gave up competitive sports. A bunch of my Presbyterian Church pals from both East and Central high schools decided to attend Hastings College in Nebraska. Hastings, like Sheldon Jackson College in Sitka, Alaska, where I worked for a summer, is affiliated with the Presbyterian Church.

I didn't have a fallback school, not even UW. I wanted to get out of Wyoming. Nebraska seemed far enough away, and with a few familiar faces, it was comfortable. Plus, I wanted to be at a smaller school, although there were likely other compatible places had I looked around.

After arriving on campus, I found there was more Presbyterian liturgy at private school, but that wasn't a voting criterium.

Chapel on Wednesday morning wasn't required, but there would be the occasional excellent program like Barbara Jordan and Dick Gregory. I was going through the motions but still didn't get the religious part of campus life at Hastings College, at least compared to some of my classmates.

Dress up family-style dinner on Wednesday night was a hassle. Fancy meals on the menu enticed us to attend.

Then there was the social engineering.

The rules disallowed freshman women from leaving campus for a few months at the beginning of the first semester. All women had to be back in the dorms by one a.m. They looked forward to daylight savings time because of springing ahead for an added hour.

There were very few minorities I got to know—a Latino, two African American guys on the football and track teams, a Chinese guy, some others, and me.

There aren't women's hours these days, but the school is still white bread, and it fits in with that middle-of-the-grain-belt-culture, which is okay. If I had to make the choice again, I would still pick Hastings.

I lived in Altman Hall, the coed dorm on campus. It was coed to the extent one side was for men, the other for women. A common basement that had the TV room, washers, and dryers connected the two wings.

Every semester, the other dorms reported many infractions around the opposite gender students in the dorms after hours and failure to return before curfew. When Daylight Savings Time ended in the fall, the women were bummed because the clocks would "fall back." They'd lose the extra hour of freedom.

Altman Hall seldom had any rule violations. Thinking something was awry, the dean of women called the dorm leadership into her office and accused us of a coverup. The Altman Angels had a code of honor and didn't monitor the halls looking for trouble.

It ended up that I went to a college where I could play, but something besides sports. I missed organized competition and joined the Hastings College speech team. I didn't compete in high school but took a speech class as an elective my senior year. The major benefit? I didn't have to watch my wrestling weight from week to week.

The speech jocks traveled as much as the football or basketball teams, mostly around the Midwest. My weekly workout was to read Newsweek and Time magazines since I competed in debate and extemporaneous speaking about current events.

After graduating during the post-Vietnam War recession with degrees in biology and political science, there weren't many employers out there identifying mammal teeth or discussing whether the confederation is a better form of government than a federation.

I applied around to graduate schools. The University of Wisconsin-Green Bay accepted me into one of the first environmental politics programs but offered no financial aid.

Being a procrastinator, I sent my paperwork in late to the UW graduate school and was accepted but on the waiting list for a teaching assistantship grant. I received a call from the registrar's office just before the fall term began, saying they had an opening, which I took immediately.

There was no career path, but the last-minute teaching job was a good first stride, even though I continued my academic missteps, creating a newfangled discipline. I melded my two undergraduate degrees into "environmental politics." Looking back, I was ahead of my time.

In 1962, American conservationist and marine biologist Rachel Carson wrote a book entitled Silent Spring. It's about the food chain reaction that happens when pesticides enter various ecosystems.

The environmental movement's inciting incident occurred in late January 1969 when one hundred thousand gallons of crude oil spilled out of a Union Oil offshore well platform near Santa Barbara, California, over a ten-day period.

Images of many miles of black beaches, some of the thirty-five hundred sea birds soaked in oil, received above-the-fold news coverage that resulted in public outrage that did not fall on deaf ears.

Less than a year later, in January 1970, President Nixon signed the National Environmental Policy Act (NEPA) into law. NEPA created the Environmental Impact Statement process to evaluate projects and offer an array of solutions.

Shortly thereafter, Auntie Hisako transferred from the US Department of Health, Education, and Welfare to the EPA. She spent the rest of her civil service career there as a budget analyst.

NEPA also established the Council on Environmental Quality (CEQ). The CEQ coordinates various federal agencies and other executive branch offices about environmental and energy policies. The initial CEQ helped inform Nixon's government reorganization that resulted in the formation of the EPA.

Environmental activists rode the NEPA tide and organized millions of concerned citizens to rally around Earth Day on April 22, 1970, on the streets, in parks, on college and high school campuses. You name the environmental malady—raw sewage in waterways, toxic waste dumps, pesticides showing up in babies—human-made disasters were making headlines.

Earth Day 1970 garnered support from divergent groups—Republicans and Democrats, wealthy and not-so-wealthy, urbanites and rural farmers, business executives and union leaders.

Because of the high level of political consensus, policy changes occurred quickly with overwhelming bipartisan support. While Nixon created some problems for himself on his re-election front, he could engage with civility when planning public policy around the environmental movement. In July 1970, Nixon merged into the

EPA antipollution, pesticide control, air and water quality programs administered by the USDA, and the DOI.

Largely based on attending Earth Day activities at St. Louis Park High School, I spent the next couple of years in Laramie figuring out the coursework for my environmental politics concentration. My research design paper was *The Earth Day Legacy: Environmental Attitudes Among College Students.*

My data showed that while college students were in favor of efforts to keep the environment clean, at the same time, students were not willing to give up Superman's American Way by doing their individual parts and changing their consumption habits.

I balanced my classwork with teaching Intro to Political Science and Wyoming Government, and later a Social Statistics class. I was big on social research and continue to be interested in designing surveys. UW paid my tuition and also a living allowance.

Before deciding to stay in Laramie, I thought about moving to Cheyenne, but my parents were okay with me staying with them, along with my sister. I think they appreciated me being around but soon realized that having another adult in the house wasn't the same as young Alan David helping clear the dinner table before running outside to play "ditch" in the dark shadows around the neighborhood.

I didn't know many people in Laramie, except for my parents' church friends. I became acquainted with my fellow graduate students, but many were married and had Laramie lives. The undergrads were younger.

After figuring out I needed to find a job, all the elective classes I took had an internship or hands-on experience associated with it.

The most practical class was Introduction to Public Relations, taught by Bill Roepke. That internship was supporting the UW Federal Energy Research Center. I still refer to the textbook Cutlip and Center's *Effective Public Relations.* The most valuable UW internship was spent blending with many Wyoming state legislators during two legislative sessions.

I commuted to Cheyenne from Laramie each day. That experience as a twenty-one-year-old had the most long-term value. My assignment was with two Joint Appropriations Committee members, easy-going Gus Fleischli from Cheyenne and stodgy Speaker of the House Warren Morton from Casper. He eventually ran for governor and was defeated by Ed Herschler in 1982.

Gus was an oilman. I met him at his office each morning, and we had breakfast at the Husky Truck Stop before we drove to the state capitol building in his white over red Cadillac Coupe de Ville. I still run into Gus now and again.

Morton's son, Bob, was a teaching assistant colleague of mine in the UW political science department. He once showed me a letter he received from his dad. Bob pulled the envelope from his backpack.

The note was formatted as a block business letter on Wyoming State Legislature letterhead stationery, typed out on an IBM Selectric typewriter, and was signed, "Sincerely, Warren Morton, Speaker of the House."

I met former US Senator Al Simpson when he was the Wyoming House Majority Whip. If there was ever a collaborative guy in public service, it was Al Simpson.

He rounded up a bunch of his colleagues and me after a committee meeting and took us to the Mayflower Café in Downtown Cheyenne, where I had my first French Dip sandwich, for whatever that's worth.

He, and later his brother Pete, took a liking to me. I learned about Al's experiences as a Boy Scout from Cody, visiting the scout troop at the Heart Mountain camp during World War II, and his lifelong friendship with Heart Mountain camp internee Norm Mineta.

Mineta was later elected to Congress in California as a Democrat and served as the US Department of Transportation Secretary in the President George W. Bush administration.

My high school, college, and grad school years were a potpourri of experiences. On the surface, nothing fit together. It turned out that it all fit together as collaborative and civil problem-solving.

TWENTY-NINE: Vietnam Guilt

World War II had been a big deal for my family, particularly in the aftermath of the Japanese attack on Pearl Harbor. My parents and their families had experiences that influenced how they raised and interacted with me.

I missed military service other than when I turned eighteen. My mom watched me climb into the red Ford Falcon before heading to the Selective Service office in the old Cheyenne airport terminal to register for the draft. It must have been after school. I was the only one who was in the office, along with the recruiter.

Registering for the draft was a tangible and personal act of patriotism. That was a rite of passage for me, but I was less aware of it than my parents. There were very few family discussions about the Vietnam War, even though TV news correspondents embedded among the troops reported about the casualty count every night on the news. Maybe that was enough.

Maybe I would have felt more patriotic had I known that my Ford Falcon was the brainchild of former Secretary of Defense Robert McNamara, who ended up serving during the JFK and Lyndon Baines Johnson (LBJ) administrations during the Vietnam War.

Before his public service, McNamara was a young upstart executive at the Ford Motor Company. Following the mid-size model Edsel debacle, he designed the Falcon, which proved to be an enormous success in 1957, competing in the compact car market with the VW Type I Bug, the Corvair, and the Valiant.

I was still in high school. My draft-deferred status was 1-H. By the time my first day of college rolled around in Hastings, the Vietnam War was de-escalating while President Nixon ordered the secret bombing of Cambodia.

The Vietnam War was politically unpopular. The mass draft was replaced by the lottery system in 1969. There was no clear enemy. The US was waging traditional warfare with fronts and rears, while the antagonists were ideological guerrillas who didn't follow the rules.

In 1973, my birth date lottery number was 275, pretty much sparing me from service. My college roommate, Sam, the same guy from Cody who went to Alaska with me, had a low lottery number in the teens and went for his physical.

By then, Nixon was planning to pull out of Vietnam "with honor." When the US negotiated its withdrawal, purple hearts, bronze, and silver stars were awarded for bravery, but the recipients were not all treated like heroes when they returned home.

Instead, while not all were disenfranchised, many veterans faced unemployment, alcohol and drug abuse, mental and physical health issues from PTSD.

Pham Dihn Nguyen, the fellow who purchased Buford, Wyoming, served as a soldier in the ARVN during Vietnamization. The United States readied for troop withdrawal and trained the local army to take over Vietnam's military defense.

Serving in the military was a part of the socialization process for young men. Eliminating the draft changed all that when military duty turned into a job. In World War II, men were teachers and plumbers, and after the war, they returned to their civilian workplaces, like Captain Miller (Tom Hanks) in *Saving Private Ryan* (1998). At the end of the movie, he was killed in action, but he eager to get back to teaching school.

There is the macroeconomics phrase, "Guns or Butter," which is an analogy for choices between defense and civilian spending and how the two can best balance the country's economic needs.

Now that there is an all-volunteer military, service is a career. Soldiers shouldn't be laid off when wars end but rather redeployed to add to the public good. When soldiers give up their guns, they can administer butter, like building roads and bridges or constructing affordable houses.

During my college years, the Hastings class schedule was 3-1-3. Three months in the fall and spring, with one month in between called the Interim. Students would take one concentrated class.

In my freshman year, I took a class about Cosmology, and as a junior, I took piano lessons, along with all the voice majors. It surprised me at the large number who didn't know how to read music. My mission was to learn, you guessed it, "The Happy Farmer," by Robert Schumann.

In my sophomore year, and upon Nixon's reelection, I chose an Interim class called "Legislators and Lobbyists."

A busload of Hastings College classmates traveled to Washington DC. It was an action-packed three weeks. We stayed at a hotel called the Alban Towers. There wasn't formal classroom work, but we spent time in the field meeting with Congressional staff members, government agencies, and lobby groups, like Common Cause.

The highlight of the class was attending Richard Nixon's inauguration on January 20, 1973. Walking back from the Capitol building after the ceremony, some of us were tear-gassed during a demonstration against the not-so-secret bombing of Cambodia.

January 22nd, the SCOTUS decided *Roe v. Wade*, and former president Johnson died. He lay in state under the Capitol rotunda while we were in DC.

In retrospect, I could have enlisted in the military. Still, after experiencing the anti-war unrest during Nixon's inauguration, his subsequent impeachment, and resignation, and listening to the Vietnam War stories that my Gillette housemate, Tom, who was awarded a Bronze Star and wounded in action, would later tell, I may have missed military experience, but I don't regret sitting that one out.

As a thirteen-year-old, I was an ardent Bobby Kennedy supporter and have wondered how the world would have turned out had he been elected president in 1968. The Vietnam War may have ended sooner. Watergate wouldn't have happened and the subsequent political upheaval.

Wars, while devastating, were cultural manifestations of patriotism. We fought the Vietnam War on TV. I saw with my own eyes the devastation of war rather than sterile and edited World War II newsreel footage before the feature down at the Paramount Theater. TV pulled the curtain back from patriotic images of heroes hoisting tattered battle flags and exposed the realities of combat.

Like Muhammad Ali, if I were drafted, I would have resisted or filed to be a conscientious objector. It made no sense for me, an Asian, to travel thousands of miles to kill other Asians.

During World War II, the level of patriotism was high. There were defined "good guys" and "bad guys." While far away from the battlefields, tenets of the American Way cast my parents and family as bad guys on the home front.

THIRTY: Reluctant Heroes—442nd RCT

My dad didn't serve during World War II. He instead was active on the home front, helping get the Skyline Nisei Club off the ground. He turned eighteen in 1941, but his doctor diagnosed him with a heart murmur. The Selective Service Board classified him as 4-F and unfit for service. The military draft was reinstituted in November 1940.

There were international tensions building between the United States and Japan. In anticipation of war, the US Department of War trained Americans as Japanese language interpreters and translators.

Before 1940, more than five thousand Nisei enlisted or were drafted into the US Army. They were mostly Hawaiians. In November 1941, the Military Intelligence Service Language School assigned sixty students to join its first class in San Francisco. Four Nisei instructors taught the sixty students. Fifty-eight were Japanese Americans.

For those serving on the mainland, individual commanders were given the option of discharging Japanese American soldiers. Commanders took away their weapons and assigned them to desk jobs or menial tasks like latrine duty for those who remained in the Army.

In 1942, the Selective Service didn't accept Nisei altogether because of their Japanese ethnicity. Meanwhile, Nisei members of the Hawaii National Guard were secretly formed into the Hawaii Provisional Infantry Battalion. The Army transported fourteen hundred soldiers to San Francisco, then to Camp McCoy in Wisconsin, and became the 100th Infantry Battalion.

The US Army formed the Board of Military Utilization of US Citizens of Japanese Ancestry comprised of military brass and the WRA. After three months, the board reported against forming an all-Japanese American fighting unit based on the "universal mistrust" of the Japanese.

The Office of War Information thought otherwise and sent a letter to FDR stating that Japanese Americans in the Army would counter allegations of racism.

FDR announced the formation of the all-Japanese 442nd Regimental Combat Team (RCT). Three of my uncles enlisted, my dad's brother Rich, Vince, who married Auntie Rose, and my mom's brother, George.

Serving in the military wasn't a priority in my family, in that there was no pressure on me to serve. I think my dad felt guilty about his non-service. My mother was more of a pacifist, and my dad was the family hawk. In 1964, Dad voted for Barry Goldwater while Mom supported Lyndon Johnson.

The Cheyenne Japanese community was most active during the 1940s to the 1960s. Nisei soldiers returned from Europe, and there was a high level of camaraderie among Japanese community members as they recoiled from the racism experienced during and following the war, which sparked the origins of the Skyline Nisei Club.

The City Café originally hosted club activities. Later, the club established a Japanese community center for events like the dinner honoring Japanese judges who visited Cheyenne in November 1950. There were thirty-nine Issei and Nisei who attended the dinner in the Japanese community center.

Cheyenne attorney George Guy, best known for defending Japanese war criminal General Tomoyuki Yamashita, invited the judges to Wyoming. He showed them around the justice system in Cheyenne.

The US military tried Yamashita for alleged war crimes committed by his troops during the Japanese defense of the Philippines in 1944. They found the general guilty of war atrocities even though there was no evidence that he approved or even knew of them.

It came out at trial that troops not under his command committed many of the crimes. Yamashita was sentenced and executed by hanging in 1946.

During World War II, Japanese Americans had to go above and beyond what was expected for minimal acceptance as model minorities. Those extraordinary actions included men enlisting in the 442nd RCT.

All commissioned officers were Caucasian, and all non-commissioned officers were Japanese, selected from the ranks of mainland troops who were already in the army. The soldiers from Hawaii on active duty before Pearl Harbor were resentful that they were passed over for the non-commissioned officer jobs.

The new recruits to the 442nd RCT joined the 100th Battalion training at Camp Shelby. The Mississippi and the Military Intelligence Language School also needed to recruit more linguists to join the 442nd RCT.

April 5th is "Go for Broke" Day, honoring Japanese World War II veterans. "Go for Broke" was the motto of the 442nd RCT. The 442nd RCT was activated in February 1943 and composed of Nisei men from Hawaii and relocation camp volunteers who trained at Camp Shelby, Mississippi.

The 442nd Infantry Regiment, the 522nd Field Artillery Battalion, and the 232nd Combat Engineer Company became the 442nd RCT. In June 1944, the 442nd RCT deployed to Italy, where they joined in combat with the 100th Infantry Battalion.

On the home front in the relocation camps, the decision to allow Japanese American internees the opportunity to enlist in the newly formed 442nd RCT caused conflict. Based on the *Loyalty Questionnaire*, fifteen hundred yes-yes boys volunteered. Many no-no boys resisted the draft and ended up in jail. The Minidoka camp saw the largest numbers of enlistees. Of the total number of 442nd RCT soldiers, point-two-five percent volunteered from Minidoka.

Maintaining morale in the new regiment was difficult, particularly among the Japanese soldiers from Hawaii and those in the army before the war who resented the recruits from the relocation camps. There were arguments and fights between "buddhaheads" from Hawaii and the "kotonks" from the mainland.

The Hawaiian soldiers came up with these monikers, referring to their dominant religion, claiming that kotonk was the sound the mainlander's hollow noggins made when they smacked the ground.

While they had differences amongst themselves, their common struggle was dealing with racism towards blacks in the Jim Crow South. The Japanese soldiers occasionally intervened on behalf of African Americans, which caused reprimands from their superior officers.

In September 1944, the 442nd RCT was sent to take part in the south of France invasion. They liberated Bruyeres and Biffontaine and rescued a battalion that became separated from its division.

The Lost Battalion is a story arc behind the movie *Go for Broke* (1951), starring Van Johnson as a bigoted commanding officer who changes his tune after fighting alongside the 442nd RCT. Robert Pirosh, who also created the TV show *Combat!* directed the movie.

The 442nd RCT joined forces with the all-African American 92nd Infantry Division in March 1945 and helped drive the Germans out of northern Italy.

The 442nd RCT was the most decorated, having earned the following awards:

- 7 Presidential Unit Citations
- 2 Meritorious Service Plaques
- 36 Army Commendation Medals
- 87 Division Commendations

442nd RCT individuals were awarded:

- 21 Medals of Honor
- 29 Distinguished Service Crosses
- 560 Silver Stars
- 4,000 Bronze Stars
- 22 Legion of Merit medals
- 15 Soldiers Medals
- 9,500 Purple Hearts

The 442nd RCT lost 650 men, over 3,700 wounded in action, and 67 declared missing in action. Of my three uncles who served, Rich earned a Purple Heart and a special citation from Military Intelligence Language School. He didn't talk at all about his time in the war, but I've wondered about the circumstances of his decorations. I knew nothing about his accomplishments until seeing the medal at his funeral.

The most decorated 442nd RCT individual soldier was from Wyoming. Toshiro "Tosh" Suyematsu was awarded a Purple Heart, a Purple Heart with an Oak Leaf Cluster, two Silver Stars, and a Bronze Star. The citation for one of Tosh's Silver

Stars when he was part of the liberation of the "Lost Battalion" summarizes his heroics:

By direction of the president, the Silver Star is awarded to Toshiro Suyematsu for gallantry in action on 22-24 October and 28-29 October 1944, near Biffontaine, France. Sergeant Suyematsu was a forward observer with the 100th Battalion during the unit's isolation near Biffontaine. When he was directed to lay a creeping barrage on the reverse side of a hill to forestall the barrage from his observation point until the rounds were just clearing the trees above him. Despite the ever-present danger of the tree bursts and a subsequent counter barrage by the enemy which came in over the ridge and bracketed him between two curtains of fire, he continued his fire mission.

Tosh moved with his parents Tsuchio "Ben" and Masa Suyematsu from Oakland, California, where Ben repaired shoes. The family moved to Casper in 1919, where Ben worked for the CB&Q railroad until the railroad strike of 1922 when four hundred thousand workers walked off the job over a national wage decrease.

After working for the railroad, Ben returned to his previous trade and set up a shoe repair shop in North Casper.

The Suyematsus were family friends on my mother's side. I don't know this for sure, but I'm guessing that since my grandfather Sakata and Ben Suyematsu worked for CB&Q at or near the Powder River and Arminto sections in Natrona County, the families grew acquainted. Tosh had two brothers, King and Taro, who I didn't know very well. I met their kids but only saw them on rare occasions in Casper.

Auntie Hisako was a friend of Tosh's sisters. Sara was a nurse in Casper, and Kiyo was a music professor at Mankato State University in Minnesota. They, like my aunt, never married and spent quite a bit of time in Cheyenne. We went on family excursions to Casper. Sara and Kiyo were both athletic and took me on my first ski outing on Casper Mountain. That was back in the day of lace-up leather boots.

Before World War II, Tosh was a student at UW when he ran out of tuition money. He quit school to join the army. He attained the rank of sergeant, but on November 30, 1941, he was demoted to buck private.

A week later, Japan bombed Pearl Harbor. He and other Japanese soldiers, including his brother, King, were assigned to desk jobs until given an opportunity to volunteer for the 442nd RCT.

After the war, Tosh returned to UW and finished his undergraduate degree before going to law school. He remained in southeast Wyoming, where he practiced law with his wife, Ellen Crowley, in Cheyenne. She served in the Wyoming State Legislature. Tosh was later named assistant US Attorney General for Wyoming.

Ted Miyamoto from Baker's Place was a member of the 442nd RCT and was decorated with the bronze star for his role in France supporting the Lost Battalion. His citation reads:

For extraordinary heroism in action on Oct. 29, 1944, near Biffontaine, France. When the forward elements of Sergeant Miyamoto's company were pinned down by fire from an enemy machine gun and supporting snipers, he fearlessly worked his way forward to the enemy emplacement. While so engaged, he was wounded in the forearm by a sniper, but disdaining medical treatment, he continued to advance until he reached a point within twenty-five yards from the emplacement; exposing himself to get a better observation, opened fire with his submachine gun, killed the two gunners and thus neutralized the position. In the two-hour firefight which followed, Sgt. Miyamoto accounted for five more of the enemy and refused to be evacuated until the initial objective was reached.

It wasn't until I started researching this book that I was grateful for the men who put their lives on the line and enlisted and joined the 442nd RCT to prove their loyalty. Their participation in the war allowed me to participate in activities that were once segregated, like playing baseball in the Cheyenne town leagues and not on Japanese-only teams.

I didn't know that Japanese players had their own leagues during the war and for many seasons after. Ted Miyamoto's brothers, Tom and Bill, played ball on an all-Japanese baseball team that competed in segregated leagues similar to the more prominent Negro League teams.

Tom caught the attention of Major League Baseball scouts, but when Pearl Harbor was attacked, his career was cut short.

THIRTY-ONE: Baseball and the American Way

There were a number of Japanese baseball teams in Wyoming. They were segregated similar to the Negro Leagues.

While I was away at college, we still lived in Cheyenne during my freshman and sophomore years. The Japanese community and my family continued to have big community events including indoor activities like samurai movie screenings and holiday parties, and July 4th and Memorial Day picnics at Holliday Park, where we played catch and fielded a few grounders away from the picnic action.

The last big family event happened when my dad's family had a big reunion in 1966. That summer, I broke my ankle sliding into second base and spent the 4th of July picnic on crutches. After that, I lost my desire to get better at hitting the curveball and quit Babe Ruth baseball.

There is a long history of Japanese baseball in the United States. World War II and EO 9066 cut short the baseball careers of many prominent Nisei players, including the Miyamoto brothers.

Baseball was one game that became a Nisei pastime at the fifteen assembly centers and ten relocation camps. That sport was a unifying activity allowed by the WRA because the game would reinforce Japanese assimilation to adopt the American Way.

Japanese baseball originated in the United States when the Fuji Athletic Club of San Francisco was founded in 1903. The Japanese Pacific Coast Baseball League was formed by the end of the decade, with teams in eight West Coast cities.

The all-Japanese leagues were segregated, similar to the Negro Leagues. By 1920, twenty teams made up a baseball league in the Rocky Mountain region.

After the bombing of Pearl Harbor, President Roosevelt received a letter from baseball commissioner Kenesaw Landis seeking his opinion about whether professional baseball should allow games to be played during wartime.

FDR wrote back what became known as the Green Light Letter, expressing that baseball is an important fabric binding Americans together. He advised that Major League Baseball should continue to play on the home front. Over five hundred professional ballplayers served, including stars like Joe DiMaggio, Ted Williams, and Stan Musial.

Following EO 9066, that philosophy spread to the Japanese leagues. Four of the ten camps fielded teams that could travel to away-games in other camps: Gila River and Poston camps in Arizona, Camp Amache in Colorado, and Heart Mountain camp in Wyoming.

The Heart Mountain camp fielded a talented team in 1944 that played an epic thirteen-game series against Gila River. The players paid their own way from the money they earned working jobs in camp.

The Arizona team made the twelve-hundred-mile road trip on an old bus that broke down several times along the way. The players wore their uniforms during the trip rather than street clothes. It was simpler to explain that they were ballplayers and not escapees from camp or spies when stopped. Gila River won the series that took about a month to play.

One member of the Heart Mountain camp team was Minol Ota. He was the camp veterinarian from Cheyenne who moved to Powell. Minol and his brother, Joe, played on the Wyoming Nisei team that won the Tristate Japanese Baseball League 1943 tournament. That team had strong West 17th Street neighborhood ties and was enshrined at the Baseball Hall of Fame in Cooperstown, New York.

Bill Matsuyama, who owned the California Fish Market, managed the team. His team included son Harry; Tom and Bill Miyamoto, who eventually owned Baker's Place; Kaye and Harry Hashimoto, and their brother, George; Paul Tani, who lived above the City Café; and Fred Futa, who lived down the block from the City Café.

By the 1960s, Japanese baseball in Wyoming was non-existent. A Cheyenne team competed in a Northern Colorado league. The Denver Nisei team included a player named Art Arita, who lived on West 17th Street in the 1940s as a child before moving to Colorado. Like other Japanese living in the interior before Pearl Harbor, Art and his family were spared relocation.

Another member of the Denver Nisei baseball club was Mas Yoshimura. He was the starting first baseman who ended up in Denver after being originally sent to the Jerome camp and later the Rowher camp.

He recalls when he and his family were transported by train from the Fresno center to Fort Logan in Denver, the train made a stop at the Cheyenne depot for a break. All the detainees were let off the train and greeted by a host of soldiers stationed along the railway platform, aiming .50-caliber machine guns at the passengers.

I played for the Cheyenne Little League Red Sox. After I broke my ankle when I was on the Babe Ruth Red Sox, my career ended until I was an adult. My dad and I played for the First Presbyterian Church slow-pitch softball team.

He was the oldest guy on the roster. I'll say he was in his early fifties. Dad played first base and was the catcher. Nobody liked to catch, and he always had a spot on the team.

"If you want to play, learn how to catch," he advised. "In slow pitch, it's easy."

He also was a good hitter and often led off. He could put the ball in play with shallow bloopers to the opposite field.

His knees and back couldn't handle the position, and I put on the mask and have been a catcher ever since, and I always played.

Dad took me to see the Yankees v. Bears exhibition game in 1964. It was thirty-one years later that I took him to the first game played at the brand-new Coors Field in 1995. It was an exhibition game between the Colorado Rockies and the Yankees.

The game wasn't quite a proper game since it was the beginning of the strike-shortened 1995 season and the replacement Yankees played the replacement Rockies.

The Rockies made the playoffs that season as the first-ever wild card team. The Rockies lost to the eventual World Series champion Atlanta Braves in a best-of-four-games series.

I gave up my Rockies season tickets after the MLB Allstar game that was played at Coors Field in 1998. I started losing interest in Rockies baseball even when the Rockies played in the 2007 World Series when they were swept in four games by the Boston Red Sox.

Since I had watched those 2001 World Series games in New York City, that experience was scratched off my list of things to do before I die.

THIRTY-TWO: Rites of Passage

Auntie Elsie was the only one of my Nisei relatives who competed in organized and competitive sports leagues. She played second base on a championship women's softball team. It was fastpitch and fun to watch because the games moved along quickly. In Lions Park, there was a regulation softball field complete with a backstop, scorers booth, an announcer, and bleachers. The women played under the lights, wore uniforms and spikes. As a kid, that was impressive to me.

The other avid sportsperson in the family was Uncle Rich. He wasn't a ballplayer but a competitive fisher. He and Hank Omoto entered fishing contests at some of the big lakes around the state. He took two huge trout to the taxidermist and had them mounted for display above the archway separating the living room from the dining area.

During the summers, he invited me and cousin Leonard to go fishing with him. We loaded up and drove to Crystal Lake and Granite Reservoir near Cheyenne. Leonard became a more avid fisher than me, taking to the deep waters near San Francisco.

The Skyline Nisei Club organized summer picnics at the lakes which were fun. I usually didn't do much fishing so Uncle Rich could use an extra pole. I was more interested in finding round, flat stones for skipping over the lake surface.

Rich worked as a meat cutter at Stop 'n Shop grocery store on the outskirts of the Japanese neighborhood. He enlisted the help of my sister and me when it came to taking inventory at the end of each month. I wasn't that great at the logic of math. I think my help was more harmful than good.

The companion business of the Stop 'n Shop was the Fix 'n Mix liquor store and bar next door, where my Yankees baseball excursion to Denver started.

Rich was also a big game hunter. I knew little about that subsistence activity of his. I still haven't developed a taste for venison, but I liked the elk steaks and hamburger when he brought that over after a big hunt.

Hunting was a family activity on my dad's side. When the war broke out, law enforcement tracked down Japanese families in town. When they stopped by Grandpa Ohashi's place, federal agents confiscated the hunting rifles. I don't know if the law enforcement agency returned them, but Rich had quite the gun cabinet where he kept various long rifles and shotguns.

We kids weren't privy to his hunting excursions. My mom made it clear that I wouldn't have been able to go along if Rich asked me, which was quite a contrast with the Wyoming gun culture.

Hunting was a way of life in Wyoming, and I think it still is. Students would get excused from school when hunting season opened up in the fall.

I viewed hunting as a rite of passage that I missed out on while growing up. Eventually, I felled an antelope while living in Lander and got that out of my system. I bought a .243 caliber Winchester with open sights from a friend named Mike for two hundred bucks and purchased a scope from Wendall over at the local camera store.

I had some previous "experience" with guns. When you consider a guy like me who could get a hold of an unregistered rifle, firearms are very accessible. Mike helped me calibrate the scope at the local gun range north of town.

While living in Gillette, Tom, the decorated Vietnam War veteran fought with the 101st Airborne and saw quite a bit of combat. He had an AR-15 semi-automatic rifle in the closet that we would take out to the back lot and blast tin cans back to the Stone Age. It was hardly target-practice and was a throwback to my youth imagining myself as Sgt. Saunders on *Combat!*

I took a hunting safety class and was as knowledgeable as any other first-time hunter. Mike was my guide. He had rules: no shooting from the vehicle or the road; I had to pick out an animal and stalk it.

We spent all morning following around an antelope buck. He finally stopped away from his herd and a hundred yards ahead. I aimed and squeezed the trigger. His knees buckled, and the lifeless carcass dropped to the dusty prairie.

Next, Mike showed me how to field dress the animal. I waited while Mike brought around the truck. We dropped it off at the processing place in Lander. I was never fond of antelope meat, but this was mild-tasting compared to some I'd tried before. That was the first and last game animal I would shoot and kill.

Mike at least made a day of it with his stalking rule. Otherwise, we could have been home hours earlier. An animal has absolutely no chance against even a small-bore rifle like mine.

I moved that rifle around from closets to crawl spaces and to basements. Finally, I traded it to a guy for some tile work on a condo remodel many years later in Boulder.

Men who fought in World War II or the Vietnam War faced some perilous times. Me felling that antelope pales to the heroics of anyone who saw combat. I wonder if there is a violence streak that people, particularly men, have pent up that needs to be released.

I imagine Uncle Rich used his big game field dressing experience at the Stop 'n Shop. Rich later worked for his brother and my uncle Jake at Pioneer Printing.

Stalking and gunning down that antelope may have been a rite of passage for me, but another form of hunting became an activity that was less equipment-intensive and more personally satisfying.

THIRTY-THREE: Fungus Among Us

Matsutake mushroom hunting was a family tradition that didn't begin until we moved to Laramie.

When we moved to Laramie in 1973, there was still family in Cheyenne, but my parents soon established themselves in Laramie. My mom was happy to leave Cheyenne in her rearview mirror.

Before my second year in college, my dad rented an apartment in Laramie, where we lived the summer before they sold the Cheyenne house. He commuted between Cheyenne and Laramie on the weekends. I didn't mind staying in Laramie on my own.

While I was in Nebraska at college, my family finally moved. It was odd to go to a different home for Thanksgiving in a different town and having to ask, "Where are the forks?"

My mom needed a change of scenery. I think she grew tired of having her family life revolve mostly around my dad's bunch. After she retired and nurtured her watercolor art business, she reinvented herself and hyphenated her name as Sumiko Sakata-O'Hashi.

As for Laramie, I never really got the hang of the place. Leaving familiar surroundings and people in Cheyenne, going away to college, and then uprooted to Laramie was a big change.

Summer in Laramie was nice, though. Like most other college towns, the students were away. I took two physics classes in summer school at UW. I was bad at math, and the two As helped my GPA. I would have likely earned Cs had I taken physics in classroom at Hastings College.

I thought summer school at UW was one of the best-kept secrets in academia. Everyone on campus was invited to an all-school steak fry at the UW science camp in the Medicine Bow National Forest.

There was a perception that summer school was for kids who had to make up classes they flunked during the regular school year. I took high school world history during the summer, which was way better than taking it in the fall. The summer I graduated from high school, learning how to type in summer school from Mr. Halverson was the most practical class I took that would be of benefit to me to this very moment.

Looking back, it mostly gave my parents a chance to build their own Japanese niche. I continued working for my dad during the summers while in college. It was tough watching my dad adapt to the rapid changes in his work life because of being uprooted.

Even though we moved only fifty miles away to Laramie and the bottling operation was similar in capacity, taking a similar production manager job wasn't exactly a turnkey operation. The equipment was newer with more bells and whistles, but the production flow wasn't efficient.

Starting the job stressed him out. He worked with a co-manager who happened to be the owner's son. He had some sort of business degree and didn't seem to have much mechanical knowledge. He eventually quit and left the company.

Being new in town, there was no familiar community to be a safety net or support network. Dad was engrained into Superman's American Way of rugged individualism, climbing to the top, working forty years for the same company.

After moving to the new job in Laramie, Dad had to restart his trajectory and again climb up the corporate ladder. Mom had excellent typing skills and landed a pretty good job at the UW College of Commerce and Industry in the Accounting Department, where she was the office manager.

We had the big family thing going in Cheyenne, but in Laramie, our new family role didn't exist until we broke into the mushroom hunting scene.

The Matsuyamas, who had the California Fish Market, were among the best Cheyenne-based mushroom hunters. Old-time Cheyenne Japanese families never disclosed their coveted areas and, thus, had the market cornered. Those families were very cliquish.

While we lived in Cheyenne, my family took a Saturday drive to Laramie, looking around for mushroom hunting grounds. We were getting close to a mother lode. At one stop, there was a disposable chopsticks paper wrapper on the side of the road. That was telltale evidence. We saw a carload of Japanese rumbling down the dirt road towards us. I think they were from Colorado.

It didn't seem right to poach mushrooms. Our hunting would have to wait. Living in Laramie was a huge benefit when it came to mushrooms. The altitude and humidity were about right for all kinds of mushrooms, and there were many hunting areas ripe for exploration.

Albany County is allegedly one of the best hunting grounds for the elusive pine mushroom, Tricholoma matsutake, a delicacy in Japanese cooking. They are quite tasty when freshly harvested, cleaned, and sautéed in butter and shoyu. I like their chewy consistency.

Armed with small gardening trowels, everyone in the party spread out to cover every square foot where the mushroom caps would poke up through the Ponderosa pine (Pinus ponderosa) pungent needle detritus.

I developed a pretty good eye and learned a few kinds of edible mushrooms like Boletus edulis, with big red caps, and Suillus americanus had sticky yellow caps and were spongier.

Digging up matsutake nurtured togetherness among family and friends. The hunts were big social events and took a good amount of planning—food preparation, gathering the tools, sorting, cleaning the finds, and cooking some up.

We had a cabin near Centennial, the home base for mushroom hunting and skiing, summer parties, and family gatherings. Now that the O'Hashis had broken into the matsutake world, that enticed kin from Cheyenne to make the hour drive to our place in the North Fork Subdivision.

Since it was the late summer, Uncle Rich came out to scout potential deer or elk hunting areas. Sometimes he hauled his boat and went fishing at Lake Hattie or Rob Roy Reservoir. If he had a successful outing, we'd have trout cooked on the grill to go along with the pan-fried matsutake.

The mushroom season was in the late summer and early fall. The ground in August and September couldn't be too wet or too dry. One week it may be too wet, but the next week perfect conditions.

When my parents first moved to Laramie, there was no family around except the immediate family. Being fifty miles from the rest of the clan in Cheyenne might as well have been five hundred miles.

That sense of isolation changed when my dad staked claims on a couple of prime mushroom-hunting areas, but after the Issei were no longer alive, interest in matsutake went by the wayside.

Not only were there generational changes in the family, but Dad was also going through a rough patch at his work. He was caught in the middle of rapid change. Luckily, that all happened toward the end of his forty-year run with Coca-Cola.

Right after the internal management of the Coke plant stabilized, it became a turbulent time for him because of changes happening with mergers and acquisitions in many businesses, like hospitals and the beverage industry.

First, a company in Wichita Falls, Texas, bought the Laramie Coke plant, which was good because they had a retirement program, at least while it lasted.

Swires, based in Hong Kong, was in a rapid expansion mode during the late 1970s, acquired a large plant in Bonneville, Utah, and soon gobbled up smaller bottling operations like Laramie in favor of converting them into distribution points.

I don't recall that Swires kept up with Dad's retirement plan. His job evolved from tedious and exact production management to organizing product delivery, which required less precision but more heavy lifting.

Dad would have had a tough time reinventing himself if he quit. Ageism isn't a new thing. In the fledgling digital era, he never turned on, let alone looked at a computer or used a cell phone.

He retired shortly after that but was hired back for a few more years because the company largely didn't want to hire other workers. Deliveries were backbreaking, and the wear and tear took their toll on him.

When he finally retired, I gave him a copy of *From Ag-ing to Sage-ing*, by Rabbi Zalman Schachter-Shalomi. This was before I became acquainted with the good Rabbi and his wife, Eve, while in Boulder. He was a big inspiration and why I continued serving many communities as a do-gooder, trying to save the world.

Dad wasn't much of a joiner but was very supportive in the background after my mom retired from UW. She was more gregarious and enjoyed group activities, like joining a quilting club and clogging dance classes.

She was a breast cancer survivor, volunteered for Relay for Life, and participated in fundraising benefit events for the local arts community and the Presbyterian Church. Dad followed along with all that.

After my grandparents and parents all passed away, as well as the other Issei and Nisei, interest waned in mushroom hunting. Going out with my elders and learning the techniques, mostly differentiating the odors that go along with finding matsutake, were rites of passage.

I couldn't tell you, except in general terms, where we hunted. I'm not even mentioning where I think the mushroom troves might be. The mental maps are going with me to my grave. Compared to a hunt for antelope, mushroom hunting is much more self-fulfilling.

Whenever I see Ponderosa pines at around seven thousand to nine thousand feet in elevation, I look for evidence of matsutake hunters, like multiple tire tread marks. These days, I've read that there are places in Scandinavia that have entered the matsutake market.

The social aspects of the mushroom hunt are gone, at least in my circles, but someone is still hunting them. The Pacific Mercantile Japanese grocery store in Denver sells them.

At one time, besides the Pacific Mercantile, there was also the Granada Fish Market that had its roots in Amache Relocation Camp in southeastern Colorado.

THIRTY-THREE: Commute for Rice

I haven't checked around Cheyenne lately, but I know no store sells matsutake. As we become more globalized, I imagine some stores sell other Japanese foods like rice. It's now branded as sushi rice. I doubt it's available in eighty-pound bags, though. Years ago, rice was packed in cotton sacks. During the Great Depression, my grandmothers repurposed the bags into dishtowels and aprons.

My grandma Ohashi was the head of her household and cooked for her sons Rich, George, Roy, and for my grandfather, plus slinging fried rice at her Highway Café.

There was always something around to eat whenever family members would drop by. She went through a lot of rice. My dad was in charge of driving her to Denver to pick up a supply of Japanese staples, particularly around the winter holidays.

The Granada Fish Market and Pacific Mercantile carried delicacies not available in Cheyenne, like tako (octopus).

The most exotic on the shopping list was canned awabi (abalone). Abalone habituates the coastal waters of California and Baja, Mexico. Abalone are also called "sea snails" and are a delicacy at two hundred dollars a can at Walmart. Give me a rubbery slice of octopus any day.

The Granada Fish Market was originally owned and operated by a former Amache Relocation camp internee, Frank Tsuchiya, from California. After the war, his business was so successful that he opened in Denver and reopened in Los Angeles.

The camp was near the Amache, Colorado, post office. Although some regional business owners were anti-Japanese, most saw Camp Amache internees as valued customers. For all practical purposes, the camp gate was open all the time, with internees free to come and go.

After obtaining his parole from Camp Amache, Tsuchiya opened a fish market in nearby Granada. Somewhere along the way, since much of the state was under Spanish rule, Granada was named after the city in southern Spain.

Before leaving California after EO 9066, he owned a similar business in Los Angeles and still had connections there. He sourced shellfish, sashimi-grade tuna (thinly sliced fresh raw fish or meat), and a variety of Japanese household pantry items such as shoyu and udon noodles trucked to Granada.

Denver University archaeological digs unearthed evidence of these connections that included shards of an abalone shell.

Amache was named after the daughter of Cheyenne Tribal Chief One Eye. Amache married a Colorado cattle producer named John Prowers. He is credited with bringing the first Hereford cattle into the Colorado Territory. The county bears his name.

In 1864, Chief One Eye negotiated a truce among the Cheyenne and Arapaho tribes and the US government. According to the agreement, tribal members would be guaranteed safe winter camping along the nearby Sand Creek.

Despite the pact, on the morning of November 29th, soldiers from the Colorado Third Calvary stormed onto the Prowers ranch and held Prowers and Amache hostage.

At the encampment along Sand Creek, the now infamous Colonel John Chivington ordered his regiment to attack the Cheyenne and Arapaho. The raid, now known as the Sand Creek Massacre, claimed the lives of one hundred and fifty tribal members, including Chief One Eye.

Before World War II, Granada was one of many small farming towns across the Arkansas River Valley, a few miles north of Camp Amache. The Atchison, Topeka, and Santa Fe Railroad established Granada as a railroad town. Geographically, Granada is on a rolling prairie basin tucked between the Rocky Mountains and the Great Plains. Despite the region's aridity, the lush fields absorb plenty of irrigation water from the Arkansas River.

Severe summer thunderstorms and tornadoes break up the semi-arid climate. Winters are cold and dry but can bring heavy snowfall. Throughout the year, high winds that sweep over the land kick up dust storms.

The Dust Bowl and the Great Depression hit Granada hard. The area remained economically depressed until World War II, and Camp Amache helped bring about an economic revival.

The camp project purchased by the WRA was entirely on private property that encompassed over ten thousand acres of the Koen Ranch and the X-Y Ranch. To create a contiguous perimeter, a dozen private farms and ranches were also included in the project area, mostly by condemnation, which caused ill feelings between the WRA and locals.

The Camp Amache population was around eight thousand internees, although over ten thousand internees came through the camp. Camp Amache was the tenth largest city in Colorado. The 2017 Granada population estimate was 496 persons.

The barracks were constructed on a low-lying hill that, during heavy rains, broke up the fast-moving water and prevented erosion and flash flooding. Like other camps, barbwire fence marked the perimeter. The WRA placed eight guard towers with soldiers with machine guns around the camp.

The first internees arrived from the Central Valley of California, the northern coast, and southwest Los Angeles. Later, over nine hundred loyal yes-yes internees from Tule Lake camp, and when the Jerome camp in Arkansas closed, around five hundred transferred to Camp Amache.

Camp Amache internees were also embroiled in the loyalty questionnaire controversy and had the distinction of the highest percentage of yes-yes internees compared to the other nine camps.

Colorado Governor Ralph Carr was the only governor who supported locating a WRA camp in his state. His cooperative approach is one reason for the lower level of statewide disdain toward the Japanese. Carr is honored for his open-mindedness with a statue of himself in Denver's Sakura Square.

The camp police department hired sixty internees to be law enforcement officers. The Amache Fire Department had three crews of internee firefighters. The forty-five-member print shop crew was prolific. The shop was set up in 1943 and produced internal camp program flyers and calendars. Training materials and over two hundred and fifty thousand color posters were printed for the US Navy.

The majority of the camp acreage was reserved for agricultural purposes. In 1943, Camp Amache farms produced about four million pounds of vegetables. Not only did the camp become self-sufficient because of its agricultural operations, but surpluses were also shipped to other relocation camps, including six hundred bushels of spinach to the Poston and Gila River camps in Arizona and one thousand bushels to the US Army.

Camp Amache internees found jobs at area farms. There was a positive relationship with area farmers and ranchers because of the wartime labor shortage. Internees were paid, but many helped as volunteers.

At Christmas 1943, Tsuchiya and the Granada Fish Market purchased a truckload of pine trees from Portland, Oregon, and donated them for each Amache Camp block mess hall.

The Granada Fish Market was so successful in serving Camp Amache, that after the war Tsuchiya opened stores in Denver and his hometown of Los Angeles. The market in Denver is long gone, but in Lower Downtown, there's now a condominium complex called the Granada Market.

Pacific Mercantile is still flourishing in Sakura Square next to the Buddhist temple. Pacific is more like a regular grocery store that stocks mostly Japanese food and sundry items.

I always liked to tag along for the ride, hoping to be treated to some gooey mochi balls filled with anko (sweet bean paste). At that time, the mochi was fresh. These days, it's available frozen, including with ice cream in the middle.

Grandma liked a restaurant called the Mandarin on 20th Street, across from the Buddhist temple and west of the 20th Street Café. That was the lunch place of choice when she wasn't in a hurry to rush back to Cheyenne, which happened on most trips.

The menu was a lot like the City Café, with short order Asian food like chop suey and my fave, pork noodles. The tsukemono (pickled cucumber salad) was as good as my grandmother's, except no sliced abalone.

As abalone became more expensive, she substituted octopus, and with octopus not readily available, kamaboko fish sausage. In a pinch, she added surimi (fake crabmeat).

Grandparents Sakata only had the two of them and didn't need to make as many trips to Denver. My mom checked with them for a list when Dad made his periodic drives for his mom.

We all had to live in two worlds. Japanese assimilated and adopted the dominant culture lifestyle. If there was anything that would lead people to think we were model minorities, it would be my family's involvement with Cheyenne Frontier Days.

THIRTY-FOUR: The Kimono Cowboy

I always have looked forward to Cheyenne Frontier Days. My sister, Lorinda, friend Carol Lou Kishiyama, and I get ready for the big parade.

CFD was, and still is, the most grandiose event in Cheyenne that happens the last full week of July and an extra weekend. Back in the day, CFD had a huge downtown presence.

For a city kid, CFD was a big deal for me. I decked myself out in a straw cowboy hat, Lee jeans, Acme boots, and a western cut snap shirt. It was a big family event.

I was a Japanese cowboy trying to buck the Japanese farmer and gardener stereotypes, not unlike all the other drugstore cowboys in Cheyenne. I didn't quite fit in with the look.

CFD is a huge ten-day outdoor rodeo held annually since 1897, the last full week in July—plus an extra weekend—and billed as "the daddy of 'em all." The event annually draws over two hundred thousand celebrants from around the world to a variety of events of interest to everyone, from cowboys to flatlanders.

If you're a vegan, healthy food eater, or animal rights advocate, CFD probably isn't where you'd want to spend your vacation days. I usually do some videography at CFD and am required to ask permission from the Professional Rodeo Cowboys Association (PRCA), which wants to ensure I, or any other professional producer, likely won't be using the footage for blatant anti-rodeo purposes.

Besides the daily rodeos that involve contests pitting men against steers, bulls, and horses; followed by the night shows; there's a non-stop carnival midway that offers rides, games of skill; and food vendors who hand out tasty turkey legs, deep-fried funnel cakes, and cotton candy.

Downtown is the location for three morning parades of floats, antique automobiles, horse-drawn carriages with riders in period dress, and top marching bands.

The local Kiwanis Club puts on free pancake breakfasts and serves forty thousand hungry rodeo-goers one hundred thousand pancakes and three thousand pounds of ham on three mornings between parade days.

In 1898, the CFD committee began inviting Native American tribal members from South Dakota and Oklahoma to participate in the Indian Village, originally set up downtown, but in 1960 moved to Frontier Park near the rodeo arena. Northern Arapaho tribal dancers and oral historians from the Wind River Indian Reservation provide the CFD tribal culture programming.

I've been to Cheyenne for CFD every year of my life, except in 2020, when organizers canceled all events because of the COVID-19 pandemic. I became embedded in the annual event. My mom's friends in her X-JWC women's club were all involved in CFD. That meant all the kids were involved, too.

During July, we all gathered at the ranch operated by Doran and Enid Lummis, along with their children, Chris, Claudia, Cynthia—we all were in high school together—and their brother Del, who is a few years younger, and the sib who I'm still the most in touch with.

Their place was on the east edge of town, where we assembled the parade float in the barn. My dad provided the Coca-Cola flatbed trailer decorated into a parade float skirted with chicken wire stuffed with paper napkins.

Mom rode on that one with her X-JWC singing group called the Dearies. Their music genre was turn of the Twentieth century—"Five Foot Two, Eyes of Blue," "Blue Moon," etc. The Dearies entertained around town in their long hoop skirts and wide-brimmed floppy hats. From their parade float, their acapella voices carried pretty well over the street noise.

My sister and I climbed onto the hay wagon, the "entry-level" float for youngsters. The float wranglers at the head of the parade coached into traditional gender roles, with the boys asked to be boisterous by yelling "Yeehaw!" along the parade route, while the girls sat quietly, smiled, and waved hankies to the adoring crowd.

There was also a wild and crazy Hell's Half Acre float in the CFD parade. At ten a.m., the beer kegs were flowing. It was a badge of honor to get on that float and still is today. The bold parade watcher would jump the float from the street.

The bar floozies flaunting their heavy makeup, alluring satiny can-can dresses, and fishnet stockings partied through downtown Cheyenne.

After the parade, the float riders arrived at the Holliday Park tent town. The would-be drunken railroad workers, cowboys, and prostitutes reveled and entertained city dude tourists.

Their vignettes about guys arguing over women or money or both and the subsequent gunfights resulted in bad guys falling to the ground and feigning death after being shot by a hail of blanks fired from their sidearms.

When I was in junior high, Cousin Matthew visited from Utah most summers. He, my sister, and I teamed up with a neighbor named Pat to sell pop at the parade.

It was an annual gig for Matthew. The extended family got together during CFD. That continued through the 1980s until my grandparents, and our Nisei parents passed away.

Subsequently, my cousins became more mobile and had fewer family reasons to return to Cheyenne.

Selling at the parade was a cottage industry for kids. The sales crews were mostly from the west side since it was so close. We east side entrepreneurs were outliers.

Over the previous few months, we saved up our weekly allowances and stocked up on grocery store-brand soft drinks like Shurfine, Cragmont, and Shasta for resale. We could have sold Coke products, but the profit margin wasn't as good even at wholesale. Besides, thirsty parade-goers didn't care about brands.

We bought bags of ice and sleeves of cups from my dad. That was before bottled water, and we provided ice in cups if requested, which none of the other sales kid crews offered.

Early on parade day, we parked the family Pontiac on Carey Avenue near Brannen's grocery store that was a great supply depot. Then, kids could sell from the street.

Now, the city government requires young vendors to get a permit, sell only on the sidewalk behind the crowd, accompanied by a responsible adult. What's the point of that? The most practical life skill I learned and retained is how to count back change and appreciate it, particularly if a young person counts back my change.

As the Cheyenne downtown lost its retail stores to urban sprawl, Brannen's, Miller's, and Safeway grocery stores closed. The state of Wyoming bought all three properties up for office space. CFD pop vendors lost their supply depots.

My next CFD parade phase happened when I was in high school. My EHS classmate, Jan Benton, organized patients who rode on the horse-drawn Civil War-era field ambulance. My high school pals, Tad Leeper, Eddie Frye, and I played wounded soldiers, and Jan was our Florence Nightingale.

We emoted in the back of the wagon as battle-weary soldiers being all bandaged up in ripped up bed sheets, moaning and groaning. We had an M-rated bedpan act that entailed a jug of water with yellow food coloring added. Jan's mom was on the CFD Parade Committee.

When the parade was over, the crowds headed for Frontier Park and the rodeo in the afternoon, the midway carnival, and night show entertainment.

When I was a kid, the CFD acts weren't extravaganzas like they are today. There were no superstars like Winona Judd or Florida Georgia Line or Charlie Daniels or Chris LeDoux.

The 1960s show talent included TV stars like Milburn "Doc Adams" Stone and Ken "Festus" Curtis from *Gunsmoke* (1955–1975). Festus spoke with an exaggerated country twang, "Safer than chitlins on a city folk's supper plate."

When he broke out of his Festus persona, Curtis was a great crooner. He was the lead singer for the Sons of the Pioneers western quartet from 1949 to 1952.

After the night show, the wild and crazy action moved to the Hitching Post Coach Rooms for indoor music and West 17th Street for partying on the streets at the Elks Club, the Blue Bird, the Mayflower, and the Crown. I didn't learn firsthand about the outdoor reveling until I was nineteen, when that was the drinking age.

Saturday, July 31, 1976, would be the last ride for my pea-green Pinto. That summer, I worked as the Glacier Basin Campground ranger in Rocky Mountain National Park (ROMO). ROMO was the radio designation for the park dispatcher.

I stayed with Rick Thamer for the last weekend of CFD. He was one of my teaching assistant classmates at UW in Laramie.

He and our mutual friend John Accardo tried to get me to stay over, but I decided to head back to ROMO that night because I had to work on Sunday at eleven thirty a.m. The Accardos lived in Cole Addition on White Cloud Road. His dad was a dentist who collaborated with my dentist, Dr. Carson, on a complicated molar extraction that entailed a chrome-plated chisel and mallet, but I digress.

The drive from Cheyenne into Colorado was uneventful, but when I took the exit off Interstate-25 and headed west on US Highway 34, a black ribbon of clouds shrouded the crimson sunset.

"Why are all these cars and RVs driving away from the park?" I asked myself as I wound my way into the "narrows" at the mouth of the steep-walled Big Thompson Canyon.

Before I made it to the small town of Drake, it was raining but just sprinkling. I reined in the Pinto for a stream of water that trickled across the road. Before I knew it, the rain poured down in buckets. My little steed slammed into a wall of water that streamed down the hillside and into the riverbed. The water soon flowed over the hood of the Pinto.

A family-filled car from Loveland coming toward me carried on into the torrent. How did I know the car was from Loveland? The license plate with the reflective LV caught my headlights as the current swept the vehicle into the canyon.

It was like when the tornado picked up Dorothy and whisked her away to the Land of Oz.

I looked with wonderment out the windshield. The wipers couldn't keep up with the rain, but my headlights lit up huge uprooted trees and big propane gas tanks as they bobbed by. I kept thinking Miss Gulch riding on her bicycle would float across the road through the deluge running down the canyon face.

I could feel boulders bigger than bowling balls clanking against the car body. My back bumper caught onto a floating port-a-potty that acted as a rudder and steered me toward the canyon wall and not into the rushing water.

After rolling down the car window, I climbed out and waded up to the highway crest. A Colorado Department of Transportation truck picked me up and dropped me at a high spot called Rainbow Lodge, where I spent the night.

Exploring the next morning, I came upon trophy-size trout washed up onto what remained of the highway. Someone covered the body of one not-so-lucky tourist or resident with a tarp.

There were rumors that Lake Estes up the road was cresting and soon to overflow the dam. A group of us climbed up the side of the canyon and waited. A Chinook helicopter eventually airlifted my band of survivors of the one-thousand-year flood to a gymnasium in Loveland, where I picked up a dry pair of socks and a cup of coffee.

The phone lines were out, and I couldn't call my family in Laramie. A great Samaritan gave me a ride to Cheyenne and dropped me off at my friend Tad Leeper's house. My parents eventually found me after first driving to Loveland to look around.

The insurance settlement was enough to get another Pinto. This one was sky blue, had better rims, a bigger engine, and an AM/FM radio with a cassette tape player. It was my first car when I lived in Gillette in the late 1970s.

By this time, Ford recalled the Pinto.

I was driving home and slowed down at the light near Ole's Pizza on Highway 14 when an oil field water truck rear-ended me.

When I looked underneath to inspect the damage, the threaded end of one bolt that holds the transmission halves together crimped up against the gas tank and, if punctured, could have sparked an explosion.

I sold that Pinto to Rick Thamer. He drove it to Texas, where he was going to law school in Lubbock. It was my last American car, and my obsession with VWs began with the sporty 1977 Scirocco.

Those are two narrow escapes I've had over the years. It seems like they come along every twenty years or so. I like to hedge my bets.

The next year, I drove the Scirocco to CFD. I met some friends from Gillette at the Atlas Motel, which is a block from the Hitching Post. I can now say that the Atlas was condemned and razed, but we tore that room to pieces.

Downtown Cheyenne was at one time a happening place during CFD. I thought about how out of control the place must have been when the railroad was being constructed, and the Cheyenne hotspot was Hell on Wheels.

West 17th Street was closed from Central Avenue for at least a couple of blocks to Carey Avenue. I remember standing in front of the Mayflower holding a Miller beer can. A cop came by and whacked it out of my hand. It clunked half-full onto the sidewalk, covered by a layer of cans.

Bikers took over the Pioneer Hotel on West 17th Street, which was a flophouse then and one now. During CFD, everyone got along with everyone.

The Mayflower burned down and made a brief comeback in the 1980s and is now a sushi place. The CFD in downtown Cheyenne today is just a shadow of its former wild and crazy self. Not everyone in Cheyenne is as CFD-crazy as me. Some locals plan their vacations around CFD and leave town.

I always found some excuse to attend CFD, particularly around obtaining media credentials to gain access when researching a story or documentary movie.

THIRTY-FIVE: Running Away to the Carnival

One CFD, I became a carny for a weekend and worked the game where contestants had to break a balloon for a dollar.

A decade or so after the big Thompson flood, I was writing a CFD-related column for the Lander WSJ. I drove to Cheyenne to pick up my press pass. The story I was writing was a first-person account of working a job at the carnival.

I picked up my media credentials and wandered over to the carnival grounds. I didn't know what to expect. The rodeo had just let out, and the late afternoon crowd streamed out of the grandstands looking for their next activity. I followed many towards the carnival grounds.

After negotiating my way past the gatekeepers, I walked around and took in the atmosphere. It had been years since I was there as a kid. After the parade, Cousin Matthew and my sister Lorinda spent some of our hard-earned cash on cotton candy, riding the Ferris Wheel, and playing a few games of chance.

I asked around and was directed to a trailer that housed the carnival administrative office. A guy named Dozer hired me on with the Bill Hames Show. He and his wife Angelyn operate a half dozen privately owned games and rides for Kelley's Concessions based in Alabama. I don't think he thought a city guy like me could cut being on my feet or talk non-stop for twelve hours at a time.

"Money," by Pink Floyd, blared from the loudspeaker by the Ferris Wheel. I slipped on the navy-blue acetate polo shirt with a circular orange and white logo over the left breast.

Dozer paired me up with a blond-haired carny named Anice. She was a born-again Christian who had a pretty hard life.

"The object of the game is to buy a dart for a dollar, bust a balloon for your choice of a small mirror. Five wins for a large mirror," Anice explained.

"Mirror" is a misnomer since the prizes are non-reflective square pieces of glass with pictures silk-screened on the back.

"I'm just part-time, a couple of nights a week. I live in Englewood and work at a print shop in Denver. I share a motel room in Cheyenne with one of the other women and her boyfriend. I used to work full time, but the guy I was with beat me up, and I left the show a couple of years ago. Dozer asked if I'd work for him again," she said while tying a knot in one of the spare balloons.

The game is really rough on the fingers. Each of the mirrors slips into a cardboard sleeve to protect the paint and prevent patron injuries. No matter how careful, I still managed to slice minor cuts where I never thought had any useful purpose, like on the index finger cuticle, which gets irritated each time a balloon stem gets tied off. My hands bled the entire weekend.

On Saturday night, another woman worked with us named Amber.

"I'm trained as a nurse and working here until something opens up in town," she said. Amber was tenderly limping around the area in obvious pain.

"It's not my foot, it's my back. I was shot in the abdomen, and it hit a disc on the way out," she said before pulling up her shirt and showing the scars. "I ruptured another disc moving a box of these mirrors and have to have surgery again."

After I arrived, Anice divided the counter up into thirds.

"Amber takes the first third. I'll take the middle, and you take the other end," Anice said with authority since it's her joint. I was the newbie and was at the end of the lineup.

There's an infinitely long imaginary line separating each section, sort of like the invisible cylinder above a basketball hoop used to determine whether a player interferes with the ball, otherwise known as goaltending.

Common courtesy is to avoid cross-hawking. Taking a fellow carny's business is counterproductive.

"If you pull that stunt on one of the guys who's traveling with the show, he'll knock the hell out of you. I'm just telling this to you for your own good if you decide to do this again," Anice advised me.

Because of my experience as a kid selling pop at the parade, I wasn't afraid of being told "No." I was oblivious to offensive remarks from jerks based on my appreciation for them at an early age at the Hitching Post.

The carnival workers I met weren't exactly from the upper crust. I was the only dark-skinned fellow there and had my guard up staying aware of potential problems that could arise around that. There was quite a bit of cussing and smoking. Luckily, the show vended no beer or alcohol on site.

I blended in with the crowd. For the most part, everyone was friendly, and I learned how to build relationships with potential customers.

"That's a nice Kiss t-shirt you're wearing, how about winning a matching mirror for your girl?" or "Looks like you spent a lot of money winning that huge panda for the little lady, pop a balloon for a matching mirror, and it only costs a dollar, a winner every time."

Occasionally, a kid would toss the dart in between two balloons. Nothing scattered a crowd faster than a loser as if we somehow rigged the game—under-inflated balloons, too much space between balloons, or whatever.

If it was a really young kid, I held him inches from the balloons to have a "winner every time." It was a cash flow business.

I took on politically incorrect character traits, being immersed in the carnival culture. Purveying those mannerisms was good for business. To this day, I break into carnival mode when I have to close a deal.

When I lived in Lander, my full-time job was working in the city administration. There was a big economic downturn when the US Steel Mine closed, laying off hundreds of Union workers. The Uranium fields also went flat when the Three Mile Island nuclear power plant melted down in Pennsylvania.

One of my jobs was to backstop the high unemployment rate by attracting new jobs to town, and assisting existing companies to expand. That was like working the carnival game, which involved keeping several business-development balloons in the air at once.

When I got busy, putting up more balloons or fetching a mirror for a winner, keeping up the endless personal chatter with everyone waiting their turn was tiresome.

I spent lag time slipping the square mirrors into cardboard sleeves. No matter how careful I was, microscopic glass shards cut my hands. Tying the balloons wore down my cuticles.

Multi-tasking is a job skill for a carny. When I'm in a store waiting for some help from a busy clerk who doesn't make eye contact, I walk away and find someone else. I didn't want my marks to wander off since all players are potential return customers.

"See you at ten in the morning," Dozer called out at closing time. We were each paid a percentage of our individual take. I inflated a hundred and fifty balloons, and my jaw ached. Angelyn handed me thirty-one dollars.

Sunday morning came quickly. It was the last day of CFD, and the crowd was much smaller. When the rodeo lets out, there's a brief surge. Monday was a workday for the locals, and many of the tourists had left for home or were out of money.

Amber called in sick and arrived late in the afternoon. I noticed she was working another joint across the way and worried that I encroached on her balloon dart game turf.

Anice and I spent the morning chatting between marks. It being Sunday, religion dominated the discussion. Anice felt that carnival witnessing was part of her calling.

By this time in my mainstream Presbyterian life, I was comfortable talking about spirituality but didn't wear it on my sleeve.

Church must have just gotten out because business picked up. There was a Shroud of Turin mirror, which was very popular, both sizes. I ended up working the entire weekend and made Dozer quite a bit of money.

The carnival grounds were suddenly quiet. It was two fifteen a.m. on Monday. The music had stopped, and it was time to strike the carnival. The women who operate each joint are the informal crew leaders and call the process the "slough."

"We'll see you next year," Dozer said while handing me fifty one-dollar bills. He hitched the dart game trailer to a panel truck and rolled out of the empty parking lot.

I'm the experiential, hands-on type. Working those long days was the toughest but most gratifying eighty-one bucks I have ever earned. I bought a billiard stick from one of the carnival vendors as a memento. Billiard sticks have a narrower shaft, ferrule, and tip than regular cues.

Writing this story, I went down into the basement to see if I still had that stick. I found it, but my nine-ball stick was missing. I decided to replace it and got a good deal on a "Sneaky Pete" Meucci stick. Sneaky Pete refers to a high-end and very straight pool cue that looks like a bar stick to not attract attention when playing serious games.

For what it's worth, I was only truly hustled once. It was a game for whiskey at the Buckhorn Bar in Laramie. Before I knew it, my opponent had blocked every pocket before running the table. I owed him a shot of Jack Daniels on the rocks.

When I get a beer at the Buckhorn, I half expect to run into Anice and Amber sitting at the bar.

THIRTY-SIX: Practical Spirituality

I get why my parents wanted my sister and me to blend in and get along. Even in middle-of-nowhere Wyoming, they had to walk around on pins and needles, having to deal with unspoken discrimination.

My parents spoke Japanese with my grandparents. I couldn't understand the conversations and asked why they didn't teach us the language.

"You have to blend in," my mom told me. "There's no reason to speak Japanese."

Blend into the background, we did. It was the path of least resistance. If there was anything that was the American Way, it was joining a Christian church.

Throughout my time in Wyoming, I stayed involved in the Presbyterian Church (UPC) to the extent that the Cheyenne UPC ordained me as an Elder. Elders are part of the governing body known as the Session, which manages the church.

We attended many church-related activities. I remember going to a potluck, and there were mostly Jell-O salads, which was okay with me. I still like green Jell-O with canned fruit cocktail mixed into it. I now make cherry Coke Jell-O salad for special occasions.

In a sense, it was integration. The church was on the "other side" of town, and kids from the other junior high feeder schools went there.

We went to church most Sundays. My parents were involved in activities like the women's circle and the Mariners social group. I'm pretty sure my mom was the main instigator of all that, and my dad just tagged along for the food.

My sister and I went to Sunday school. My ulterior motive was the possibility of Jesus trading cards given out at the end of class. We both sang in the choir. The youth choir performed in the early service and the adult choir during the main event at eleven a.m.

Later in the afternoon was youth fellowship. Those groups were fun with not much emphasis on Christianity-related stuff. The mission was to make it home before *Batman* came on TV.

When it came to summer church camp, the one closest to Cheyenne was called Skyline. It was fun and a way to know kids from other parts of the state.

A few kids bullied me. I was small, and kids would pull on the sides of their eyes to make them slanty and feigned nonsensical Asian-sounding noises, which was annoying.

I did have allies, but they didn't seem to know how to, or were uncomfortable with reacting to racist incidents. One summer, it scared me to go to the shower, so I didn't for the entire week. Instead, I plunged into the nearby ice-cold pond.

The Cheyenne UPC pastor, Bob Walkley, was the Skyline Camp manager. He never mentioned anything to me, but Bob must have said something to them based on how some of the campers' actions towards me changed.

I was artistic and had that going for me. When it came to the arts and crafts activities, I excelled, which was a hedge against being bullied.

UPC's brand of Presbyterians didn't emphasize the "Jesus Saves" drills: Sins=Hell, and Good=Heaven. It was mostly about the liturgy of church life, such as my sister's baby christening (they baptized me).

All the 3rd graders received a free Bible. I still have mine but had it rebound when I wore it out. Well, I actually dropped it off the top bunk at camp one too many times. High school graduates received a pocket-size Bible, which is still in the box.

Then there was catechism class. The head pastor, Rev. Pattison, conducted the sessions. We listened to the questions and repeated the answers in the booklet. "What is the chief end of man?" was the question I had to learn for the final exam that happened before the congregation.

When I went off to college, I wasn't flamboyant but came to think about "What would Jesus do?" instead of telling people if they don't "believe" they are destined to hell.

Besides being a Presbyterian, my mom got her to wish to live the American Way with one-point-five kids, a dog, two cars, and a ranch-style house in the suburbs. She settled for two kids, a re-homed dog, the house, a car under the carport, and a pickup parked out front.

This was quite a departure from her childhood. She and her family grew up in a clapboard Orpha section supervisor's house in rural Converse County, Wyoming, just off Fort Fetterman Road.

Fort Fetterman is located a few miles north of Douglas and is now a Wyoming State Historic Site. The US Army established it in 1867 to protect settlers traveling to Montana on the Bozeman Trail.

The fort was named after Captain William J. Fetterman, who was killed in combat, along with eighty other soldiers. The Arapaho, Cheyenne, and the Lakota warriors led by Red Cloud and Crazy Horse outmaneuvered the over-matched US Cavalry.

We visited Orpha a time or two. Joe and Lucy Shinmori were childhood friends of my mom. They all went to school in the Orpha one-room schoolhouse.

Most of my mom's childhood friends were the children of railroad workers called section hands. Many traqueros were immigrants from northern Mexico.

Governor Luis Terrazas of Chihuahua, in 1881, drove a silver spike completing a rail line linking Mexico and the United States, which allowed immigrants transport to the United States and coincided with the West's construction and completion of the transcontinental railroad.

The dominant immigrant labor force that laid track in the Nineteenth and Twentieth centuries was from Mexico. Despite low wages compared to their American coworkers, and discrimination, immigrant laborers became permanent residents, not by law but by fact.

Mom spent time at her Mexicana friends' homes. She learned how to make flour tortillas. I surmised they were from northern Mexico because flour tortillas are more particular to the states like Sonora and Chihuahua. The recipe is simple. Mix flour, water, salt to taste, and lard. The kneaded dough is flattened and cooked in a pan or griddle. The key ingredient is lard.

Growing up, flour tortillas were our other bread. Mom made a dish from vermicelli (thin wheat noodles) mixed up with tomato sauce, ground beef, maybe some chopped onion. I later learned from my colleagues when I was working in Zacatecas, Mexico, the dish was called fideo, the Spanish word for vermicelli. Then we rolled up the fideo in the flour tortilla.

After grad school, I bade my family a fond farewell and moved to Gillette sight unseen. My first stop was with a group of guys renting a house at 611 Kendrick Avenue.

I sought stability and checked out the First Presbyterian Church. The pastor was Reverend Rubesh. In the course of small talk, since I was a former elder in the Cheyenne church, we had acquaintances in common. Rapid community growth didn't spare the Gillette UPC.

I felt a bit obligated to get more involved since Rev. Rubesh desperately needed more volunteers, particularly to teach Sunday school classes. I agreed to take on junior high school kids.

While in Gillette, I again had feet in two worlds. One was based on my staid American Way upbringing as a model minority. The other was my 3003 Club risky lifestyle. I was conflicted, but it was fulfilling. There was some overlap, though. Gillette was a tiny town at the time, and I attended church with several of my younger friends, which supported me.

After my stint in downtown Lander living above the Ace Hardware store, I was a long-term house sitter for another Alan. He taught various wilderness survival courses for the National Outdoor Leadership School (NOLS) with its international headquarters in Lander.

He would leave town for months at a time for NOLS and kept the place up. Alan was also a devout Christian and lay biblical scholar. I was reasonably familiar with the basic premise of Christianity but wasn't so interested in the subtleties and literal interpretation of the scriptures. He introduced me to the Evangelical Presbyterian Church (EPC).

That was a big change. The EPC came about in the 1980s. There were members of the UPC who became spiritually disenfranchised with the church that became spiritually liberal. In the early 1970s, the UPC Council on Church and Race granted twenty-five thousand dollars to the Black Panthers and ten thousand dollars to the Angela Davis defense fund.

Those stances split the Cheyenne UPC to the extent that the conservative members broke away and started the Highlands Church built in the Cole Addition near the community pool. My parents stuck with UPC. As it turned out, the more biblically literal EPC brought about an "Aha" moment for me that strangely made my Christian belief system more tangible.

When I was a kid, my parents didn't expose me to other religions. I know both sets of my grandparents practiced forms of Buddhism. Grandparents Sakata converted to Episcopalian. Auntie Hisako followed in that practice and was a prominent member in her various churches.

The Presbyterian Church attracted my mom, and Dad followed along.

I occasionally would observe Grandma Ohashi praying when we were at the cemetery decorating graves in the Japanese section of the Lakeview Cemetery on Memorial Day.

Other than the Matsukawas in Salt Lake City, none of my other Nisei relatives expressed much about their spiritual beliefs. I attribute that to their treatment during the war and potential backlash from exhibiting any cultural expressions like Buddhism.

I, too, just went along. I learned nothing about Eastern religion until I was an adult living in that Buddhist cooperative house in Boulder. Even then, it was in very general terms.

There would have been a more supportive community if I lived in more diverse places like California, Hawaii, or even Denver. As I was coming of age, that was around the time the Cheyenne Japanese neighborhood and community members dispersed.

My family members were the only minorities in the congregation. Later, Bob and Larry Walters and their mom started to attend. Mrs. Walters was from Japan, and her sons were hapa (half Japanese). We were all active in church activities.

As a kid, one of the main reasons I went to Sunday school was for the swag like Bible verse rulers, cookies, and trading cards—Jesus cards. The First Presbyterian Church was one of the larger protestant churches in Cheyenne.

My Sunday school teacher had a lesson and then passed the cards around. I'm pretty sure the girls didn't know what to do with them. Probably wrecked these paper treasures by gluing them in a scrapbook.

I'll trade this Mantle for your Jesus.

Most of my trading card collection consists of baseball cards. My favorite Jesus card is a 1965 baseball card of Jesus (heh-zoos) Alou. He and his two brothers, Matty and Felipe, all played for the San Francisco Giants. Baseball factoid: In 1963, during three games, the trio played together in the same outfield.

Jesus began his career in 1959 with the Hastings Giants, which played in the short-season Class D Nebraska State League. While I was in college, the Hastings

College Broncos baseball team played at Duncan Field, constructed in 1940 as a WPA project.

While at Hastings, I became interested in author Erich Von Däniken and his book *Chariots of the Gods* (1968). Basically, it's about beings from other dimensions who, the author believes, are angels, based on literal Bible interpretations.

The alien angels spoke to biblical characters like Moses and Elijah through burning bushes, pillars of fire, and other supernatural media. The chariot that Jesus will ride when he returns at the end of the world will be a UFO.

Ancient aliens still have a following. The Bible categorizes angels from archangels at the top to Satan at the bottom and several categories in between. There are cable TV shows dedicated to the topic.

Supposedly, a constant unseen battle is waged between good and evil. Since I'm more into the tangible, the aliens/UFO/angels model made some sense.

I'll skip through time.

Since college, I have put all this supernatural stuff in the back of my mind. It wasn't normal small talk among my friends. While in Gillette, a 1980 story ran in the *Casper Star-Tribune* about strange lights in the sky bouncing around at the Morton Pass Farm owned by Pat McGuire and his family.

The farm is at the mouth of Sybille Canyon between Laramie and Wheatland on Highway 34. I called the reporter about it, and even as a journalist, he was awe-struck.

A TV show called *That's Incredible* (1980–1984) hosted by actress Cathy Lee Crosby, singer John Davidson, and former New York Giants and Minnesota Vikings quarterback Fran Tarkenton.

The show sent a crew to Wyoming for a story about the UFO phenomenon happening in this remote space alien stage in southeast Wyoming.

"We have to go there," I said to a group of my friends.

The story is whacky and more involved than what I'll write here, but hold on to your aluminum foil hats.

A world-renowned paranormal psychologist from the UW named Leo Sprinkle specialized in alien abduction experiences and, through hypnosis, regressed McGuire to the time he said aliens took him aboard their UFO several years earlier.

He claimed to have been in touch with the Archangel Michael and given instructions to drill a big well on his property and begin farming.

Despite geologic reports that there was no water, the well he drilled was a gusher, over eight thousand gallons per minute.

The state of Wyoming approved Pat for a low-interest loan to purchase irrigation equipment, even though hydrology studies said the sagebrush country would remain dry and unproductive due to lack of water.

He flew the Israeli flag over the water well pumping station in homage to Archangel Michael and his other alien abductors. He said the aliens wore Star of David belt buckles. He also sported one on the belt that held up his Wranglers.

After reading the newspaper story, my UFO entourage drove down and met the That's Incredible crew. The nocturnal lights weren't as active as a few weeks earlier, but there were some to be seen, which I photographed.

Those who didn't witness it can explain the phenomenon away, but I believe my own observations and this was some weird stuff.

On my way from Gillette to visit my parents in Laramie, I usually stopped at the McGuire's place through the early 1980s. One day, the access road was closed.

After that, I lost touch with Pat and his family. Over time, I heard UW ended up with the farm. Pat died in 2009.

When I was working at the CFD carnival that Sunday morning, I had a conversation with Anice. I wanted to find out what a conservative Christian thought about my far-out ancient alien interpretations of biblical history.

"What do you think about UFOs—Unidentified Flying Objects?" I asked. I told her about the UFO experience I had when I was living in Gillette and drove with a group of friends to the Morton Pass Farms a few miles north of Laramie.

"They are of the devil," she said without hesitation. "They are the messengers of Satan."

I explained to Anice that I had read books on the topic of angels as aliens. One was *Angels: God's Secret Agents* (1975) by Billy Graham. It puts good and evil angels into context and mentions the UFO phenomenon, and I can't help but make the same comparisons with what I saw on those hills on Highway 34 that summer.

Graham asserts that some Christian writers speculate UFOs could be a part of God's angelic host who preside over the physical affairs of the universe, which may explain supernatural occurrences. Anice was skeptical and said she'd do more research. I wrote down the book title for her, but we agreed to disagree.

A few years later, after I moved to Lander, I was in Cheyenne for some reason. I saw that Billy Graham was speaking at Frontier Park. It was free, so I went over to listen.

It was the biggest religious event I'd attended, at least until I went to see Pope John Paul II at Cherry Creek Reservoir in 1993.

Now that was a crowd. I've only taken Catholic communion one time, and it was at that papal mass.

Rev. Graham didn't talk about angels or UFOs, but he's one inspiring speaker. I was compelled to give a few bucks when his minions passed the hat. To get a tax deduction, the church had to send you a receipt back in those days.

A few weeks later, the *Evangelical Free Church* minister and his wife invited me to their house. They were young and personable. My minister was notified by the Billy Graham organization that I was at the Cheyenne gathering.

I had forgotten that I wrote that as my home church on the offering envelope. He and his wife asked me over to talk, presumably, about my faith and all that. I'm not the overly zealous type, and it surprised them that I went to see Billy Graham.

Our small talk gravitated to Graham's book about angels, and I told them my aliens-as-messengers-of-God story.

Like my CFD carny friend Anice, they looked at me as if I was nuts but were aware of Graham's work. The topic didn't come up again.

I'm still an avid trading card collector and plan to hold on to them, just in case. I don't want to be standing at the pearly gates, and Peter says, "Welcome to heaven, but where's that Jesus card collection you've been saving?"

By the way, man's chief end is to glorify God and enjoy him forever.

THIRTY-SEVEN: Assimilation

I began my career as part of the Wyoming Human Services project team. My colleagues included Felix Sowada and Charlie Anderson. We had a common interest in climbing. This is atop Devil's Tower.

I wouldn't be where I am today without practical internships. When I was an intern at the carnival, I lived in Lander, where I landed my second job in the city government. That carnival experience closing deals by building strong relationships brought together my sense of entrepreneurship.

I ended up working for municipalities because of fate. I knew little about public administration until my first job at Gillette.

After graduating from Hastings, finding a full-time job was in the back of my mind, but I didn't know how to go about it. I've always been pretty good about change management, so I wasn't too freaked out about having student loans to repay, no roof over my head, and being stuck somewhere between Nebraska and Wyoming.

When I went off to college, Grandpa Sakata gave me a check for one thousand dollars along with a speech in Japanese. He then translated and told me that being a hard worker won't be enough. Getting an education in anything is important, but I would have better success if I got to know people.

This was a throwback to his days with the railroad when he kept his job after Pearl Harbor was bombed. I took him at his word and began my next journey back to Wyoming. I sat out the post-Vietnam War recession at the UW grad school.

My major coursework at UW included many elective classes with an internship or hands-on experience attached to them. I was walking through the Student Union and came upon a sign-up table. The sign read something like, If You Want a Job After Graduation, Join the Wyoming Human Services Project.

The WHSP was my ticket, with no looking for work and no job interview. The state was pulling out of an oil and gas bust in the mid-1970s. Congress amended the Clean Air Act in 1977, tightening the sulfur dioxide emission standards. That made Wyoming coal more desirable than high-sulfur eastern coal. On top of the regulatory changes, soft coal became a desirable fuel source because of its relative ease of extraction—surface mining.

Wyoming boomed again.

The WHSP curriculum taught students using a multi-disciplinary approach, some creative and effective ways to develop social programs that could ease the negative impacts of rapid population growth in rural areas during the coal boom in the Powder River Basin that includes parts of southeast Montana and northeast Wyoming.

The region supplied about forty percent of coal in the United States, but that has since tailed off because of competition from lesser expensive oil and methane gas.

The social problem the WHSP team was in town to reverse was known as the "Gillette Syndrome." It was a typical boomtown stereotype of a bunch of rough and tumble single guys from Texas who lived out of their beat-up pickup trucks, dug coal by day, and partied hearty at night in a tiny town where they fought over women—the eligible ones were single moms living in trailers, or still in high school.

The WHSP team members were from differing academic disciplines. Diverse perspectives would result in well-rounded impact mitigation and community development strategies. It was an early form of analog crowdsourcing.

The job exposed me to consensus decision-making before it became trendy.

My cohort consisted of an attorney, a social worker, parks and recreation staff, and myself, a political scientist working in the city administration. Our team spent half of our hours with our agency job placement. We collaborated during the rest of our time with community-based organizations helping solve problems resulting from rapid population growth.

I initially got to know Rev. Rubesh. He was part of the Council of Community Services project that continues today. The council coordinates social services around Campbell County. It originated from an idea by a tall and rotund police officer named "Tiny," who wanted to maximize the amount of charitable food and cash given to transients to encourage them to get out of town.

Volunteering for Rev. Rubesh at the Presbyterian Church, I blended into old Gillette but at the same time began to lose any sense of my past, to the disappointment of my mother. She expected me to blend in, but instead, I was more conspicuous.

I previously mentioned Tom, the decorated Vietnam War veteran with the AR-15 rifle. He was a deputy county attorney. Tom, WHSP lawyer Phil, and I chipped in on the house we bought using Tom's GI Bill veteran housing benefit.

Our place was the gathering spot for a crowd of young and upwardly mobile professionals and was known as the 3003 Club, which was our street number on Foothills Blvd.

I came to learn that I had lived a sheltered life in the suburbs of Cheyenne. Maybe there was debauchery happening around me, but I may have been oblivious and not paying close enough attention. I was a late bloomer once I got into the real world.

My parents weren't the rowdy types. Once in a while, they would be invited out to parties by the owner of Cheyenne Beverages, which included Coors beer distribution, in addition to soft drinks. They attended but weren't comfortable with the Country Club crowd. Many of that ilk went to college and had the subsequent learned behaviors around drinking and partying.

One summer, our Cole Addition house was brimming with guests. My mom prepared Japanese-type food like teriyaki wings and maki sushi when it came to entertaining. Those were always a big hit.

The Shinmoris were in town and attended the party. My dad's boss and his wife were there too. By this time, the basement was finished, and he stored liquor behind the bar constructed out of two huge display-stand size Coors cans. From upstairs, I poured some "76" lemon-lime soda—the local brand, bottled by Coca-Cola—into a glass of ice.

I wondered what all the fuss was about and poured myself a High Ball with the Seagram 7 on top of the small fridge. It went to my head quickly. I had more fun than usual with the Shinmori kids. The next morning, I woke up with flu-like symptoms and slept it off the rest of the morning. My parents suspected nothing because Alan David was such a good boy.

That experience was a lot like when I first started hanging out with my 3003 Club housemates. I had smoked a little pot in Laramie with my fellow grad students, but that wasn't a lifestyle like it was in Gillette that revolved around watching movies, playing strategic board games, and listening to music.

I mentioned before how my taste in music was narrow, with my favorite records being those by Burt Bacharach, Dionne Warwick, and other easier listening musicians.

One of my housemates was a guy from Boston named Bob. We had a love-hate relationship and still do since he's a Red Sox fan and I'm a Yankees fan.

He was quite the audiophile and the only person I knew who had seen the Beatles live. His dad worked at the Suffolk Downs racetrack in 1966, and Bob got in to watch.

He and I spent hours mixing music on cassette tapes. I don't even know if Wyoming radio stations played the tunes Bob collected—Patti Smith, Steely Dan, Boston, Styx, Talking Heads, Grateful Dead, New Riders of the Purple Sage, et al.

I wish I had those tapes back. It was before technology was commonly available to convert analog data from tapes into digital form. Something about the recorded sounds of scratches, pops, and skips gave the tape mixes character.

Another one of my housemates was Jim. He was one of the high school football coaches and played linebacker for the UW Cowboys. After I moved from Gillette, he returned to his roots in Detroit, Michigan. We kept in touch.

In 1981, I was in Detroit for a meeting. I think it was the National League of Cities conference. Jim got a couple of tickets to see the Rolling Stones at the Pontiac Silver Dome. I consider that the "disco Stones" era—"Start Me Up" and "Hang Fire" are two tracks off that album. Iggy Pop and Santana were the opening acts. Carlos Santana was good. Iggy was booed off the stage.

I've since seen the Stones five more times in Denver.

That was a memorable trip for a small-town kid. Jim took me to a White Castle hamburger stand. "Buy 'em by the sack." Now I buy 'em in the frozen food aisle.

We were noshing while walking, and I came upon urban wildlife. It was a rat the size of a cocker spaniel sitting up waiting for hamburger bun crumbs to fall to the sidewalk.

The 3003 Club was my first taste of living in an intentional community, as bizarre as that sounds. We had a consensus decision-making process, "BBQ or Tacos," and believe it or not, there were disagreements, "Cheez Whiz, not grated cheese?"

My pals and I embodied the "Gillette Syndrome." This was my first job, and I was making more money than I had ever made in my life and nowhere to spend it.

We lived the rural version of *St. Elmo's Fire* (1985). We all had excessively too much fun for a gang of young professional whippersnappers in the most conservative county in the state. The risky lifestyle I led back then is now legal in some form in most states, but not in Wyoming.

I'll leave it at that. To paraphrase the tagline from this Oscar-winning movie, "The events depicted in this story took place in Gillette, Wyoming. At the request of the survivors, the names have been changed. Out of respect for the dead, the rest has been told exactly as it occurred."

WHSP placed me in the Gillette city administration as a grant writer. My big boss was Mike Enzi, who was mayor. He was a visionary for Gillette and, rather than let rapid growth randomly change Gillette, he assembled a team of young upstarts to manage the transformation.

Enzi worked his way through the state legislature and was eventually elected to the US Senate. He suddenly passed away after a freakish bicycle accident in late July 2021. My friends got our band together and had fun reminiscing about the good old boomtown days.

Governor Ed Herschler appointed Mike's wife, Diana, and me to a couple of terms on the Wyoming Private Industry Council that dealt with distributing US Department of Labor workforce training funds.

Gov. Ed was a gruff but personable guy. He answered his own phone and smoked Philip Morris Commanders. Bars stocked Cabin Still whiskey, not knowing when Gov. Ed might stop by to shoot the breeze.

Mayor Enzi's direction to me was to bring as much federal and state money into Gillette as I could.

"If Gillette doesn't apply for it, some other place will," he advised.

Since my first job, I've been a fundraiser for forty years, and that's a philosophy and a life skill I continue to hone today.

My legislative internship turned out to be a valuable life skill. I ended up back in Cheyenne as a lobbyist for the city of Gillette. Mayor Enzi was very aggressive and turned me loose to raise thirty million dollars for the Madison Water Project.

I lived at the Hitching Post Inn for a month, talking lawmakers into approving the funds because they were obligated to serve the good people of Gillette—the "Energy Capital of the Nation."

That it was. Gillette was the fossil fuels industry headquarters that paid millions in severance taxes, which funded schools and public infrastructure for the entire state.

Convincing the lawmakers really took little doing. The sponsor for the bill was Representative L.J. Hunter.

I spent quite a bit of time in Gov. Ed's office to be sure he would sign the legislation. It wasn't a slam dunk with the railroads chasing me down the court.

Ed Herschler typified politically purple Wyoming. He was an FDR Democrat from Kemmerer on the southwestern edge of the state in Lincoln County. Gov. Ed is the only three-term governor. He first defeated Dick Jones in 1974, riding the Democratic tide that swept the country after Watergate.

His "growth on our terms" mission during the 1970s energy boom resulted in some of the country's toughest state-sanctioned environmental impact regulations. He barely defeated John Ostlund from Gillette in 1978. Four years later, he won his unprecedented third term over my legislative mentor, Warren Morton.

Representative Hunter was a pharmacist and provided me with boxes of medicine bottles that I filled with water that smelled like rotten eggs with bits of scaly carbonate floating around in the fizzy water, and then placed them on each legislator's desk.

The major roadblock was UP railroad lobbyist Jack Knott, who needed me to convince him that the city of Gillette wouldn't be selling or allowing others to use the Madison formation water to transport coal in a slurry pipeline. That would be obvious low-cost competition with coal cars rumbling to Texas power plants. It turned out Jack was the father of one of my high school crushes.

Efforts were underway by Energy Transport Systems, Inc. (ETSI), led by a guy named Frank Odasz. His story was about a massive pipeline between Wyoming and Texas that would deliver a slurry of pulverized coal mixed with brackish Madison formation water to fuel power plants.

The city of Gillette project proved the Madison water was drinkable. The water issue was the least of ETSI's problems compared to obtaining a right-of-way through four of the largest landmasses in the country—Wyoming, Colorado, Kansas, and Texas.

Knowing my way around the Hitching Post Inn from my days as a busboy gave me a sense of confidence since I was very familiar with the surroundings.

Because of my legislative internship, I knew my way around Wyoming's state government. I became pretty good at lobbying for a young guy and did so for subsequent legislative sessions on behalf of the Wyoming Association of Municipalities.

While I didn't realize it, I came to learn that my grandfather was right. Getting a job or any advantage was more about, first, "who I knew," then "what I knew."

Remember family friend Secretary of State Thyra Thomson? Wyoming operates on the commission form of government. The top elected officials—Governor, Secretary of State, Superintendent of Public Instruction, State Treasurer, and State Auditor—all serve on various boards and commissions that ultimately decide about various aspects of the state government.

Back then, the Farm Loan Board granted and loaned state funds for local government capital projects—roads, fire stations, water plants, etc. Whenever I would appear before the board, Mrs. Thomson would invariably ask how my grandparents and family were doing, much to the chagrin of the other local government representatives in the room. I could always count on her support for my projects.

THIRTY-EIGHT: The Music Man

After some professional success, having way too much fun, not to mention chasing UFOs, I left Gillette's fast-paced and free-wheeling life to work in the Lander city administration in the early 1980s. Things moved a lot slower in Lander, nestled at the foot of the Wind River mountains in Fremont County.

Rather than coasting in from Gillette, I had to slam on the breaks and downshift to first gear when the Great Fremont County Depression hit.

The 1979 Three Mile Island nuclear power plant meltdown in Pennsylvania stopped further Fremont County uranium mining. When the Chernobyl reactor melted down in Ukraine seven years later, that disaster didn't exactly quell public perceptions about the harms of nuclear power.

Jeffrey City, located sixty miles south of Lander, was a bustling uranium boomtown that had a population of forty-five hundred that included mining families and those working in support services.

In the early 1930s, Jeffrey City was a family homestead known as "Home on the Range," which is also the name of an abandoned motel. The town was later renamed for Dr. Charles W. Jeffrey, a big advocate for uranium mining during the Cold War.

In 1957, Western Nuclear Company established Jeffrey City as its bustling town with schools, recreation facilities, stores, restaurants, and bars. When the uranium industry went bust in the 1980s, the downturn resulted in ninety-five percent of the citizenry heading out of town. The 2010 census lists the population at fifty-eight.

Compounding that was the closure of the US Steel iron taconite mine south of Lander in 1983. Relative to the county population, the job loss was devastating.

Following the bombing of Pearl Harbor, the US Steel Geneva Mill in Vineyard, Utah, became a potential strategic target. The US military believed that building an inland mill would be protected from any enemy attack.

The iron ore mine near Cedar City, Utah, was the primary source of raw material but soon became insufficient to keep the Geneva mill operating at full capacity. A secondary source identified was a large reserve at what became the Atlantic City taconite mine south of Lander.

Although the war had ended, the Wyoming open-pit mine and short line railroad to the Geneva mill began construction in 1960.

The steel market softened, and US Steel closed the Atlantic City mine and shifted the Geneva mill source to a taconite mine in Minnesota. In October 1983, the mine's five hundred employees south of Lander were out of work.

When I arrived, there was a housing shortage because Lander was very stable. The first place I lived was in the Faust Apartments above the Ace Hardware store. That was well before mixed-use urban living was trendy.

McRae's drugstore was two doors down, the Grand movie theater across the street, my bank at the end of the block, and the Safeway behind my city hall office was five hundred feet away.

I didn't drive around town much for a year. To this day, I now realize how my past living arrangements, in a Lander mixed-use apartment, a Gillette co-op house, living in the dorms, and a close family life as a kid influenced why I became hooked on the high-density mixed-use urban lifestyle.

My work evolved from strictly city planning into facilitating economic development and creating a good story for Lander.

Thanks to Auntie Amy, who dragged me along to the theater in Salt Lake City, my economic developer role model was the flim-flam music man, Professor Harold Hill. After he convinced the good people of River City, Iowa, to purchase musical instruments for the boys to play in the newly formed town band, the young players would learn the music using the "think method."

To paraphrase Professor Harold Hill: You got trouble in Lander City and what you need is a Centennial celebration. This was my self-imposed tagline.

Modeling the think method for the Lander community was successful. People would stop me on the street and tell me about a business idea or a guy they knew looking for a place to move his business.

For the think method to work, there has to be something immediate that has a quick turnaround and a tangible outcome. Like most cities, there are multiple possible centennial dates. How about 1884, when Lander was established by land survey? With Lander, that could have been when the townsite was designated as part of the Fort Laramie Treaty in 1868; or when Lander was incorporated in 1890, which would have been a big competition with Wyoming's statehood date.

It was a stretch but was timely in 1983 and fit with a "back to the past" economic downturn narrative. The event resulted in short-term success and long-lasting but unnoticed effects. The Lander City Council appointed the Lander Centennial Committee. The celebration nurtured a high amount of entrepreneurship.

The centennial began a year before with a save-the-date kickoff. Lander celebrated for twenty months until July 1985. The committee sponsored a contest to pick out a centennial logo that could be product licensed.

There were commemorative plates, silver and bronze coins minted, a centennial Winchester rifle, shirts, and limited-edition lithographs based on a painting by Jerry Antolik, a limited run of Coca-Cola cans with the logo. My friend, Robin, at the Pioneer Museum, came across a box of centennial memorabilia and was seeking additions to the collection.

During this time, the city of Lander started a survey to designate the Main Street core area as a historic district. A part-time weed and pest control seasonal employee named Nancy was kept on staff and given the task to develop and process the district survey.

The Wyoming State Historic Preservation Office and the US National Park Service added the Lander Historic District to the National Register of Historic Places in 1987.

There was pushback from a few Main Street business owners about "creeping socialism" and government taking of property rights. Despite the protests, the City Council pushed the application ahead, and the rest is history.

I remember the first time I re-visited Lander twenty years later. There were banners and signs welcoming tourists to Historic Downtown Lander. I heard later that the Wyoming Department of Transportation paid for big improvements to Main Street, in part because of the historic district designation.

The 1884 date also stuck. The *Wikipedia* entry for Lander has the founding date as 1884, rather than 1890, the incorporation year.

I also literally became a music man.

The photographer at the paper, Tom Stromme, entangled me in many new interests, including working on VW air-cooled engines. He had a Type I orange VW convertible and an orange Type III VW camper van.

My first Type I was an orange 1965 VW bug that overheated, which stopped after sealing up the engine compartment. That was a good car that I should have kept.

My mom located a 1965 VW Karmann Ghia in Torrington. I bought it, but it turned out to be a lemon. It was on blocks more than it was on the road.

Tom was also an avid garage sale attendee, and one Saturday morning he pounded on my door. "I think you should buy this violin I just saw," he said.

I wrote a newspaper story about the local Suzuki violin school run by a woman named Becky. We went over, and the fiddle was still there, and I bought it.

"You should take lessons," Tom said about the instrument that had provenance. It once was owned by local fiddler Quentin Roberts.

I contacted Becky about enrolling in her school. Out of all her students, I was the tallest one. The Suzuki teaching technique is based on the idea that if kids in Japan can learn a complicated language like Japanese, they can learn how to play the violin. I credit my knowing how to read music with how rapidly I learned.

In the mid-1980s, Becky and her husband Mike ended up moving for some reason or other. She asked if I felt like I could take over her teaching practice. I agreed and ended up with a dozen or so of her students and some of my own. The business was good enough to rent a studio downtown.

I eventually became too busy with my real job and turned the business back to Becky, but I continued playing. By this time, Becky had also established an orchestra, and a few of us would occasionally perform at a local bar called the Hitching Rack.

Since then, I take art forms where they wouldn't normally be found. The Hitching Rack was the Lions Club after-meeting hang out. Once a month on

Wednesday evening, my string trio, two violins, and viola, enraptured the otherwise rowdy bunch with some Mozart.

I brought with me from Gillette the WHSP collaborative approach to problem-solving. To this day, my decision-making methods revolve around the multidisciplinary think method.

In Lander, that included two groups of dedicated citizens. The city Economic Development Commission and the private sector LEADER Corporation.

The city applied for state grants, and LEADER loaned small amounts of seed money into projects. Both groups helped with some smokestack chasing to entice businesses to relocate, but the most success happened with local businesses expanding and counseling aspiring entrepreneurs.

In 1983, my grandmother Sakata planned a big family gathering to honor her brother. I had taken little time off other than a day or two around legal holidays. Thanks to one of my Lander friends, a trip to Peru would give me a taste of Latin American politics while reconnecting with my cultural past and family roots.

THIRTY-NINE: Peruvian Cousins

Half of my mother's family was Peruvian. We attended a family reunion in Lima.

Half my mom's family is Peruvian. Her uncle was being honored for some reason or another in Lima. My grandmother organized a family trip to Peru for the award ceremony in October 1983.

On the surface, my having Peruvian relatives may seem unusual, but Peru was the first Latin American country to establish diplomatic relations with Japan in 1873. Part of my grandmother's Iwasaki family immigrated to Peru, and my grandmother ended up in Wyoming after she married my grandfather Sakata.

During World War II, Peru cut off relations with Japan and considered an internment program of its own but chose to deport over a thousand Japanese Peruvians to the United States, primarily to three camps in Texas nearest to the port in New Orleans.

Unlike the WRA-managed camps, the three detention centers in Texas at Seagoville, Kenedy, and Crystal City were constructed and administered by the Immigration and Naturalization Service (INS) and governed by the Third Geneva Convention of 1929—Relative to the Treatment of Prisoners of War.

In the early 1900s, the US government was mainly interested in keeping immigration in check to protect American workers from less expensive foreign labor. Immigration management was a matter of commerce.

In 1903, Congress transferred the Bureau of Immigration to the Department of Commerce and Labor—now separate departments of Labor and Commerce. In June 1933, the INS was established.

In 1940, the INS was transferred to the US Justice Department to deal with potential enemy aliens as the United States moved closer to involvement in World War II.

The American Red Cross monitored the INS to ensure the camps met enemy alien detainee treatment standards. The Geneva Conventions set standards around the quality of food, size of living quarters, and amount and type of clothing that each detainee can possess more than what may have been issued.

The INS, like the WRA, designed the camps to be much like stand-alone communities with food stores, auditoriums, a hospital, places of worship, a post office, bakery, barbershop, beauty shop, school system, a Japanese sumo wrestling ring, and German biergartens.

In April 1942, the first ship named the US Army Transport (USAT) Etolin left Callao, Peru, with nearly a hundred and fifty Japanese men. During that first trip, the Etolin picked up Japanese deportees from Colombia before heading for San Francisco. The INS denied them visas and passports, classified them as enemy aliens, and detained them at assembly centers.

Other ships, including the Swedish charter Steam Ship (SS) Gripsholm, the SS Shawnee, and the SS Frederick C. Johnson, transported Japanese from Peru to Panama before heading to the United States. The ships docked in New Orleans.

In April 1942, the INS took over a women's prison facility in Seagoville, Texas, and converted it into a detention center located twenty miles southeast of Dallas.

Most of the detainees were Japanese, and Germans were deported from Latin America to the United States. Women and couples without children were sent to the Seagoville center, men to the Kenedy center, and families with children to the Crystal City center.

The Seagoville center detainee population in July 1942 consisted of a handful of German men and forty German and Japanese women. The number of detainees increased over the following months.

Most women detained were classified as "voluntary" because they agreed to join their interned husbands in other camps around the WRA camp network. The detainees were permitted to possess personal items like hot water bottles, clothing, sewing supplies; creature comforts like rugs, curtains, cushions, and small electric appliances such as irons.

The Seagoville center population changed primarily as a result of detainee repatriation to Germany and Japan. In June 1942, the US Department of State (DOS) repatriated fifteen hundred Japanese from Seagoville and other internment camps. By August 1944, the camp's population dwindled to around three hundred and eighty, mostly Germans.

By September 1943, nearly all Japanese Latin American detainees at Seagoville were repatriated to their home countries, with some families transferred to the Crystal City center. The Seagoville center closed in May 1945.

The INS, in March 1942, repurposed a twenty-two-acre Great Depression-era Civilian Conservation Corps (CCC) site into the Kenedy Detention Center in Kenedy, Texas, located in Karnes County, which is sixty miles southeast of San Antonio.

The CCC was a voluntary public work relief program that operated from 1933 to 1942 in the United States for unemployed, unmarried men during the Great Depression.

The CCC was a major part of President FDR's New Deal that provided manual labor jobs. Workers conserved natural resources and constructed federal, state, and local government public works projects in rural areas, including Wyoming.

There were numerous CCC projects in Wyoming, including roads in Yellowstone National Park, facilities at Glendo State Park, and numerous public works projects around the state.

The US Congress ended the program in 1942. The need for the massive work relief program declined with the World War II military draft.

There were two thousand Japanese, Germans, and Italians deported from Latin America processed through the Kenedy center.

The initial wave of Kenedy center detainees arrived in April 1942 from Latin America and included over six hundred and fifty Germans and Italians. Within the following two months, six hundred more German and Japanese detainees arrived.

Over time, the Kenedy center detainees separated themselves into ethnic "clans" such as the Germans from Guatemala, the largest clique. Conflicts grew among the various groups.

Towards the end of 1942, the US Army focused on guarding hundreds of thousands of prisoners of war captured from the Axis nations of Japan, Germany, and Italy. The INS was given greater authority to house potentially dangerous enemy aliens and US citizen Axis sympathizers at internment camps and detention centers throughout the US.

Needing more space, the remaining Kenedy detainees were released, repatriated, or transferred to other camps. The camp was closed in September 1944 and converted into a German and Japanese POW camp.

INS leased over two hundred acres of land for the third site to build a detention center at Crystal City, located in Zavala County, fifty miles from Mexico, and was originally a migrant labor facility site. In the 1920s, Crystal City's population boomed when migrant farm laborers came across the border to work area farms.

The camp detained mostly Japanese and Germans deported from Latin America and interned Japanese Americans transferred to Crystal City from other WRA assembly centers. By the end of 1945, the Crystal City center held a little more than thirty-four hundred mostly Japanese and German internees.

Peru developed a strong wartime relationship with the United States during World War II. Riding the wave of anti-Japanese sentiment in Peru strengthened its western hemispheric defense.

The relationship resulted in Peru obtaining loans from American banks to finance a steel processing plant. In exchange, Peru allowed the US military to operate an airbase at Talara, a strategic location to defend the Panama Canal from attack.

I don't know why my great uncle and his family were allowed to stay in Peru. They owned property in Lima in a remote town called Supe in the Barranca

Province on the Pacific coast. In 1983, Supe didn't have running water, and rudimentary electrical circuits were easily overloaded.

I have Peruvian cousins named Carlos, Juan, and Pedro. Pedro moved to the United States and now lives in Florida. Recently, he was in Colorado for a job-related conference. We met up briefly and took a whirlwind drive to Estes Park. We're in touch on Facebook.

Pedro was unsure why his family was allowed to stay in Peru rather than relocated. When the economy went bad in Peru, some of my cousins went to Japan, where they faced discrimination because they were not native-born.

I spoke fluent Spanglish, but the common language among us was Japanese. Questions would be asked in either English or Spanish, then translated into Japanese then the response given in either English or Spanish.

My aunts prepared the Peruvian food Japanese style. We had a lot of ceviches (raw fish marinated and cured in lemon), also with shoga (ginger) and shoyu. The Chinese food restaurants are called chifas. I've read that there are now Japanese-style nikkei Peruvian restaurants.

During my time in Peru, 1983 was a turbulent time with the Communist Shining Path guerrilla fighters on a rampage. The terrorists slaughtered hundreds of tribal people who lived in the mountainous regions.

One of my Lander friends and colleagues was a retired Foreign Service diplomat named Dave Raynolds. He and his wife and daughter owned a bison ranch in Sinks Canyon. I mentioned to him that I was taking a trip to Peru. "When you're on one of those Peruvian buses, sit next to someone with a chicken. If a terrorist gets on board, grab the chicken and blend in with the rest of the passengers," he advised.

I didn't experience chickens on the bus, but while flying to Iquitos on a side trip to the Amazon River headwaters, the Fawcett Airlines jet stopped on the taxiway to let on a passenger lugging a box full of peeping chicks who sat down in my row. "I have a friend who works in the US Embassy in Peru—Frank Ortiz. I'll call ahead and let him know you're coming," he mentioned on his way out the door.

In 1983, the chaos in Lima and the long lines of would-be asylum seekers extending around the US Embassy looked like a scene out of that Sissy Spacek and Jack Lemmon movie called *Missing* (1982) about a journalist who disappeared during the overthrow of Salvador Allende in Chile.

As a precaution, I went to check-in at the Embassy. We went to the head of the long line and were greeted by a young Marine sitting behind a glass window that was a foot thick. He buzzed us in to meet Frank Ortiz.

It turned out Frank Ortiz was the US Ambassador to Peru. He and his staff were madly packing up and getting ready to leave in the midst of domestic chaos. We only had time to exchange some small talk before we were ushered out.

The next morning, the newspaper headline was something about Frank Ortiz being recalled and the embassy closed by the DOS because of the political and social unrest.

I flew out on AeroPeru. The trip to Miami was exhausting. I landed late and booked a room at an airport hotel where I slept for a few hours before boarding a domestic flight back to Denver and the commuter flight to Riverton. That's the same route I traveled when I met Mrs. Honkawa.

My friend and newspaper colleague Diana, who accompanied me to the Heart Mountain camp the first time, picked me up at the Riverton airport. The time-zone difference was three hours later. I didn't have jet lag, but it was good to get back to the day-to-day grind.

FOURTY: Bison and the Arapaho

After I returned from Peru, there were a few economic development successes with existing business expansion, a new hospital, and renewed optimism with the Lander Centennial celebration.

There was a mayoral change, and the public sector lost its challenge. I decided to give free enterprise a try.

A business that I had helped get established in Lander had an opening in the finance office, and I signed on with them. They manufactured steel parts on a just-in-time basis for an exercise equipment company. The company was not yet stable and eventually went out of business after a pretty good beginning.

This would be the story of my life after leaving a steady and cushy government job. Because of my ability to pick up pieces, floundering groups would hire me to resurrect projects and develop new approaches, but when all the money was gone . . .

At that same time, I went through an unfortunate marriage with a business partner while in Lander, which further proves that I'm better helping others get started from the outside than working with people who think they know what they are doing from inside their business.

I'd always been on an even keel, but if my life was ever in upheaval, it was after that failed business experience and related disruption in my personal affairs. But everything seems to work out for the best.

When I was still with the city of Lander, Gov. Ed appointed me to the Uranium Mill Tailings Task Force that dealt with leaching radioactive contaminants in Fremont County and the eastern edge of the Wind River Indian Reservation. One of the task force members was Northern Arapaho Business Council Chair Gary Collins. My friendship with him and the subsequent connections I made with the Northern Arapaho Tribe would reconnect me with my Japanese cultural roots in a roundabout way.

I arranged a meeting with US Senator Al Simpson, who helped get federal legislation passed to clean up the mess.

There was a local politician who stumbled into the meeting with a constituent. The good Senator Simpson chewed out the two for disrupting our meeting.

Afterward, the gate crasher took credit for putting the mill tailings meeting together. Years later, he apologized to me about that. He later explained it as a political lie that got out of control. At least he felt guilty about it.

Around that time, and I was reinventing myself, I received a life-changing phone call from the Northern Arapaho Economic Development Commission (EDC) chair Ernie Sun Rhodes. He asked if I'd be interested in working for the EDC.

After a couple of stops and starts, I began what would be the start of a decades-long journey with the hinono'eiteen (Northern Arapaho Tribe) and my friendship and working relationship with Gary that continues to this day.

Being immersed in a population of people who looked more like me also reconnected me to my Japanese roots. After thirty years of contact with the Northern Arapaho, I'm often asked how I've maintained a strong relationship with the tribe.

"I look Arapaho, I'm not related to anyone, and I can't vote," is my usual response. "I'm a Japaho."

The cultural upheaval the Japanese experienced during and after World War II is minor compared to how manifest destiny affected Native Americans.

I learned about manifest destiny in my high school US history class taught by Mr. McIlvain. I didn't have a practical understanding of it until I worked for the Northern Arapaho Tribe. The Northern Arapaho and sosoni'iiteen (Eastern Shoshone) tribes share the Wind River Indian Reservation.

I'd say that many people don't realize that federally recognized tribes are sovereign nations and have a direct relationship with the US government that's spelled out in the US Constitution. Federal funds, for example, flow directly to the tribes and don't filter through state governments.

The Shoshone and Arapaho tribes have separate tribal governments but share and manage the reservation as a joint tribe. Over the years, this arrangement caused conflicts since the two tribes didn't get along that great before the Indian Appropriation Act in 1851 created the reservation system.

Every morning for four years, I made the sixteen-mile commute from Lander to Ethete, which translates to mean "good" in the Arapaho language, where the tribal government is located.

If you haven't had occasion to spend time among Native American tribal members, that's an experience everyone needs to have. It was a good fit for me. The Arapaho are collaborative, and it takes a while to gain consensus from several interests, including spiritual leaders, elected officials, and the tribal members-at-large.

The Northern Arapaho proposed some controversial projects like Monitored Retrievable Storage (MRS). In 1991, the US Department of Energy sought a state or Indian tribe to store spent nuclear power plant fuel rods shipped to a facility where they would be stored.

There were workshops for prospective MRS hosts about how to look to the future, which was thousands of years from the present when culture and languages changed.

It turned out, fear of environmental damage stopped the project that, theoretically, would have created a steady labor force for twenty-four thousand years, the half-life of Plutonium-239.

A group of private businessmen picked up the MRS ball but didn't get very far with the idea either. A friend from Gillette became the US Department of the Interior Solicitor General and, up until January 20, 1993, helped move the project through the bureaucracy. The project timing wasn't the best after Bill Clinton defeated President George H.W. Bush. My friend was soon out of a job when the guard changed.

Wyoming has always had a largely pass-through economy: value added to fossil fuels at out-of-state power plants, livestock finished in out-of-state feedlots, the Transcontinental Railroad moving people across and out of Wyoming.

Wyoming's wild and wooly West story as an isolated place where more antelope and deer play than people, attracts big projects fitting for the wide-open spaces like the Heart Mountain relocation camp in northeast Wyoming.

The SCOTUS in 1989 upheld a Wyoming Supreme Court ruling and awarded the Eastern Shoshone and Northern Arapaho tribes 500,717 acre-feet of 1868 pre-territorial rights—the best and most senior rights.

When I was working for the Northern Arapaho Tribe, one of the staff directives was to use water and keep as much of it as possible from flowing downstream.

The six hundred-acre Arapaho Farm was one of those projects. The enterprise consisted mostly of fallow ground that was put under plow and hand irrigated. Well before that experience, I self-identified as a farmer.

One summer, my sister and I spent a month irrigating sugar beets on the Shinmori farm near Orpha. That's how I got to know their kids, Bobby, Kathy, and Jay, who taught me how to hand irrigate.

Early each morning, we went out to move water around the fields using arced plastic tubing of various diameters. The idea is to use the siphoning effect by filling each tube in the ditch so there's no air. I would cover one end with the palm of my hand and lift it over the ditch berm into the sugar beet furrow.

Spreading around irrigation water became a life skill for me. I was not good at it, but the Arapaho farm manager was surprised I knew how to irrigate. We created quite a few jobs by hand irrigating rather than spreading water with more efficient gated pipe and center pivots.

In addition to the tribal farm that adds some value to water, bison reintroduction used water. The first efforts began with a traditional bison ceremony that coincided with a summer school class session chronicled in National Geographic magazine in November 1994. Here it is going on thirty years later, and I'm still working on that Arapaho culture project.

The Sixteenth-century bison population that ranged around North America is estimated to have been thirty million animals. But to put our hands on one bison for this traditional bison ceremony was quite the ordeal.

A guy named Ed, who was the tribal insurance agent, and I hauled a horse trailer behind his pickup to Lame Deer, Montana, to pick up a bison promised by the Northern Cheyenne Tribe. After arriving, the herd manager had culled one, but it roamed back into the hills. The next stop was the Crow Agency, where a bison was available, but that herd retreated into a canyon before we arrived.

We rambled back to Lander, where we started and ended up purchasing a bison from a herd that ranged around Sinks Canyon and was owned by Dave Raynolds and his family.

Following that sort of successful hunt, I've been involved with many of the same tribal members to return bison to the Northern Arapaho tribe. That effort is marked by a similar bison ceremony organized in November 2016.

The bison were hunted nearly to extinction in the Nineteenth-century, with fewer than one hundred animals in the wild by the late 1880s.

To find one bison for this similar bison ceremony was a bureaucratic nightmare.

Wyoming is home to three public and sort-of free-ranging public bison herds. The most well-known is in Yellowstone National Park. The bison range should be much bigger than the boundaries of the park. The herd population expands faster than the US National Park Service (USNPS) can contain it by natural mortality and predators.

They wander out onto non-federal lands, causing conflicts among state wildlife and agricultural agencies, environmentalists, and ranchers who fear a bacterium carried by bison called, *Brucellosis abortus,* will infect their herds and cause spontaneous abortions. According to the USNPS, there has been no documented case of *B. abortus* being transmitted between bison and cattle.

Ironically, culling the Yellowstone bison to seed and expand Great Plains tribal herds is the best solution. The USDA Animal and Plant Health Inspection Service (APHIS) between LaPorte and Fort Collins, Colorado, has a small quarantine facility that has produced a herd that now roams around on the Soapstone Prairie Natural Area managed by the city of Fort Collins and the Red Mountain Open Space managed by Larimer County.

APHIS is the US government agency that manages birds at airports to prevent their collisions with airplanes. The service has vegetable-animal sniffing dogs that monitor passenger check-in lines for illegal critters and plants smuggled in and out of the United States. APHIS also has a research branch that designed a way to keep prairie dogs from chewing up underground nuclear missile silo wiring.

There are two herds managed by the state of Wyoming at Hot Springs State Park in Thermopolis and Bear River State Park near Evanston. We received word of a "dry" bison cow from the Thermopolis herd. She was unable to reproduce and would eventually be sold.

After trying to work through channels, Wyoming Arts Council folklorist Annie Hatch coordinated a ten-minute meeting with some higher-ups in the state government.

To the chagrin of the state park superintendent, the result of that whirlwind meeting freed up that bison cow for our ceremony. At market, the bison had an estimated value of one thousand dollars that was lost to the state park coffer.

During manifest destiny, bison were commodities. They ran wild and were hunted for their skins and other body parts with the animal carcasses left on the ground to be scavenged by coyotes and wolves. After the animals rotted, bounty hunters piled mass quantities of their bones on railroad cars and shipped them back east for processing into carbon black, fertilizer, and to be powdered to manufacture fine bone china.

Bison herds roamed and lingered in pastures to graze, making them easy targets for hunters more interested in their body parts than their spiritual significance. The US Army condoned the unfettered extermination of bison herds. It was typical for one hunter to quickly kill a hundred and fifty animals or more without moving from his blind.

Fewer bison meant more range for cattle driven up from Texas. Removing the Great Plains tribal members' main food source, which was also the center of tribal spirituality, would pressure them onto reservations.

The bison cow we were given for the Arapaho ceremony was a commodity. Is the animal considered a "wild animal" or "domestic livestock?" If wild, will the Game and Fish Department require that bison have been inoculated against Brucellosis? If domestic, would the state Department of Agriculture require a permit to haul the load?

It really didn't matter.

The day of the ceremony, an early model Wyoming state government pickup truck hauling an ancient desert-khaki painted Bureau of Land Management (BLM) surplus horse trailer kicked up dust as it rambled slowly on the dirt road to the Ethete Rodeo Arena.

The driver backed up to one of the catch pens, and his helper, who happened to be an EHS classmate of mine named Roger, unloaded the animal. I signed for her on a scrap of paper, and we were set.

I contacted all the reservation schools, more as a courtesy, about the event. Just after the bison arrived, much to my surprise, a caravan of Yellow Dog school buses came from two directions and converged at the rodeo grounds. Hundreds of school children were off-loaded to take part in the sacred event.

The night before the ceremony, Harvey Spoonhunter, one of my former bosses, invited me over to his house for a sweat where we would be, among other things, praying for the bison. Sweat lodges are domed huts that are covered with blankets and tarps to hold in the heat.

He and his brother, Marlin, placed roundish river rocks into a fire pit and heated them with red hot embers. The hot stones were carried into the sweat lodge on a shovel blade and dropped into a pit. Harvey blessed a container of water and poured it over the rocks before the door was closed, creating a lightless and humid atmosphere.

The next day, after the Hot Springs State Park wranglers dropped off the bison, William Ignatius John "Iggy John" C'Hair was the tribal elder who presided over the ceremony.

"Alan, killing a buffalo is on my bucket list," he said to me. "Can I have the honor?"

Who was I to argue? After Iggy John gave a blessing honoring the bison, and the Eagle Drum sang a song, my colleague, Gary, gave him instructions about where to aim his .30-06 caliber long gun. He squeezed the trigger. The rifle cracked, and she dropped in her tracks. The bison was dressed in the traditional way, supervised by one of the elder women.

One of the tribe's top priorities places primary emphasis on reversing assimilation. According to Iggy John, the missing arc in the circle of life is the bison.

For a non-tribal member, I found the event very uplifting to watch the busloads of students who anxiously gathered around Iggy John and the bison to see and hear how the bison was dressed out for subsistence and ceremonial purposes.

Even before the wars waged by the US government against Native Americans, including the Northern Arapaho, tribal members were subjected to US government-sponsored Americanization efforts.

Whatever pain and suffering Japanese in the United States experienced during and following World War II was nothing close to the plight of Native Americans.

The United States was booming. With mass immigration from Europe, there was growing public support for standard education based on a set of cultural values and norms presumably held by all citizens, including immigrants and Native Americans.

Between 1790 and 1920, the US government forced cultural assimilation of Native Americans to culturally become Anglo-American. George Washington formulated a policy that encouraged a "civilizing" strategy.

When the wars against the tribes ended in the late Nineteenth and early Twentieth centuries, traditional religious ceremonies were outlawed. There are numerous books and movies about Native American children forced to enroll in boarding schools where they abandoned their cultural traditions, were required to learn English, and to attend a Christian church.

The Dawes Act of 1877 broke down the traditional collaborative tribal structure into one of individuals consistent with the American Way. That act gave each tribal member US citizenship and an allotment of their reservation land to theoretically provide a sense of ownership and turn Great Plains nomadic people into sedentary farmers.

The transcontinental railroad enabled more settlers to move further west, and along with that, bison numbers declined because the railroads wanted bison eliminated. Herds of bison damaged locomotives when trains failed to stop in time to avoid animals on the tracks. Bison could delay trains from moving for days.

Railroads hired commercial hunters, including William "Buffalo Bill" Cody, to shoot bison and, as a side benefit, provide a food source for their laborers.

Bounty hunters soon arrived in masses. They boarded trains that would slow down so the hunters armed with long rifles could climb atop the railcars or fire shots at the herds from their passenger seat windows.

This one bison cow from Hot Springs State Park was more regulated than the thirty million slaughtered in the Nineteenth century.

The Eastern Shoshone Tribe recently established a herd on the west side of the reservation. Much to my surprise, a few miles away, the Northern Arapaho received ten head delivered from the National Bison Range in Montana. I heard there are talks underway to de-commoditize the animals and merge the two herds into one.

Towards the end of my formal tenure on the Wind River Indian Reservation, a bunch of Arapaho artists led by Eugene Ridgely, Sr. wanted to create a cultural conduit to pipe their artwork and culture back to their ancestral homelands in Boulder, Colorado. Art galleries on the Pearl Street Mall in the 1980s were plentiful, and the owners opened up wall space for Northern Arapaho artwork.

I commuted from Colorado to Lander for a couple of years. That drive was a dangerous one during the winter. I-80 extends from Washington DC to San Francisco except when severe winter weather strands travelers on a ninety mile stretch between Laramie and Rawlins.

Winter is a growth industry for Wyoming. When all the hotels fill up, and tractor-trailers line the truck stop parking lots, the Wyoming Department of Transportation closes the road. I've been caught on that stretch pounding through snowdrifts and zero visibility after the road was closed behind me.

That's a lonely drive. Anyone who can navigate the I-80 "Snow Chi Minh" trail between Rawlins and Laramie on winter roads covered with black ice and ground blizzards can drive anywhere.

I grew up in treacherous winters. Snow drifted in our Windmill Road front yard as high as the roof. That was nothing compared to the blizzard of '49. My dad told stories about driving to work during that series of storms. Our East 10th Street home was near my dad's work at the Coke plant. He was dedicated to his job. Regardless of the weather, he always went to work. As the supervisor, he felt obligated to the company.

He woke up to a freezing morning. His Ford pickup started but drove to work in reverse because the frigid temperatures froze the gear box. He told me to learn how to drive backward with a standard transmission. I ended up being a pretty good parallel parker.

That snap of cold weather in 1949 is considered one of the worst weather events in the northern Great Plains. The first storm began January 2nd and continued through January 5th with heavy snow, strong winds, and below-zero temperatures. Twelve people reportedly died in Wyoming during the blizzard.

I was the Arapaho artist advocate and was able to keep the cultural pipeline viable for two summers. The venture wasn't sustainable because the project management was largely a volunteer effort and I didn't make the drive during the winter. On top of that, several Boulder galleries closed their doors.

After working with the Northern Arapaho tribal members and their challenge to renew their language through reverse assimilation and reclaim their traditional homeland, I realized how my parents tried to protect me from racism. Since Pearl Harbor and eighty years of assimilation, not one Japanese American has turned White.

FOURTY-ONE: Cohesion and Dispersal

I recalled the July 4th and Memorial Day picnics organized by the Skyline Nisei Club. It finally occurred to me that the main reason my parents took me to those events, while enjoyable, was because those club events were safe times and places where the Japanese could interact with one another.

The moms prepared food like it was New Year's Day in the summer. The events were the Cheyenne version of the Bon Festival, the Japanese Buddhist version of Day of the Dead.

In Japan, the Bon Festival was based on the lunar calendar and celebrated in early to mid-August. After the western calendar became more common, the summer events evolved into times when families reunited, honored their family members, visited cemeteries, and cleaned up gravesites.

When I was young, the picnic fare included American standards like hot dogs, hamburgers, potato salad, and Japanese food. Moms packed their food in classic square enameled wooden boxes, but tapuru waru (Tupperware) became the standard by this time.

There were all kinds of maki sushi rolled in nori (seaweed paper) with fancy fish, like unagi (eel).

Nigiri sushi, the small wads of rice with pieces of fish or crustaceans on top, wasn't part of the table. Those didn't meet the "working class" standard in that raw fish items weren't practical for a bento (lunch) box. I didn't try nigiri until I was an adult.

There were musubi (rice balls) with a bit of umeboshi (pickled plum) in the middle. As an adult, I developed a taste for musubi and maki sushi made with SPAM.

SPAM is chopped-up pork meat that is reconstituted and canned in a rectangle shaped can. As a kid, we always had a can around the kitchen. I didn't learn that it was a World War II food staple and included in C-rations. I read soldiers consumed a hundred and fifty million pounds of SPAM during the war. I keep a can of SPAM around for emergencies.

The fancy specialty items were inari made from abura age (thinly sliced deep-fried tofu pouches), stuffed with seasoned rice. They are very labor-intensive to make.

Each family had their own teriyaki chicken marinade—some more sugary, some with ginger, some thicker, some thinner. My mom made thinly sliced teriyaki flank steak that was good. Flank steak was once a cheap cut and is now very expensive.

If it was Memorial Day, after the first food go-around, we all went to the Japanese area of the Lakeview Cemetery and decorated gravestones.

On July 4th, we made sure to finish up at the picnic grounds in time to make a stop at the fireworks stand before heading to the Kishiyama place to blast off firecrackers.

The 1970s was a time of transition in the Japanese community, including with my family. The Skyline Nisei Club became less active as the Issei generation passed away along with many traditions, like the summer picnics and gatherings at the cemetery.

When the Memorial Gardens opened on the east edge of Cheyenne, my family bought in as charter members. It's one of those headstone-less cemeteries sprung up all over the West on the outskirts of towns. They were easy to mow and maintain, with plenty of room to expand.

All my family members' plots are out there. That move away from the urban Lakeview Cemetery also coincided with the Cheyenne Japanese scattering away from Cheyenne, particularly from downtown.

Having that cemetery plot is one thing that will keep me coming back to Cheyenne. Very few of the out-of-town cousins visit Cheyenne anymore. Jake and Jeanne's daughters, Alison and Leslie, are the only cousins who still live in Cheyenne.

For the record, if I don't get around to updating my will, I want some of my ashes scattered in Crow Creek on the east side of Central Avenue that flows alongside I-80. Crow Creek was the original military settlement that evolved into Cheyenne. Dad and I hiked around the sandstone cliffs and explored animal dens. My heirs can scatter the remainder of the ashes on or bury them under the family plot in the Memorial Gardens.

I keep threatening to get the few Sansei cousins and friends still in Cheyenne and ask my out-of-town cousins to return for a reunion. It seems like the only time I see my cousins these days is if there is a funeral. Soon those will be our memorial services. Before those become too frequent, we talk about a cousin reunion, including the primas de las Peru.

FOURTY-TWO: Civility Lessons Not Learned

I started the story out by relating my recollection about what I was doing on 9/11, and my mom's observation about the backlash Muslims would experience. She was right about that.

Like the Japanese in 1941, in the days, weeks, and years following 9/11, elements of American society turned against Muslims and people who look like Muslims. Shortly after the attack, the FBI, without charge, detained more than one thousand Muslims and Arabs. The US government again reorganized its immigration agencies and policies. They expanded their purview further beyond labor and commerce to national security.

Thousands of Muslim immigrants were subsequently deported from the United States. This action riled up Aya Medrud.

People of the Muslim faith have a long history in the United States, much longer than Asians. It's estimated that between ten and twenty percent of people brought to colonial America to be enslaved were Muslim.

There are records of Muslims who fought on the American side during the Revolutionary War and three hundred Muslims who fought for the North during the Civil War.

Based on their long history in America, there were no federal laws passed limiting the immigration of Muslims, as happened with the Immigration Act of 1924 that limited the number of Asians entering the country.

Wyoming isn't without its controversies involving Muslims. The Powder River Basin is home to around two hundred residents who self-identify as Muslim, with around thirty who live in Gillette, my former stomping grounds.

When I was in Gillette, I can't say I ever came across any Muslim people. Northeast Wyoming has a long history with Muslim immigrants dating back to 1909 when Zarif Khan moved to Wyoming from Afghanistan.

Numerous accounts chronicle the experiences of Kahn, who became known as "Hot Tamale Louie" because he sold the steamed cornmeal snacks on the street to passersby and eventually opened a storefront in downtown Sheridan.

Louie's customers respected him and his business and supported his application for naturalization as a United States citizen, which was approved.

Meanwhile, the Immigration Act of 1924 brought about several lawsuits seeking to strip citizenship from previously naturalized people. Someone reported Louie. In 1926, by a long stretch of the 1924 act, immigration authorities declared Louie to be Asian and reversed his citizenship status. In 1954, he reapplied for naturalization, which was approved.

Most of the Muslims in Gillette are descended from Khan. In 2015, a group of local Muslims decided to purchase a home and convert it into a mosque. That caused an uproar between a local movement called "Stop Islam in Gillette" and the townsfolk.

The protests and rallies raised the eyebrows of law enforcement agencies, including the FBI. The short-lived conflict caused Gillette to boil, and now it is just simmering.

There was a conciliation between the Stop Islam group advocate Matt Colvin and the mosque organizer Aftab Khan. Wyoming Public Radio, the state's National Public Radio affiliate, set up a conversation for a segment entitled *Time Heals All Wounds: Breaking Bread, Finding Common Ground After Angry Mosque Incident.* The upshot of the conversation was, the two advocates agreed to disagree.

Intentional actions like the WPR radio program that brought people with divergent perspectives together are what can better institutionalize civility in the public discourse of controversial issues. The challenge is for individuals to shed Superman's American Way and become more collaborative.

Since 9/11, and continued oppression toward Muslims and people who look like Muslims, it doesn't seem that much was learned from the Japanese experience in World War II as xenophobic history is repeating itself. The facts, of course, are much different, but the cultural pushback is similar.

A week after his 2017 inauguration, President Donald Trump issued EO 13769, Protecting the Nation from Foreign Terrorist Entry into the United States. This was the first in a series of EO and presidential proclamations banning Muslims from entering the United States.

The subsequent presidential administration rescinded these orders but while in force, they deepened the cultural divide evidenced by nationwide protests about institutionalized xenophobia toward Muslims.

Recall the World War II signs and blatant slogans that unified American people against the Japanese: "No Japs Here" and "Slap a Jap."

During the COVID-19 pandemic in summer of 2020, racial strife hit a crescendo for African Americans following the murders of young men and women by law enforcement officers.

Anti-Asian sentiments manifested themselves when individuals and groups hid behind the excuse that COVID-19 originated in China. They hurled racial epithets and committed random and intentional acts of violence toward Asians of any ethnicity.

The Immigration and Nationality Act of 1965 may have done away with immigrant discrimination on paper, but it did little to change the minds of Americans who desire ethnic homogeneity since fewer Europeans are crossing the US borders compared to the enormous immigrant influx from Latin America, Asia, and Africa wanting to join the American Way.

FOURTY-FOUR: Civility and Superman's American Way

Al Simpson was in Boulder a few years ago. We were guests of a mutual friend named Oak Thorne at his Ecological Institute fund raising event.

There's nothing inherently wrong with Superman's American Way that touts individual prosperity and equality for all. But what if the means of achievement changed from winning and losing to collaboration, from assimilation based on exclusion to acceptance by intentional efforts that bridge cultural divides among diverse people and xenophobic America.

During World War II, Superman fought the Axis powers—Japan, Germany, and Italy. The good-over-evil comic book stories sent a mixed message.

At one time, comic books had a bad image. While these inexpensive and periodic publications were extremely popular among young people, critics looked down upon them. Societal police blamed comic books for causing juvenile delinquency and the formation of gangs.

Comic books were the decadent video games of their day. I read a blog post on the DC Comics website about how in 1949, DC Comics, to contrast with that negative public perception, wanted to send the message of inclusion and equality to its readers and collaborated with the National Social Welfare Assembly (NSWA) on a public service announcement comic book series featuring Superman.

The public backlash resulting from the World War II relocation of Japanese Americans was of concern for the NSWA, particularly after the war when Japanese resettlement began.

The NSWA Committee on Japanese Americans published bulletins about conflicts around employment rights, housing availability, and legislation that codified discrimination toward Japanese Americans, such as the various Alien Land Acts that prohibited property ownership by Japanese. The NSWA partnership with DC Comics was a natural fit.

In 1950, in one of his public service announcements, Superman reminded us that his American Way was actually one of civility and cultural inclusivity.

". . . and remember, boys and girls, your school—like our country—is made up of Americans of many different races, religions, and national origins. So, if you hear anybody talk against a schoolmate or anyone else because of his religion, race, or national origin—don't wait, tell him that kind of talk is un-American!"

How might we reengage Superman to remind us about his inclusive American Way?

Individual civility: On a personal level, the only person I can change or control is myself. My social change bar is set at the "grocery store line" standard. That means a time when random shoppers waiting in line to check out hear an offensive or disrespectful remark from a fellow shopper. The bystanders turn around and confront the perpetrator and become an ally to the victim who received the brunt of the taunt.

Conversations about race and ethnicity are not easy. I'm hesitant to say something and unintentionally making an inappropriate remark or reference. Psychological research has found that biased views about race and ethnicity result from life-long socialization.

The United States continues to evolve into a more diverse and multicultural society. The Pew Research Center administered an Implicit Association Test (IAT). The IAT is a method that quantifies hidden biases by measuring how individuals relate positive and negative words with races and ethnicities. The Pew study investigated the subconscious bias of whites and Asians towards one another.

Half of the white sample preferred whites over Asians. The Asian sample, which has assimilated to be the model minority, was as likely to show a bias favoring whites over Asians (38%) as they were to regard Asians more favorably than whites (42%).

Bringing about social change is tough work, and I've had friends drift away over it. It's a vulnerable place, but individuals must be willing to change. If I'm not willing to get out of my comfort zone, I can't expect others to do so either, which is why I try hard to walk my talk.

It's hard work to unwind the recordings in your head and reflect upon how Superman's American Way affected how you became who you are today. It's okay to make mistakes as you change your perspective about people different from yourself.

It's a continual challenge for me to know people unlike me, but it's a way to create a quiet movement that civilly engages people one person at a time rather than reacting to what you may experience. Social change doesn't happen only by "liking" posts on Facebook, ranting, chanting, raving, and waving signs at rallies that make for good photo ops.

Individual change is an ongoing march. Take small steps. Who do you sit next to in church? Sit next to a stranger. Who do you invite out for coffee? Go out of your way and ask someone you haven't seen in a while.

Neighborhood civility: I don't think it's hyperbolic to say that the results of manifest destiny that led to discrimination and racism towards Japanese relate to the consequences of urban sprawl. The West 17th Street Japanese community and the rest of downtown Cheyenne slowed down in the 1960s and 1970s.

The Japanese experienced a cultural shift largely between 1924 and 1944, and over time, assimilation was normalized with acceptance of the model minority moniker that clumps all Asians under the same stereotype.

The ten new Lotus townhouses in the Nishigawa neighborhood were sold and occupied on the 500 block of West 17th Street.

I randomly bumped into a guy from Cheyenne at a baseball game in Denver. We got to chatting about our Cheyenne connections. He mentioned the Nishigawa Townhouses and was unaware of the Japanese community in his West 17th Street neighborhood. He was surprised about my connection to the development. John Dinneen passed on a link to the Beyond Heart Mountain documentary, a companion to this book.

On a micro-scale, the decline of downtown Cheyenne was partly due to the displacement of the Japanese as a result of discriminatory laws that erased the culture of the community coupled with razing many historic buildings with untold or forgotten stories of their own.

National civility: A national movement can be scaled by individuals with living experiences, such as mine. I'm an advocate for intentional community housing arrangements and particularly a fan of the collaborative secret sauce. Cohousing communities have as their premise one that reinvents Superman's American Way through acceptance of individual differences, including all perspectives, decision making by consensus while working towards the community good.

Organizations such as the Cohousing Association of the US consist of thirty thousand people living in over one hundred and seventy existing intentional communities and another hundred and sixty in formation.

Cohousing community members look to repurpose abandoned buildings or go stick-built on vacant property. Cohousers, in collaboration with local communities, can create a neighborhood story by working with the current residents and businesses and agreeing upon a narrative that defines the acceptance of existing neighbors or new ones. That narrative informs investors and how their participation can revitalize, redevelop, or develop neighborhoods consistent with community norms, expectations, culture, and history.

While making the last edits to my story, I happened to be visiting friends from Cheyenne who also lived in the Cole Addition and moved to Sun City West near

Phoenix. It's an age-restricted place that reminded me of growing up in the suburbs, except all the residents are old with grown children instead of young families with elementary school aged kids.

I may end up returning to my past in a senior citizen suburb, if I don't watch it.

FOURTY-FIVE: Reconnecting My Family Roots

After snapping out of a deathbed illness in 2014, I readjusted my outlook on life. I've been more intentional about getting my various "bands back together," including reconnecting with my family roots. That put me on the path to write this book.

After my Issei grandparents passed away, my Nisei parents, uncles, and aunts were freer to westernize their lifestyles. I have no surviving aunts and uncles. It's just my sister and our cousins, now. All of us have gone our separate ways, forged lives of our own, and built new family traditions.

Recently, I visited cousin Milton in San Francisco over a Memorial Day weekend and visited the graves of Auntie Rose, Uncle Vince, and cousin Carolynn.

We toured some haunts from our younger years on the streets of San Francisco. Godzilla Sushi was where I ate sushi in a restaurant for the first time, and my first strip joint, the Condor Club, made famous by the overly-buxom Carol Doda and her Condorettes. That bar was where Milton introduced me to Galiano Stingers—Galiano and peppermint schnapps on the rocks. Clint Eastwood as *Dirty Harry* (1971) cruises down Broadway and slowly passes by the Condor Club.

We talked about a family reunion of sorts. Most of my Sansei generation first cousins are still on the right side of the grass. The surviving cousins and their families are scattered around the country: Hawaii, Washington State, California, Utah, Wyoming, Kansas, and Indiana.

I'm thinking that rather than a face-to-face meet-up, for starters, we could have a virtual reunion using one of the live stream conferencing services.

Auntie Joan and Uncle Tom were long-time Greeley, Colorado, residents. Both were in their eighties and recently passed away. I missed Joan's memorial several months ago, but after returning from California, I drove up to Tom's service held near Loveland. I didn't know anyone outside of my cousins since they were mostly Tom's millwright colleagues and friends.

I'd been out of touch with my cousins, for the most part. I met a few of their kids, but when they were very young. It was good to see cousins Margo and Gary, who are still in Greeley. Even though they are only an hour away, they all have families and lives of their own, and we have grown apart on a day-to-day level. Bobbi is in Hawaii and Kathy in California.

We do have in common our childhoods and memories of growing up with a strong extended family. But in the big picture of things, those were experiences that helped us be who we are today. When we do meet up, we'll be bonded by our recollections and remembrances about our days when we were younger.

"Now we're orphans and the family elders," Bobbi lamented. "How did that happen?"

I think all Baby Boomers have similar thoughts about generational succession. I knew I was getting old, but I didn't think it would happen this fast.

FOURTY-SIX: Reinvented Traditions

Christmas was and still is my favorite holiday. I adopted Kentucky Derby Day as a new holiday when I became old enough to horse race gamble and drink mint juleps.

When I was growing up, my family always had a big Thanksgiving get-together at our place in the Cole Addition. Grandma Ohashi usually had a spread on the south side. There was no shortage of turkey.

Since my emancipation, and me going off to college, I haven't found a new Thanksgiving groove, nor have I for any of the other holidays, for that matter. Since college, Thanksgiving became a second-tier holiday for me.

Floundering around holiday traditions became even more prevalent after my parents died. I go along to visit one of Diana's daughters, Amanda, and her family. That seems to be different each year. Maybe variety is a sign of the times.

In college, we would get out for fall break, maybe starting Wednesday after classes and then the long Thanksgiving weekend. I think I was on campus for Thanksgiving two years, invited to a classmate's home for another, and carpooled back to Wyoming once. Randy was the only Cheyenne classmate who had a car.

I liked being on campus during breaks. There were very few kids around. It was like having the place to myself. That makes perfect sense to me now that I figured out I'm an introvert.

While in Gillette, I remember I was planning to drive to Laramie one Thanksgiving, but a big snowstorm along the Snow Chi Minh trail prevented my travel. Tom and I were both stranded at the 3003 Club. We went down to the 7-Eleven at the bottom of the hill and picked up frozen steaks and other convenience store food to round out our feast.

The great thing about living in America, Christmas can be celebrated in many ways. When my sister and I were young, my parents, particularly Mom, wanted to inculcate us with a family tradition. We put up a tree, but it didn't seem like it was around a particular date. The decorations were the hand-blown delicate glass ones from Germany. The tinsel was made out of strands of some lead alloy that was carefully placed one piece at a time on each bough twig and disassembled with as much care and stored on a card in the original box for reuse the following season.

On Christmas Eve, particularly when my sister and I were older, we went to the midnight Presbyterian church service. There was no opening of a present that night. Everything always waited until Christmas morning.

When I was in grade school one Christmas, Santa Claus was over at our new next-door neighbors. Santa turned on the carport light, the beams of which shined directly into my bedroom window. That signaled to me that his visit to our house was done, even if it was three o'clock in the morning.

I was up and inspected around the tree. Luckily, I held a high degree of delayed gratification. My dad came out and reminded me that the action wouldn't start until six a.m. and that I might as well go back to bed. When I did, I lay there in anxious anticipation.

Dad covered my bedroom window with large cardboard Coca-Cola advertising placards to obscure Santa's traipsing around at the neighbors in subsequent years.

We ripped into the packages after opening the stocking stuffers that always included an orange that had worked its way down to the toe. As a kid, I wasn't much into asking for things and was happy with what I received, even socks.

One of my most "useful" gifts was the spring-loaded bazooka that shot the blue plastic rockets. My friends all wanted to be in my squad when we played *Combat!*

The bazooka was a ground-to-ground anti-tank weapon with a steel tube braced on top of the shoulder that shot Rocket Propelled Grenades (RPGs).

A radio comedian named Bob Burns is credited with coining the term "bazooka," which was what he called an improvised musical instrument made from a length of pipe with a funnel stuck on the end.

After we picked up the living room, we loaded into the car along with a favorite gift or two and trekked over to my grandparents to round out the day. I do recall firing that bazooka around my Grandparents Sakata's place, which wasn't a very good idea.

Even as an adult, I made it to Laramie for most Christmases. The tradition evolved to a Christmas Eve standing prime rib roast dinner.

Neither my sister nor I had children. Mom hung on to the family traditions as long as she could. I didn't realize the importance that young children play in forming traditions, particularly around holidays. Amanda's son, Mason, is now getting older and those Christmas mornings will change.

New Year's Day was definitely Japanese style. My mother and grandmother put out big spreads of maki sushi, a steamed Pacific lobster, Good Luck sake (rice wine), and New Year ozoni (good luck soup) served with globs of unsweetened mochi. I make a pot of ozoni, but that tradition hasn't gained much traction.

My dad died in August 2003 after a long bout with some undiagnosed progressive lung disease that I suspect is what made me sick shortly after I turned sixty. While on my back in a hospital bed, my surgeon finally diagnosed me with a septic ulcer and rolled me into the operating room for emergency surgery. The next week, I was in surgery again for lung biopsies.

The pathology lab sent my tissue samples off to various laboratories. It was the one at the University of Michigan that figured out I had Pneumocystis pneumonia (PCP). Maybe it was genetic.

After Grandparents Sakata and Auntie Hisako passed, my mom paid for a family pilgrimage to Japan. We were guided by one of her cousins. My dad was stricken by very evident shortness of breath when he couldn't walk up one of the tall buildings we visited on the tour. After that, his lungs deteriorated for ten years until he was on his hospice bed in Cheyenne. I'm pretty sure, had thoracic photography been available, my dad would have had a different lung disease diagnosis and treatment regimen.

This was the first time I was laid off, but I was set to start a new job in Denver. My mom and sister took some time off from the hospital, which gave Dad and me some time together. I won't call it quality time because it was far from that. Over the years, I made frequent trips to Laramie other than for holidays attending UW sporting events or meetings in Cheyenne and Laramie. During those visits, I spent time with my parents. That was quality time.

I mentioned that Monday would be the first day at my new job. I offered to stay, but he insisted that I return to Colorado. "I'm not going anywhere," he said.

"I'll be back after work," I responded. My sister called and reported that he passed that Monday, August 18, 2003.

Mom died the following December, on the 2nd, at home in Laramie of a brain aneurism. That was the end of the O'Hashi family name and traditions, as I knew them.

The torch was passed when my father died. The rituals of carving the turkey at Thanksgiving and the standing rib roast on Christmas are now my responsibility. More rites of passage.

My Christmas traditions have changed, too. I've rationalized sipping oyster stew on Christmas Eve since I took papal mass from Pope John Paul II in 1993 at the service held near Cherry Creek Reservoir in Denver. I adopted the ritual from my movie-making colleague Michael Conti, who said it has something to do with Catholics not eating meat on Fridays. I do roast a standing prime rib either on Christmas Eve or on Christmas. Both are largely activities I do on my own.

When I turned twenty-one, a started a new holiday tradition that does appeal to my friends. My birthday in 1953 fell on the seventy-ninth running of the Kentucky Derby, the first Saturday in May. My dad had money bet on the favorite horse, Native Dancer. Long shot Dark Star ridden by Henry Moreno won the race.

Since I got out of college, I've had a birthday event on Derby Day that involves mint juleps and, when possible, some off-track betting. Mint juleps are cocktails made from bourbon, simple syrup, mint, and crushed ice. Online betting is now allowed, making it unnecessary to watch the race at an off-track betting parlor.

These days, in the cohousing community, when my birthday falls exactly on Derby Day, that means a big blowout with women wearing the wide-brimmed elegant hats, BBQ, Derby pie, and horse race gambling.

As for the O'Hashi/Ohashi family reunion, maybe we'll get around to it next Derby Day or maybe a summer or two after that at the very latest.

No matter what your memories are from growing up, I hope they are fond ones. Do what you can to keep your stories and traditions alive.

FOURTY-SEVEN: What Do I Know?

My vast store of general knowledge does have limitations. In addition to threading my experiences and recollections through the story are historical details about the four years and millions of dollars spent by the US government constructing and managing fifteen assembly centers and ten relocation camps to contain a hundred and twenty thousand people.

Having been a news source, my accuracy benchmark is eighty-five to ninety percent; and as a journalist and writer, I strive for between ninety and ninety-five percent accuracy. Please let me know if you have beefs with any of my information, its accuracy, interpretation, and/or perspective.

One of the problems when talking about race and ethnicity is a lack of a common language which is why references end up being derogatory slang terms. The Perpetual Immigrant stereotype also feeds into this lack of understanding. Japanese, Indonesians, Chinese, Koreans, et al. are all clumped under "Asian."

I referred to various tribes and struggled with how to refer to them. The terms I considered were Indigenous People, American Indians, and Native Americans. I settled on Native Americans, even though that can be construed to be anyone born in America. I think "Indian" is a misnomer, and Indigenous People sounds jargony. When possible, I referred to specific tribes rather than with the general term.

If you have further questions that *Beyond Heart Mountain* may have brought up, the most comprehensive compilation of the Japanese American World War II experience is included in the *Densho Encyclopedia*, which is a publicly accessible website and is pretty well vetted.

As for other information, being a seasoned journalist, I cross-referenced at least two credible sources available on the World Wide Web to fill in some details about events and people I recalled.

Much of the information about the 400 and 500 blocks of West 17th Street in downtown Cheyenne is from the original manuscripts of the Japanese chapter in *The History of Cheyenne*, edited by Sharon Lass Field in 1989. My mom, Auntie Hisako, and Auntie Elsie were in charge of compiling the Japanese family histories that ended up in my inherited files.

Cross-checking those, I found some inconsistencies and verified information with online sources, as well as other conversations with family members.

The Special Collections Room at the Laramie County Library has city directories and phone books spanning the past century, which were useful to determine where residents lived, and businesses thrived.

The LeClercq Jones Collection is a great photographic record of downtown Cheyenne from the mid-1970s through the 1980s, which also was very helpful.

Ancestry.com and *Newspapers.com* are great resources for finding detailed information about people, places, and dates. If you don't think you have a digital footprint out there, forget about it. I'm amazed how much data pops up, even with straightforward search terms.

I can't forget Wyoming State Archive reference archivist Suzy Taylor, who can put her finger on just about any obscure file in the mysterious back room at the Barrett Office Building in Cheyenne.

I also drew from personal conversations with my cousin Milton Ichiyasu, my sister Lorinda, coattail cousin Carol Kishiyama Hough, high school friend Bob Walters, childhood friends Randy Suyematsu, Brian Matsuyama, Terie, and Linda Miyamoto.

Interviews with Carol, Bob, Brian, and Terie were part of a documentary based on Beyond Heart Mountain that aired on *PBS* in December 2021.

I don't know if many of the details would have surfaced if it weren't for social media. I made several queries about the *West 17th Street* neighborhood on Facebook.

No matter what your memories are, I hope they are fond ones.

DENSHO ENCYLOPEDIA RESOURCES

Heart Mountain Relocation Camp
https://encyclopedia.densho.org/Heart_Mountain/

Tule Lake Relocation Camp
https://encyclopedia.densho.org/Tule_Lake/

Pomona Assembly Center
http://encyclopedia.densho.org/Pomona_(detention_facility)/

Minidoka Relocation Camp
https://encyclopedia.densho.org/Minidoka/

Tulare Assembly Center
https://encyclopedia.densho.org/Tulare_(detention_facility)/

Gila River Relocation Camp
https://encyclopedia.densho.org/Gila_River/

Rowher Relocation Camp
http://encyclopedia.densho.org/Rohwer/

442nd Regimental Combat Team
https://encyclopedia.densho.org/442nd_Regimental_Combat_Team/

Seagoville Relocation Center
http://encyclopedia.densho.org/Seagoville_(detention_facility)/

Kenedy Relocation Center
http://encyclopedia.densho.org/Kenedy_(detention_facility)/

Crystal City Relocation Center
https://encyclopedia.densho.org/Crystal_City_(detention_facility)/

Camp Amache
http://encyclopedia.densho.org/Amache_(Granada)/

ABOUT THE AUTHOR

Alan O'Hashi is a documentary movie maker and writer based in Boulder, Colorado. He's a whole brain thinker who boarded many ships on his way to becoming a creative entrepreneur.

Made in the USA
Middletown, DE
19 March 2022